Behavioral Economics
FOR
DUMMIES®

by Morris Altman, PhD

John Wiley & Sons Canada, Ltd.

Behavioral Economics For Dummies®

Published by
John Wiley & Sons Canada, Ltd.
6045 Freemont Blvd.
Mississauga, ON L5R 4J3
www.wiley.com

For general information on John Wiley & Sons Canada, Ltd., including all books published by John Wiley & Sons, Inc., please call our warehouse, Tel 1-800-567-4797. For reseller information, including discounts and premium sales, please call our sales department, Tel 416-646-7992. For press review copies, author interviews, or other publicity information, please contact our marketing department, Tel 416-646-4584, Fax 416-236-4448.

For technical support, please visit www.wiley.com/techsupport.

Wiley publishes in a variety of print and electronic formats and by print-on-demand. Some material included with standard print versions of this book may not be included in e-books or in print-on-demand. If this book refers to media such as a CD or DVD that is not included in the version you purchased, you may download this material at http://booksupport.wiley.com. For more information about Wiley products, visit www.wiley.com.

Library and Archives Canada Cataloguing in Publication Data

Altman, Morris

        Behavioral economics for dummies / Morris Altman.

Includes index.

Issued also in electronic formats.

ISBN 978-1-118-08503-5

        1. Economics—Psychological aspects. 2. Finance, Personal—Decision making. I. Title.

HB74.P8A58 2012   330.01'9   C2011-907846-5

ISBN 978-1-118-08969-9 (ebk); 978-1-118-08970-5 (ebk); 978-1-118-08971-2 (ebk)

Printed in the United States

1 2 3 4 5 RRD 15 14 13 12

WILEY

About the Author

A former visiting scholar at Cornell, Duke, Hebrew, and Stanford universities, **Morris Altman** is currently professor of behavioral and institutional economics and head of the School of Economics and Finance at Victoria University of Wellington. He is also professor of economics at the University of Saskatchewan, where he was head of the Department of Economics from 1994 to 2009. Recently, Morris was elected Visiting Fellow at St. Edmund's College, Cambridge University, and was a Visiting Scholar at Stirling University in Scotland and an Erskine Fellow at the University of Canterbury, Christchurch, New Zealand.

Morris was elected and served as president of the Society for the Advancement of Behavioral Economics (SABE) from 2003 to 2006. In 2009, he was elected president of the Association for Social Economics. He is editor of the *Journal of Socio-Economics* (Elsevier Science) and former Associate Editor of the *Journal of Economic Psychology,* where he remains on the editorial board.

Morris has published over 80 refereed papers on behavioral economics, economic history, methodology, and empirical macroeconomics and four books in economic theory and public policy and has made over 150 international presentations on these subjects. He is currently completing three books on related subjects and is researching endogenous technical change, the linkages between economic justice (human rights), power, and economic growth and development, as well as the importance of altruism, ethics, and reciprocity in economic theory.

Morris is also leading major projects in experimental economics. One examines the role of prices, incomes, and social variables in determining consumer demand. Another investigates the conditions under which improved working conditions affect effort inputs and how this might impact unit costs and profitability.

He currently lives in Wellington, New Zealand, with his wife, Louise, and their daughter, Hannah.

Dedication

To my wife, Louise Lamontagne, and our daughter, Hannah Altman, for their love, inspiration, and patience.

Author's Acknowledgments

I am very grateful to Robert Hickey of John Wiley & Sons, who got me involved in this exciting project. He carefully helped me work through a detailed template for this book, which has become its backbone. I would also like to thank Elizabeth Kuball, my project editor, for keeping me on my toes throughout my tight schedule and making very helpful suggestions that have contributed to improving the rhetoric, style, and content of this book. I'm sure that without Elizabeth's interventions, there would be no book. I'd like to thank my technical editor Nathan Berg of the University of Texas at Dallas for his many helpful comments and suggestions. Louise Lamontagne, my colleague and collaborator of over 30 years, read through the manuscript, making critical comments and suggestions that added much to this book's value. Hannah Altman played a critical role, always encouraging me to tackle this difficult but exciting project and adding a few hot tips of her own.

Teaching behavioral economics over the past decade has contributed immensely to the quality of this book. It gave me the opportunity to read deeply into the literature. Difficult and sometimes seemingly simple questions from my students forced me to think through concepts in behavioral economics in much more nuanced fashion than I might otherwise have done. Also, many of students' research papers in behavioral and experimental economics helped enrich my understanding of the field.

I've been thinking about and researching behavioral economics since the early 1980s, when I was working through, deconstructing, and reconstructing x-efficiency theory in my doctoral work in economic history. I'll always be appreciative to the late Harvey Leibenstein of Harvard University, the pioneer in this line of theoretical reasoning, for his mentoring and encouragement even though I was clearly heading for a road that he was not a great fan of. I also owe thanks to Professor Harold (H. R. C.) Wright, my McGill University teacher and mentor, who gave me the freedom to think and develop my own thoughts. Also of foundational importance from my McGill days are Paul Davenport, Chris Green, Jack Weldon, and Athanasios (Tom) Asimakopulos. It was Tom who enticed me out of political philosophy into economics where, he insisted, you really can make a difference. I must also thank John Tomer, a close colleague and friend on the behavioral economics bandwagon for 20 years, whose pioneering research pushed me into thinking about behavioral economics from different and interesting perspectives.

Publisher's Acknowledgments

We're proud of this book; please send us your comments at http://dummies.custhelp.com.
For other comments, please contact our Customer Care Department within the U.S. at 877-762-2974,
outside the U.S. at 317-572-3993, or fax 317-572-4002.

Some of the people who helped bring this book to market include the following:

Acquisitions and Editorial

Project Editor: Elizabeth Kuball

Acquiring Editor: Robert Hickey

Copy Editor: Elizabeth Kuball

Technical Editor: Nathan Berg, PhD

Project Coordinator, Canada:
  Pauline Ricablanca

Editorial Assistant: Katie Wolsley

Cover Photos: © iStock / Marcello Bortolino

Cartoons: Rich Tennant
  (www.the5thwave.com)

Composition Services

Project Coordinator, U.S.: Kristie Rees

Layout and Graphics: Jennifer Mayberry,
  Corrie Socolovitch, Laura Westhuis

Proofreaders: Debbye Butler, Dwight Ramsey

Indexer: Estalita Slivoskey

John Wiley & Sons Canada, Ltd.

  Deborah Barton, Vice President and Director of Operations

  Jennifer Smith, Publisher, Professional and Trade Division

  Alison Maclean, Managing Editor, Professional & Trade Division

Publishing and Editorial for Consumer Dummies

  Kathleen Nebenhaus, Vice President and Executive Publisher

  Kristin Ferguson-Wagstaffe, Product Development Director

  Ensley Eikenburg, Associate Publisher, Travel

  Kelly Regan, Editorial Director, Travel

Publishing for Technology Dummies

  Andy Cummings, Vice President and Publisher

Composition Services

  Debbie Stailey, Director of Composition Services

Contents at a Glance

Table of Contents

Chapter 4: Why Incentives and Markets Matter, but Money Isn't Everything 65

Part II: Understanding Choice 89

Chapter 5: Exploring the Limits to Free Choice. 91

Chapter 6: Quick and Simple Heuristics and Real-World Decision Making 107

Chapter 20: Ten Decision-Making Lessons from Behavioral Economics 333

Introduction

*B*ehavioral economics is all about making our *economic models* (the tools we use to understand and explain economic behavior) more rigorous and realistic, by building them on solid empirical foundations. It brings into the analytical mix psychological, sociological, neurological, and institutional factors. It adds breadth and depth to economic analysis. Although behavioral economics has grown in prominence over the past two decades, many conventional economists still smirk when it's mentioned. They see behavioral economics as a bunch of mumbo-jumbo, pop psychology — but nothing could be farther from the truth.

Unlike conventional economics, behavioral economics is devoted to understanding economic phenomena based on actual human behaviors. Behavioral economics doesn't assume that people must or even should behave in a way that's deemed rational by conventional economics. The fact is, more often than not, people behave in ways that *aren't* consistent with the conventional wisdom.

From the perspective of behavioral economics, people aren't expected to know everything, to calculate everything in any great detail, or to be narrowly selfish. They *are* expected, however, to be influenced by the world around them — especially by friends, family, past decisions, culture, and religion. People also are expected to be influenced by how the brain is structured: People's decisions are affected by their limited abilities to acquire and process information and, therefore, by the need to develop decision-making shortcuts (known as *heuristics*). Behavioral economics recognizes that people are not all the same. They have different tastes, wants, desires, and bargaining power, all of which can have important implications for the choices they make. It is in this unconventional world that people make decisions — and this is the world that behavioral economics is interested in understanding.

About This Book

This book introduces you to a wide array of important economic issues, in a refreshingly new light. From business cycles to asset bubbles, from savings to investments, from ethical behavior to fairness, from how choices are made to economic outcomes, from emotions to stoic calculating in decision making, from overconfidence to underconfidence, from love of money to the importance of certainty and status, behavioral economics has something important to say.

This book introduces you to the theories of behavioral economics. It fills you in on how behavioral economics differs from conventional economics, as well as where the two overlap. Economics isn't an either/or situation — plenty of what conventional economics has to say is valid and useful. Behavioral economics just adds some more tools to the economic toolkit, helping you make sense of why people make the decisions they make.

Keep in mind that this book is a reference, which means you don't need to read the chapters in order from front to back. It also means that you aren't expected to commit what you read to memory — you can return to this book again and again, to find the information you need.

Conventions Used in This Book

You don't need a degree in economics to understand this book, but knowing the few conventions I use will help you navigate to the information you need:

- ✔ When I introduce a term, I *italicize* it and define it shortly thereafter (often in parentheses).

- ✔ I place web addresses in `monofont` so that you can easily spot them. **Note:** When this book was printed, some web addresses may have needed to break across two lines of text. If that happened, rest assured that we haven't put in any extra characters (such as hyphens) to indicate the break. So, when using one of these web addresses, just type exactly what you see in this book, pretending as though the line break doesn't exist.

- ✔ I tend to use *we* and *our* to refer to economists, and *people* and *their* to refer to the population as a whole. For example, I may say, "We can use this information to study people's decisions." It's not that economists aren't people (although some non-economists may beg to differ); it's just that I want to make the writing as clear as possible.

What You're Not to Read

Technically, you don't *have* to read anything in this book — you won't be quizzed on it. But, assuming that you want to find out about behavioral economics, your understanding of the subject won't be seriously impaired if you skip the following:

✔ **Material marked by the Technical Stuff icon:** Of course, if you have the time, or if you feel really hungry for juicy technical stuff, you'll find these paragraphs interesting. (For more on this and other icons, turn to "Icons Used in This Book," later in this introduction.)

✔ **Sidebars:** These gray boxes may contain historical information, more info on particular economists, technical details, and so on. Sidebars are interesting, but they aren't essential to your understanding of the topic at hand, so if you just want to know what you *need* to know, you can skip them.

Foolish Assumptions

I don't assume very much about the readers of this book, but I do assume the following:

✔ I assume that you're interested in how real people behave in the real world and what we can learn from their behavior.

✔ I assume that you have an interest in economics and economic events, but that you're a wee bit frustrated by the tall tales often told by economists about economies and economic issues, as well as the predictions that economists make.

✔ I don't assume that you have a degree in economics, but you may be a student in an economics course or you may be thinking about taking an economics course.

✔ You may have heard about behavioral economics and wondered what all the fuss was about.

✔ You may be a businessperson, someone involved in public policy, or an investor, and you want to use the behavioral economics toolkit to make smarter decisions.

If you see yourself in any of these descriptions, this book is for you!

How This Book Is Organized

This book is divided into five parts. Here's an overview of what each part contains.

Part I: Introducing Behavioral Economics: The Science of Making Real-World Choices

In this part, I introduce some of the key concepts of behavioral economics. I also explain why realistic assumptions matter for constructing economic theories and analyses. I fill you in on the importance of psychological, sociological, institutional, and physiological factors for developing these assumptions and models. I talk about the role of the brain's architecture when it comes to model building and decision making. Finally, I cover how behavioral economics enriches the conventional economics toolbox (which focuses on relative prices and income as key determinants of the choices people make). Basic economic incentives matter, but on many important occasions, they tell only part of the story.

Part II: Understanding Choice

In this part, I examine the role and meaning of free choice in economic decision making. Conventional economics assumes that people's choices are made in a vacuum, but behavioral economics says otherwise. Here, I explain the impact that history, culture, norms, peers, gender, family, labels, and the framing of options have on people's choices. I also discuss the conditions that are necessary in order for people to make choices that reflect their true preferences (given the constraints they face). I elaborate on unconventional tools that people have developed to make decisions. I explain how these tools sometimes produce errors and biases in decisions, as well as when and why these tools produce superior results to the decision-making procedures recommended by conventional economics. Finally, I discuss the important role that emotions and intuition play in the decisions people make.

Part III: Growing the Economic Pie: The Economic Importance of Ethics, Well-Being, and Culture

This part deals with the role of a variety of economic variables in the payment of taxes and criminal behavior, but it's not only about economic rewards and punishment. I also discuss why social welfare, unions, minimum wages, and the like don't have to have the negative effects that conventional economics predicts. A lot depends on workers' preferences and how workers are treated in the labor market and inside the firm — both of which are largely ignored in conventional economics. The fact is that the work environment can have a big impact on productivity and, ultimately, on the wealth of nations.

In this part, I also discuss the role of ethics in decision making, productivity, and what's produced in the marketplace. Contrary to what conventional economics says, ethics can stimulate productivity while being consistent with firms competing in a global economy.

Finally, I explain the important role played by institutions and government policy in affecting economic behavior and economic outcomes.

Part IV: When Bubbles and Busts and Inefficiencies Are Possible: Some Behavioral Insights into the Strange World of Economic Reality

This part deals with topics that are near to the hearts of many behavioral economists and always hot in the press. Here, I delve into the reality of inefficient markets and asset bubbles and busts. I also discuss the causes and importance of these bubbles and economic inefficiencies for the economy. I explain the importance of psychological and institutional variables to the generation of business cycles, recessions, and depressions. I also fill you in on labor market behavior over the business cycle. Finally, I explain what behavioral economics has to say about happiness. Conventional economics would have you believe that happiness is simply a product of more income and wealth, but behavioral economics recognizes that factors other than wealth and money are critically important to a person's happiness.

Part V: The Part of Tens

This wouldn't be a *For Dummies* book without a Part of Tens. In this part, I discuss some of the implications of behavioral economics for public policy. I fill you in on experiments that provide insight on how and why people behave in certain ways and what this implies for economic theory and our understanding of decision making and decision-making environments. Finally, I point out some insights that behavioral economics has for consumers to help them make better decisions.

Icons Used in This Book

Icons are the little images in the margins of this book. Their purpose is to draw you to certain kinds of information. Here's what the icons mean:

The Tip icon marks anything that'll help you understand a concept more easily.

You don't have to commit this book to memory — there is no final exam at the end of this book — but when I tell you something that's important for you to remember, I flag it with the Remember icon.

When I discuss core economic concepts that are important to behavioral economics (or to the subject at hand), I mark the material with the Econ 101 icon.

Throughout this book, I illustrate key concepts with examples from the real world, and when I do, I flag those paragraphs with the Real World Example icon.

When I have a go at some more complex, technical material, I flag it with the Technical Stuff icon. If you're the sort who reads instruction manuals from cover to cover, you may find this material particularly fascinating. Otherwise, you can safely skip anything marked with a Technical Stuff icon, confident that you aren't missing anything essential to the topic at hand.

Where to Go from Here

You can start reading this book pretty much anywhere — let curiosity be your guide. Use the table of contents to pick a chapter that grabs you, or turn to the index to find subjects you've always been interested in. Chapter 1 is a good starting point, because it provides a road map for the rest of the book. Chapter 4 is particularly useful if you're interested in the connections between conventional economics and behavioral economics. For some background on the neurological underpinnings for decision making, check out Chapter 3. Chapter 2 is a good launching pad if you're interested in how economic models are built and how these analytical engines function (and sometimes fail). Wherever you start, you'll find useful information on how psychological, social, and institutional factors affect people's economic decisions.

Part I

Introducing Behavioral Economics: The Science of Making Real-World Choices

The 5th Wave By Rich Tennant

In this part . . .

Behavioral economics is about understanding how real people behave in real-world settings. In this part, I examine the role that assumptions play in developing robust economic theories and economic analyses.

I also discuss the role of the brain's architecture in this part. The decision-making process and people's choices are hugely impacted by how the brain is structured and how it evolves into adulthood.

Finally, I consider the role of incentives in motivating people's behavior. In behavioral economics, as in conventional economics, economic incentives matter — the difference is that in behavioral economics, what affects people's decision making is much more complex and nuanced.

Chapter 1

Decoding Behavioral Economics

- -

- -

*B*ehavioral economics is all about developing economic analyses for real people in the real world. It's about making economic models more robust, more accurate, and more practical. But behavioral economics, like its conventional bedfellow, is very much concerned with incentives, costs and benefits, cause and effect, and economic efficiency.

Behavioral economics enriches the conventional economics toolbox by incorporating insights from psychology, neuroscience, sociology, politics, and the law. We end up with more vibrant and revealing economic analyses based on more realistic assumptions about how individuals behave in the real world and the real-world circumstances that influence the decisions they make. In behavioral economics, people aren't calculating machines. Instead, they're decision makers driven by both passion and reason. This type of enriched economics provides us with a better understanding of individuals' economic behavior and their societies.

Making Wise Assumptions

All economists — conventional or not — make assumptions about people in order to do their economic analyses. But in conventional economics, the realism of assumptions doesn't count for much. Assumptions are supposed to be all about prediction, and building models requires economists to simplify reality. Conventional economists figure they just need to get the basics down pat — they don't need to describe in detail the apple market to build a model of the apple market.

Behavioral economists, on the other hand, believe that too many of the assumptions in conventional economics are not only simplifications of reality, but also simple-minded and often downright wrong. Behavioral economics says that these unrealistic assumptions often lead to weak and sometimes inaccurate economic analyses and are misleading guides for public policy and private practice.

Why reality matters

One of the originators of behavioral economics, Nobel Laureate Herbert Simon, argued that economic models require realistic simplifying assumptions. Realistic assumptions are necessary in order for economists to build models that help explain not only the causes of actual human behavior but also the institutional framework in which real people make decisions. We need models that not only predict well but also explain well, models that tell us something about cause and effect.

For example, if we start with the assumption that all economic outcomes are efficient (which conventional economics assumes), we'll never notice any inefficiencies, and we'll assume that people's choices are producing efficient outcomes. Our assumptions can blind us from engaging in rigorous economic analysis.

To construct rigorous and meaningful scientific models, our simplifying assumptions have to capture important, realistic elements of how people behave and the decision-making environment they're in. We have to get our psychology right in order to construct rigorous models that tell a plausible story. But behavioral economics is much more than psychology. Models also need to make assumptions that take into account norms, peer pressure, culture, religion, differences in tastes and preferences, power relationships, gender, and past behaviors. Plus, assumptions need to capture the reality of the legal and overall incentive environment, which can differ across communities and societies.

Why incentives matter — even in behavioral economics

Conventional economics focuses on the effect of economic incentives like prices and income on people's decisions.

It's true that behavioral economics is fixated on the psychological, sociological, and institutional underpinnings of modeling assumptions, but behavioral economics doesn't dismiss the importance of economic incentives.

Incentives do affect people's decisions. It's just that, often, incentives aren't enough to tell a good story about economic phenomena.

When behavioral elements are left out of standard models, choices can end up going in the opposite direction of what the standard theory predicts. For example, people sometimes do buy more when the price is high or do less work when new monetary payoffs are introduced. Economists need to enrich the traditional economics toolbox — but we can't ignore the importance of economic incentives to the decisions people make.

Making Sense of Choice

Conventional economics assumes that people are calculating, omniscient, self-interested, and focused on maximizing their wealth or income. Behavioral economics is unapologetic about expanding on this conventional decision-making toolkit.

Conventional economics offers us a model that prescribes how people should behave to get ideal results. The conventional model also tells us (or so it's assumed) how people behave, on average.

For behavioral economics, it's important that we be able to not only describe but explain how people make choices. It's also important for us to get a handle on how most people will behave, and how they make particular decisions given particular circumstances.

Maximizing versus satisficing

Almost no one maximizes, carefully calculates cost versus benefit, operates with perfect information, or carefully forecasts into the future the implications of current decisions, especially with any degree of certainty. People engage in what behavioral economists refer to as *satisficing* — they do the best they can to get the best possible results they can, given the psychological, physiological, and environmental constraints they face.

If conventional behavior is considered to be rational, then behavioral economists refer to the way in which people actually *do* behave as *boundedly rational*. Being boundedly rational often involves decision-making shortcuts, or *heuristics*. Some behavioral economists argue that using heuristics typically results in errors and biases in decision making. Others argue that heuristics often generate superior results, given that people are human, not machine-like decision makers.

The effect of emotions

Emotions play an important role in people's decision making, and behavioral economics incorporates this important fact of life into its decision theory. Emotions are assumed to be unimportant for decision making in the conventional economic model.

Some behavioral economists believe that emotions interfere with people's capacity to make smart decisions. But other behavioral economists believe that emotions and intuition can play an important positive role in the decisions people make, with emotions and intuition building on memories of past experience and understandings. Emotions and intuition have their upsides and downsides — but they're definitely part of the decision-making process (despite what conventional economics says).

The avoidance of loss

Sunk cost Phenomena

In conventional economics, people are particularly concerned with maximizing income and wealth. But behavioral economics recognizes that people aren't only willing to trade off some income to reduce the risk of making money. On average, people tend to really despise losses and even despise giving up on lost causes. And people often are willing to sacrifice some income and wealth to avoid losses, to stick with what appears to be a lost cause, to gain some certainty, and to avoid ambiguous outcomes. This all is referred to as *loss aversion*. People do what it takes to make themselves more satisfied — but however important money is to them, maximizing money and wealth given the risk involved doesn't appear to be the only thing that matters.

Most people will also gladly sacrifice some income and wealth to help others or to punish people they consider to be cheats and free riders. They get a happiness spike by being nice to good people and by punishing the "bad guys." This isn't to say that people are willing to sacrifice everything — but when you go with the conventional assumption that people are focused solely on maximizing their income and wealth, you're overlooking a key part of human behavior.

How options are framed

Conventional economics says that people aren't influenced by trivial changes in the manner in which options are framed. For example, conventional economics says that if people want to donate their organs after they die, they'll arrange for that to happen no matter what — and if they don't become organ donors, it's because they didn't really want to.

But the fact of the matter is that people are affected by how options are framed. For example, if the default option for organ donation is to *not* donate at death (in other words, if you have to make some kind of effort to become an organ donor), most people won't. If the default option is to donate (for example, if organ donation is the rule, and you have to make an effort to indicate that you *don't* want to donate), most people will donate.

Very often, opting for the default is just one less obstacle to cross when making decisions. In a world of uncertainty, defaults also signal what is the right thing to do.

However you look at the issue, framing is important. And because of its importance, how options are framed becomes very important to the choices people make and to economic outcomes that can have considerable implications for society at large, such as retirement savings.

Paternalism versus free choice

In conventional economics, people's choices are always the best choices, and we should leave well enough alone, unless people's choices are causing harm to others or where individuals don't bear the entire costs or benefits of their choices. So, crime should be regulated and so should pollution. But the fact that people don't behave as conventional economics recommends raises the issue of whether most people can make choices that are in their own best interest. Some behavioral economists recommend that governments intervene to nudge people into making choices that the experts perceive to be in people's best interest. They argue that these choices are the choices people would make if they knew better — in other words, the experts' choice is people's preferred choice.

But many behavioral economists argue that even if governments trust the individual to do the right thing, they need to arm decision makers with appropriate tools so that they'll make the best possible decisions. This means making sure that people have accurate information, the means to locate and understand the information, and the power to make decisions. If a woman has no power to decide how many kids she'll have and no information on contraception, she can't make choices that are in her best interest. Nudging is not required here. Governments only need to provide citizens with the capability to make good decisions.

The role of social context in decision making

People don't make decisions in isolation from society or, at a more micro level, in isolation from family and friends. They don't behave as if they're operating in a hermetically sealed room. They're influenced by what their friends and family think and do and by what those outside their group do. People are affected by social norms, by culture, by religion. Their decisions also can be significantly influenced by those they identify with — their level of happiness is impacted by their desire to fit in. Current decisions also often are influenced by past decisions — by friends or enemies people have made, by whether they smoked or did drugs, by whether they fell in love with learning or sports.

The fact that people are influenced by the world around them doesn't mean that economic incentives aren't of any consequence. Nor does it mean that social context precludes choice. Instead, traditional economic factors must be placed in a broader context. People's decisions are enriched by the ebb and flow of noneconomic variables. These noneconomic variables affect how and the extent to which people respond to economic variables. They make our economic models more rigorous.

Relative positioning

According to conventional economics, people's *relative position* (for example, how one person's income or status compares to another's) is not supposed to influence their choices or level of well-being, but it does. Increasing income or wealth makes most people happier. But very often, how people are doing relative to other people also has a major impact on their level of happiness.

And very often, how income is growing relative to what it was before is just as important as, if not more important than, the growth of income in absolute terms. Sometimes people are even willing to sacrifice some income or wealth to improve their relative positioning.

Also, if people's incomes are not growing but their relative position is deteriorating because others are experiencing a boost to their income, many people would prefer to block income improvements to others, just to maintain their superior relative standing. Better to be rich in a society of beggars than in a society where most people are pretty well off.

Growing the Economic Pie

The size of the economic pie is affected by nonmonetary factors, often by factors that are assumed to be bad for the economy by conventional economics (such as being fair and ethical). Some behavioral economists argue that sometimes the striving for fairness introduces rigidities into the market for good, rational reasons, which can have good or bad effects, depending on circumstance. The bottom line is that we can't properly model macro economy without introducing a constellation of nonmonetary variables into the mix.

People tend to retaliate against unfair behavior and reward fair behavior when and where possible, and this can have tremendous consequences on how productivity is determined and how different levels of productivity are sustained over time. Fairness has no such effect in conventional economics. But the advent of what are referred to as *x-efficiency theory* and *efficiency wage theory* opened the door wide open to the reality that how hard and smart people work very much depends on how fairly they're treated.

Unlike in the conventional wisdom, effort is not fixed. The economic pie often grows with some good doses of fairness and ethical behavior inside the firm. Nasty societies tend to be poorer. But being fair costs money. So, both fair and unfair societies can subsist side by side. Either way, being fair or ethical can be sustainable, even in highly competitive market economies.

Consumers often get a happiness jolt from being fair, buying ethical products, and shopping in ethical stores. Many people are even willing to pay a higher price to get what they want, creating a market for higher-priced ethical products. But more often than not, competition makes ethical output cost competitive. Ethical firms are induced into becoming more productive, allowing them to cut costs and reduce prices.

Deciphering Bubbles and Busts

Behavioral economics and a related field, behavioral finance, have lots to say about economic efficiency and economic bubbles. Markets can be seriously inefficient, causing opportunities for gain for some and opening the floodgates to humongous economic losses on both individual and social scales. Conventional economics insists that markets are efficient. But simply assuming away market inefficiencies results in weak and misleading analyses and dangerous public policy recommendations.

Inefficient markets and investment behavior

Financial markets are said to be *efficient* if asset prices reflect the fundamental or intrinsic values of the real assets that they represent. In conventional economics, this is what asset prices are supposed to do. But they don't in the real world, where history is overflowing with examples of asset price and commodity price *bubbles,* in which these prices deviate enormously from their fundamental levels.

Behavioral economics has documented and analyzed these realities. Sometimes bubbles are a product of rumor, escalated by investors following the crowd. Then there is the inevitable crash. And, yes in the long run, asset prices and commodity prices converge to their fundamental values. But behavioral economics, by recognizing the reality of inefficient markets, is building the capacity to understand them and to discern whether limiting the extent of bubbles and crashes is possible. And these crashes can potentially drive otherwise healthy economies into serious economic crisis, unless saved by the visible hand of government.

Emotions, intuition, animal spirits, and business cycles

Cycles in the real economy are part and parcel of healthy capitalist production. But the extent of deep and severe economic recessions or depressions or the great heights of economic prosperity can't be explained by economic variables alone.

Behavioral economists have introduced *animal spirits* (people's expectations of what may happen in the future) to help explain business cycles. In this way, emotions, intuition, and social context are introduced into the modeling of business cycles. Traditional emphasis on consumer, firm, and government spending, saving, and investment behavior; interest rates; and exchange rates remain important. But the states of mind of the consumer, investor, and politician also are critically important to explain movements in total output and unemployment. If most people believe that the economy is going to hell in a handbasket, then dropping interest rates to zero won't have much effect. And if workers are depressed, both current and future productivity can drop significantly.

Understanding Happiness: Money Isn't Everything

The more money people have, the happier they should be. Money buys happiness, according to the conventional wisdom. But this easy linkage between money and happiness, which still serves to inform economic theory and public policy, is not unequivocally supported by the facts. To the contrary, a multitude of research has examined in great detail the relationship between income and happiness, as well as the noneconomic determinants of happiness or life satisfaction. What's clear is that increasing income is of *some* importance to happiness, especially in low-income economies and especially among the poor in all countries. But there are also some very real diminishing returns — more income per person produces smaller and smaller gains in happiness. Also, what people do with their money, how government spends their money, and the extent of people's political freedom all have great effects on people's level of happiness.

Two countries with the same level of per-capita income, but with different systems of education, healthcare, levels of trust, security, and governance, will end up with different levels of happiness. For example, people in the United States are, on average, less happy than people in less wealthy economies, such as Canada. This doesn't mean that reducing per-capita income in the United States won't dramatically reduce the level of happiness of Americans. But the evidence suggests that if the Americans spent their money differently, especially in the public sector, they might very well be happier than they are today, especially the American middle class and the American poor.

Chapter 2

Getting Real about Assumptions

. . . .

In This Chapter

▶ Understanding economic models

▶ Unveiling how traditional economists regard assumptions

▶ Introducing reality to economic analysis

▶ Uncovering the meaning of rationality

▶ Knowing why assumptions matter for economic inquiry

. . . .

*B*ehavioral economics differs from conventional approaches to economics in one key way: In behavioral economics, the realism of assumptions matters big time. Behavioral economists pay special attention to how realistic their psychological, sociological, and institutional assumptions are. Many contemporary behavioral economists pay particular attention to the psychological assumptions introduced into economic models and how these assumptions help explain economic behavior.

In behavioral economics, realistic assumptions are critical in building economic models that help us analyze the world. Such assumptions also allow us to better understand how people behave when making decisions — which types of decisions result in poor or superior economic performance, for example.

In conventional economics, on the other hand, the realism of assumptions doesn't matter. What matter most to a conventional economist are the predictions produced by the model, no matter how far-fetched the psychological, sociological, or institutional assumptions may be.

In this chapter, I explain why realistic assumptions are important for economic analysis. I also discuss why individuals typically don't behave the way conventional economics assumes they do, and why this is significant for economic analysis and public policy.

Defining an Economic Model

An *economic model* is a simplification of the economic world that is designed to help us better understand and explain various aspects of the economy. It's supposed to be bare bones, focusing on the basics. Economic models are built upon *simplifying assumptions* about the real world. For this reason, a model is not supposed to describe or explain all aspects of economic or social life. When an economic model helps explain the price of iPods, for example, there is no need to describe, even in simplified form, the market for apples or the market for light bulbs. These two other markets aren't important to understand the market for iPods. You describe only what's important to the problem at hand.

Also, an economic model is supposed to be logically consistent. A model can't assume that increasing demand always makes prices rise *and* always makes prices fall. A model can't claim that narrowly selfish behavior increases a nation's wealth *and* decreases a nation's wealth. Two claims that can't be true at the same time are logically inconsistent. But you *can* assume that, in a logically consistent fashion, selfish behavior increases a nation's wealth under *some* circumstances and reduces a nation's wealth under *other* circumstances.

Overall, a model should be built in a logically consistent fashion. This is something that both behavioral and conventional economists agree on. Also, models aren't written in stone and are supposed to be tested against the facts on the ground and modified and even tossed into the trash if they fail to provide us with reasonable explanations. Too often, this important last step is not taken in conventional economics and is a source of much criticism from behavioral economists.

Behavioral economists are not opposed to model building, simplifying assumptions, or even logical consistency. But behavioral economists often challenge how conventional economic models are built. Too often, conventional models don't lay solid foundations for rigorous economic analysis.

In this section, I discuss how conventional economic models are built. I contrast this with how behavioral economists construct economic models. For behavioral economics, the realism of assumptions is critically important if we want to better understand how the economy functions and what causes what in the economy.

Explaining economic phenomena

Few economists would disagree that economics is about explaining and understanding economic events. Why don't people save enough for retirement? Why do some people smoke and others don't? Why are some countries rich and others poor? Why do people hold on to poor investments? Why do people purchase financial assets at a price that is way above the economic value of the corporations that issue them?

However, today, many economists focus on building economic theories that are mathematically elegant and logically consistent but that have little connection to the real world. They often make the argument that real-world applications are there to be had if we look hard enough. The problem is that little attention, if any, is paid to the real-world connection, and the focus of research is the mathematical building blocks of the research. Also, the behavioral assumptions underlying the theory are hardly ever discussed in any detail. Assumptions are made that others have made before. Often, tradition is more important than realism. What counts for these economists is whether the model is logically consistent with these assumptions, not whether the assumptions have any connection to the real world.

In behavioral economics, the focus of the theory — however mathematically oriented it may be — is to explain and understand economic events. Behavioral economists pay special attention to how the theories underlying psychological, sociological, and institutional assumptions help us to better understand the economy and the behavior of individuals who form the basis for economic outcomes. The assumptions we make are thought to be key to shedding light on the choices people make and their consequences for individual and social well-being.

Making simplifying assumptions

Economic models can't be completely descriptive or completely realistic. The whole point of building models is to abstract from reality, focusing on factors that are most relevant and crucial to analyzing the question at hand.

For example, if you were interested in analyzing the market for the BlackBerry or the iPhone, constructing a model that includes a discussion of the market for apples and oranges would be a waste of time (and even confusing). However, you *would* want to elaborate upon the market for cellphones. You would want to make assumptions about why people buy and sell cellphones and what motivates them to purchase smartphones like the BlackBerry and the iPhone.

In both conventional and behavioral economics, there is no debate that sim-plifying assumptions is a lynchpin of model building, good theory, and rigor-ous economic analysis. In other words, you can't and don't have to describe everything — just the basics. But in the conventional economics approach, the litmus test for a good model is whether it produces good predictions.

These predictions are not crystal-ball-type predictions. As economist Deirdre McCloskey has pointed out, if economists could predict the future, they would all be rich. Sadly, for most economists, this is not the case. Economists are even worse than meteorologists at predicting future events — and they don't dress any better either.

The type of predictions that economists make help explain economic events that have already occurred. Good theories are able to "predict" the price of oil yesterday using a particular model. Economists then use this model to help us understand when and whether it's most likely that the price of oil will increase sometime in the future and some of the likely effects this may have on the economy.

Discovering the irrelevance of facts

Most conventional economists argue that if the predictions work, it makes no difference what assumptions you make about human behavior or institutions. In fact, replacing realistic assumptions with unrealistic assumptions that generate better predictions is just fine from a conventional perspective. The realism — or even the abstract realism — of your assumptions is of no conse-quence to the quality of the economic analysis.

Milton Friedman of the University of Chicago pioneered this approach to economic modeling in the early 1950s. Friedman was awarded a Nobel Prize for his research in monetary economics. Friedman went so far as to argue that efforts to build models using relatively realistic simplifying assump-tions are "fundamentally wrong." He maintained that our assumptions can be wildly unrealistic and still be the right stuff for economic models. Friedman provided a now classic example of what he meant by unrealistic assump-tions, using the analogy of expert billiard players. He argued that we can predict perfect shots by assuming that the expert player behaves as if he or she knows and applies the mathematical formulas consistent with producing perfect shots. Friedman admits that this assumption is wildly unrealistic (it doesn't even represent a simplification of reality), but it predicts the perfect shots very well. Therefore, assuming that billiard players are expert math-ematicians makes for good theory.

As with Friedman's billiard-player model, conventional economics pays little attention to how the expert billiard player *became* an expert and a champion. In fact, a training program for billiard players concentrating on math and engineering courses would not produce expert billiard players.

However, following from the conventional approach, if a country would like to produce champion billiard players, it should select possible champs on the basis of math proficiency. Sounds weird, but many economists I've talked to believe that this would be a good idea. This approach is partly a product of the belief of many economists that logic (especially in its more mathematical form) is the be all and end all of economics.

However, champion billiard players are a product of a good eye, the ability to focus, and a lot of practice. Modeling expert billiard players more realistically would generate great predictions of the perfect shot — as good as Friedman's wildly unrealistic assumptions. But the more realistic behavioral assumptions provide a superior, more truthful *explanation* of events.

Behavioral economics makes the point that economics is not only about prediction, but also about explaining economic events. Often, the two are closely related.

Understanding the role of math in model building

Economics has become increasingly math oriented over the past few decades, and many behavioral economists have a strong focus on math when presenting their arguments. But what clearly distinguishes behavioral economics from the rest is that most behavioral economists at least attempt to draw their assumptions from reality.

Math is a language that helps build precise and logical models. (These models can be done in plain English, too, but the math helps.) Using math doesn't tell us if an economic model is based in fantasy or reality, though. You can determine the answer to that question only by checking out the assumptions. **Remember:** Math-based models can be just as fantasy-based as non-math-based models.

Many contemporary economic models are more concerned with the logic or core math fundamentals than with anything else. Such models often introduce or change assumptions with little concern for the realism of the assumptions. What counts is the logic of the argument. In this case, building a model on completely unrealistic behavioral assumptions is fair game. The problems posed don't need to have any real-world application.

The economist may try to prove mathematically why firms are efficient under certain conditions that are completely unreasonable. There may then be debate on whether another set of unrealistic assumptions makes more sense or whether there is a mathematical error in the model. What matters here is that the math is technically correct. Reality is of secondary or even tertiary significance. Economist Deirdre McCloskey refers to this as *blackboard economics;* this is the economics of logical deduction and mathematical proof.

For behavioral economics, the math is of secondary importance. Math is simply one tool in the behavioral economist's toolbox. What counts most of all is whether our assumptions and the models built upon the foundations of those assumptions help us to better explain economic events.

An elegant math-economics model that tells us little about economic reality is of little use in behavioral economics. It can't tell us much about why some countries develop and others don't, why some people smoke and others don't, why some people save and others don't, why some families are large and others are small, why some banking regulations work and others may contribute to economic crisis, and why some people buy products simply because the rich and famous do.

For example, the standard conventional economic take on minimum wage is that it must produce more unemployment because it increases the cost of labor for a firm. But as Nobel Laureate George Stigler of the University of Chicago, writing decades ago, pointed out, this bad economic consequence can be expected to take place because we make a very specific simplifying assumption about what happens behaviorally inside the firm. We assume that minimum wages can't and don't positively affect workers' and managers' incentive to work harder and smarter. If they did, minimum wages wouldn't necessarily have negative effects on the economy. Research in recent years suggests that minimum wages often have the positive effect on efficiency that conventional economics assumes can't occur. For this reason, the starkly negative picture that conventional economics paints of minimum wages has to be taken with at least a few grains of salt.

In a related example, conventional economics tends to assume that all folks working in the firm are doing the best they can (or at least that they can't do any better). Following from this assumption, conventional economics argues that economic efficiency is a given. If there are problems with firm performance, it can't be located in the realm of inefficiency. This potential source of problems is simply assumed away. One door is closed, by assumption, to further economic investigation.

Herbert Simon and the importance of realistic assumptions

In stark contrast to Milton Friedman (see "Discovering the irrelevance of facts," earlier) Herbert Simon championed the perspective that the predictions of economic models are highly sensitive to our assumptions about decision making. Better assumptions tend to yield better predictions. And, Simon argued, the simplifying assumptions of behavioral theories "constitute a direct refutation of the argument that the unrealism of the assumptions of the classical theory is harmless." Simon was awarded a Nobel Prize in 1978 for his pioneering contribution to the then nascent field of behavioral economics.

Simon found that, too often, the predictions of conventional theory are assumed to be correct because the simplifying assumptions are presumed to be correct. He also argued that because conventional economics tends to pay scant attention to the realism of simplifying assumptions, it tends to ignore the fact that good assumptions can generate predictions that are as accurate as bad assumptions. But good assumptions make for good analysis. Unrealistic assumptions make for mediocre and misleading analyses.

Another example: For decades, Bernard Madoff ran the largest Ponzi scheme in history, with a multitude of international connections. The success of Madoff's Ponzi scheme was based in part on the assumption that conventional economics makes about financial markets — mainly, that the markets should self-regulate. One assumption is that big fish like Madoff would be so afraid of losing their reputation that they wouldn't engage in fraudulent activities. But Madoff did, and his investors lost billions of dollars in the process. Obviously, Madoff's behavior wasn't driven by a fear of losing his reputation. And you can bet he's not alone.

Because regulators assumed that leading investors and their employees would behave in a particular way, a relatively lax regulatory environment was introduced. Had more realistic behavioral assumptions been driving the regulatory predictions of investor behavior, a different regulatory environment may have been constructed.

A Ponzi scheme promises high legitimate returns on investment. But it actually provides such returns by making payments out of the capital provided by new and existing clients. As long as there is enough new capital flowing into the Ponzi scheme and there are no excess calls on current investments, the Ponzi scheme is sustainable. The Ponzi scheme investors typically reap significant economic returns, with no clue that the fund has no economic foundation. When the bubble bursts, fortunes can be lost and individual investors can be utterly destroyed, their lifelong savings vaporized.

Considering cause and effect

Two factors or variables are positively correlated with each other if high values in one variable are related with the high values in another. There is a negative correlation if low values in one variable are related to high values in another. Correlation is statistically measured by a correlation coefficient that is between 0 and +1.0 or −1.0. A correlation coefficient of 0.90 tells us that two variables are positively and highly correlated. The price of oil is normally *negatively* and highly correlated with the demand for oil — as the price of oil goes up, the demand for oil goes down.

Very often, cause and effect is confused with a positive relationship between factors. Two factors may be positively related without one of these factors causing the other. For example, unemployment insurance payouts tend to go up when the unemployment rate increases. There is a strong correlation or statistically strong relationship between these factors or variables. But this doesn't mean that unemployment insurance *causes* unemployment.

You can have a strong correlation between two variables without there being any cause-and-effect story in the background. The fact is that, as the unemployment rate increases, more people draw on unemployment benefits. An increasing unemployment rate results in greater unemployment benefit payouts.

To get to the roots of causation, you have to understand how different variables may connect to each other. Don't confuse correlation with causation.

Watching out for spurious correlations

When economists don't pay much attention to the validity of the assumptions they make in building their models, they can easily fall victim to *spurious* (false) correlations. Spurious correlations are only statistical in nature, and there is no causal connection between the variables.

You may have a very high positive correlation between the amount of rainfall in Manhattan and the number of garments manufactured there, or between the amount of rainfall at Wall Street and the movements in the Dow Jones Industrial Average. But these are probably spurious correlations. To appreciate that these correlations are spurious, you must have a solid grasp on the realities that underlie garment manufacturing and the New York Stock Exchange.

High correlations are often spurious — they're only *suggestive* of causation. Getting your assumptions right helps you distinguish between spurious correlations and actual causation.

Contemplating Conventional Economic Assumptions and Real-World Alternatives

The basic model of the conventional economics actor, commonly referred to as *Homo economicus,* is characterized by a number of very strong behavioral assumptions. These assumptions form the basis for key economic predictions. They also underlie many conventional economists' explanations of events and serve as an important tool to distinguish between correlation and causation. But these simplifying assumptions have been critiqued quite severely by behavioral economists as being highly unrealistic.

Conventional assumption #1: People's preferences are stable and consistent

Among the key assumptions that conventional economists make is that people's preferences are stable and won't change or flip. If you prefer an orange to an apple, you won't suddenly prefer an apple to an orange. Also, conventional economists assume that people's preferences are consistent. If you prefer an orange to a pear and you prefer a pear to an apple, you'll prefer an orange to an apple.

Behavioral economists argue that there is strong evidence suggesting that preferences are *not* always stable and consistent. A classic example of this from behavioral economics is that many people prefer not to save for retirement when they're young, but later in life many of these same people regret their decision because their preferences flip toward increasing savings. By the time they decide that saving is important, it's too late to do very much about it.

The fact that preferences can change in this fashion means that economists need to allow for this type of behavior when constructing models and try to understand why such behavior occurs. Doing so will produce higher-quality economic analysis. When it comes to savings, allowing for the fact that preferences aren't always stable or consistent helps economists better understand why and when many people don't save adequately for retirement, even though they have the resources to do so.

Conventional assumption #2: People are solitary decision makers

Conventional economists also assume that our preferences are not influenced by other people (including relatives and friends), social norms, or the media. In other words, economists assume that people make decisions as if they were making them in a bubble. They don't even expect your past decisions and the past decisions of others to influence your current decisions.

Behavioral economists have long argued that these simplifying assumptions are the wrong ones to make about decision making. People typically make decisions in a social, historical, and institutional context, and this context affects their decisions. Change the context, and you may very well change people's decisions.

When we recognize that people don't make many of their decisions as if they were living in a bubble, we need to start thinking about how norms affect people's preferences and choices.

Norms or, more specifically, *social norms* are defined differently by different people. But one useful definition is that social norms represent a standard for what is good, normal behavior. When people do good things, they feel good about themselves; when they do bad things, they feel bad about themselves. Social norms affect people's behavior independent of prices and incomes because of how they affect people's spiritual well-being and level of happiness. In a society where the social norm is volunteering, more people will volunteer. If the social norm is to tip for service, more people will tip. If the social norm is to treat minorities badly, more people will do so.

For behavioral economics, social norms represent an important additional determinant of people's preferences and choices. They're another important building block for rigorous economic theory.

Conventional assumption #3: How people form preferences doesn't matter

Not only does conventional economics all too often make incorrect simplifying assumptions about preferences, but it also argues that how people end up with these preferences is not important. What *is* important is that these assumptions produce top-notch predictions. Behavioral economics would add, with some forcefulness, that explanation is what's critically important. Prediction without explanation is not very useful.

But understanding how people's preferences have evolved to be what they are helps economists to understand what determines those preferences (and changes in preferences). This information also can help economists appreciate why, very often, preferences differ from one individual to the next, and why preferences can change. Your preferences may initially differ from those of your spouse or partner, and that may affect your choices. But over time, both your preferences and your spouse or partner's preferences may change, and that, too, may affect your choices.

Conventional assumption #4: People have the same preferences

Conventional economists tend to assume that individuals have the same preferences — we're all assumed to be pretty much the same. This idea is referred to as the *representative agent model,* and it's yet another simplifying assumption that's supposed to work well in predicting economic behavior.

Nobel Laureate Gary Becker of the University of Chicago, one of the key movers and shakers of conventional economics, now argues that this type of simplifying assumption often fails to provide a sound basis for rigorous economic models. Behavioral economists would agree with Becker's argument. In behavioral economics, whether you assume identical preferences depends on the issue you're trying to model and understand. Often, this requires the assumption that preferences may be not only different but also conflicting.

The black box of the household

One area where it's assumed that preferences are the same is in the household. Conventional economics assumes that all members of a household are identical and that one person's preferences (typically, the husband's) has preferences that represent the preferences of everybody else in the household (the wife and children, for example).

Of course, this assumption ignores potentially serious conflicts in preferences and the very real possibility that actual choices made by the household represent the wants and desires of only one person within the household. It also sidesteps the issue of how households make decisions. Explaining economic decisions in a household where women have few rights is quite different from explaining economic decisions in a household where men and women are equal before the law and in the culture and custom of society. In a rights-based society, economic decisions can be quite different than they are in a society where men's rights trump women's.

The black box of the firm

A key focus of conventional economics is that firms maximize both profits and productivity. How a firm achieves this dual goal is often beside the point. The underlying assumption is maximization. The simplifying assumption is that the firm acts as one (the *representative agent*) to maximize profits and productivity.

Conventional economics recognizes that conflict can exist within the firm and that conflict requires resolution. This internal conflict is referred to as the *principal-agent problem.* The agent is delegated to act on behalf of the principal. The agent could be the worker or the CEO. The principal could be the manager, the board of directors, or the shareholders. But the agent may not naturally do what the principal wants. Part of the conventional economic perspective looks at what should be done to get the agent to maximize profits or productivity on behalf of the principal.

Behavioral economics raises the issue of when, what, and where firms maximize. It doesn't assume that maximization is what firms (workers, managers, and owners) naturally do or want to do. Behavioral economics also raises questions of what individuals do inside the firm to achieve their objectives. One important related question is why firms don't maximize productivity.

When a firm doesn't maximize its profits and productivity, it's very often related to the fact that conflict exists within the firm and that managers and owners are more interested in their own material and spiritual well-being than in the immediate interests of the firm. As long as the firm's costs and profits are good enough to keep the firm in business and shareholders satisfied, that's all that matters.

Conventional assumption #5: People are all maximizers

Conventional economics assumes that people are all maximizers — in fact, this statement is something of a mantra to the conventional economist. But this assumption is meaningless unless some substance is added to it. There are two critical focal points of the maximization assumption:

- ✔ **People set out to maximize — and actually succeed in maximizing — their individual level of material well-being.** A key ingredient to maximizing the size of the economic pie is the assumption that people attempt to maximize their well-being, but this isn't all: They're supposed to focus on their material well-being. All people should be wealth maximizers if they want to maximize their well-being and level of happiness.

People aren't expected to turn down options that will increase their wealth or income. Moreover, conventional economics assumes that only wealth maximizers are rational.

Based on an abundance of evidence, behavioral economics challenges the assumption that people are only wealth maximizers and that those who *don't* maximize wealth are somehow irrational.

✔ **Firms maximize their profits and minimize their costs through the decisions and resulting action of owners, managers, and workers.** Another key ingredient to maximizing the size of the economic pie is the assumption that firms maximize returns and thereby maximize productivity and minimize costs. According to conventional economics, firms have no choice but to behave in this fashion, especially if markets are competitive. If this is your working assumption, then firm performance is not an important topic of conversation. There is no need to discuss what's happening inside the firm when you assume that firms are maximizing profits and minimizing costs from the get-go.

But this assumption also has been challenged by behavioral economists. The evidence suggests that this type of maximization is not typical. Even with a lot of competition, many firms aren't doing their best to maximize productivity — yet they still survive. Behavioral economics maintains that this type of common non-maximizing behavior is important, and assuming it away does considerable harm to economic analysis.

Behavioral economics argues for more realistic simplifying behavioral assumptions that produce better predictions and explanations of economic phenomena.

Herbert Simon argues that people simply don't have the capacity to maximize, so they do the best they can given the neurological, psychological, and environmental constraints they face. Simon refers to this as *satisficing behavior.* In a sense, people *are* maximizing, but not in the fashion assumed by conventional economics. Other behavioral economists argue that satisficing behavior often produces better results than maximizing behavior.

Simon argues that the world is awash with non-maximizing behavior, at least in the sense meant by conventional economists. He argues:

> In the biological world at least, many organisms survive that are not maximizers but that operate at far less than the highest achievable efficiency. Their survival is not threatened as long as no other organisms have evolved that can challenge the possession of their specific niches. Analogously, since there is no reason to suppose that every business firm is challenged by an optimally efficient competitor, survival only requires meeting the competition. In a system in which there are innumerable rents, of long-term and short-term duration, even egregious sub-optimality may permit survival.

Vernon Smith, the founder of modern experimental economics, goes so far as to argue:

> In fact it is shown that firms that maximize profits are the least likely to be the market survivors. My point is simple: When experimental results are contrary to standard concepts of rationality [such as maximization], assume not just that people are irrational, but that you may not have the right model of rational behavior. *Listen to what your subjects may be trying to tell you.* Think of it this way: If you could choose your ancestors, would you want them to be survivalists or to be expected wealth maximizers?

In other words, many conventional assumptions not only offer a poor description of behavior, but also provide bad advice on best-practice economic behavior.

Conventional assumption #6: People have perfect knowledge

Another key assumption of conventional economics is that people have perfect knowledge of the following when making decisions:

- **Alternative opportunities that are relevant to the decisions they make:** This kind of knowledge is sometimes referred to as *unbounded knowledge*. Conventional economics assumes that when you make a decision, the decision incorporates all relevant data that's out there in the information universe. People simply don't have the time and resources to obtain this type of information, so they make satisficing decisions based on more limited information.

- **How their decisions will affect the future:** Conventional economics assumes that people are able to forecast into the future the consequences of their actions. And it's assumed this is the case even if the future is highly uncertain. Once again, behavioral economics points out that people don't have the time, resources, or ability to forecast into the future. They can make only educated guesses, based on imperfect information, knowing and sometimes not knowing or appreciating that their guesses assume that future circumstances typically change in unpredictable ways.

- **How they'll think and feel in the future:** Conventional economics assumes that people's opinions don't change as they get older. In other words, when you make a decision today about investing in your education, not only do you know the consequences of your decision, but in the future, your opinion about your past decision will be no different from when you made it. Conventional economics assumes that your preferences remain unchanged.

As you probably know from experience, who you are today is often quite different from who you used to be. And your present self has no way of knowing (with any degree of certainty) who your future self will be and what your wants and desires will be down the road. How many hippies and anti-materialists from the 1960s became the exact opposite in adulthood? Who would've seen that coming? Certainly not the young people milling around the Haight-Ashbury singing folk songs 50 years ago.

Conventional assumption #7: People have unbounded computational capabilities

Intimately related with the assumption of unbounded knowledge (see the preceding section) is the assumption that people have unbounded computational capabilities. Conventional economics tends to assume that people are able to do a multiplicity of computations to arrive at decisions that meet their needs in the best way possible.

In the real world, not only do people lack the brain capacity to process information in this manner, but most people don't have the knowledge to do such calculations even with help from calculators or computers.

Behavioral economists, on the other hand, argue that you can predict and explain decision making better if you don't assume that people are endowed with unbounded computational capabilities. And this assumption is fact based: Realism works better than fantasy in the realm of assumptions.

Herbert Simon introduces the term *bounded rationality* to define smart behavior that works within the neurological, psychological, and institutional bounds of the human condition. We find ways to make decisions given the real-world constraints we face. Assuming unbounded computational capabilities is misleading with respect to explaining decision making and even predicting the outcomes of people's boundedly rational choices.

Behavioral economics finds that most people use experienced-based *heuristics* (decision-making shortcuts) to make their decisions (because they can't practice the unbounded computational behavior assumed in conventional economics). These heuristics provide, in many environments or circumstances, a sounder foundation for economic analysis than the assumption of unbounded rationality. People actually don't have to do all the computations that conventional economics prescribes in order to make good or even great decisions. (For more on heuristics, turn to Chapter 6.)

Milton Friedman returns: The unbounded computational manager

Conventional economics assumes that, to survive in the marketplace, managers must be doing their best to maximize the returns to their firms. Some economists assume that managers will do their best (regardless of the state of the market) and that incentives will be built into the firm's employment environment for managers to do so. Given these assumptions, Milton Friedman provides a classic example of unbounded computational capabilities. Friedman maintains that:

> . . . firms behave as if they were seeking rationally to maximize their expected returns . . . and had full knowledge of the data needed to succeed in this attempt; as if, that is, they knew the relevant cost and demand functions, calculated marginal cost

and marginal revenue from all actions open to them, and pushed each line of action to the point at which the relevant marginal cost and marginal revenue were equal.

Now, Friedman does admit that real business-people don't actually behave in this way. They don't "literally solve the system of simultaneous equations." However, Friedman argues that these false assumptions generate predictions that are consistent with a firm maximizing its returns.

Friedman and many conventional economists pay no attention to whether more realistic behavioral assumptions generate the same or better predictions. They ignore whether certain behavior causes certain outcomes. All they care about is prediction.

Conventional assumption #8: People have willpower

Conventional economics assumes that people have the willpower to make the choices that they really want to make. If you overeat, smoke cigarettes, drink, or do drugs, conventional economics argues that these choices all represent your true wants and desires, your true preferences.

You do drugs or buy designer watches or eat junk food because that's what you really want do given prices and your income. You may want a $2 million yacht, but that's just not going to happen given your salary as a waitress. But you did buy those cigarettes, which reveals your preference for cigarettes given the price of cigarettes and your income.

Behavioral economists, among others, ask whether people have the willpower to choose what they most prefer. If you're lacking in willpower, you aren't making choices that reflect your true preferences and you'll end up making choices that don't enhance you happiness or well-being.

If you want to lose weight, but you buy that great-smelling hot dog sold by a street vendor, this may suggest that you aren't revealing your true preference when purchasing the hot dog. If you smoke, even though you say you want to quit, this choice also may suggest a weakness of willpower. How about buying an expensive watch even though you're trying to save money? Some people would say that this also represents a weakness of will. The same is true if you've become addicted to drugs or gambling — you *want* to break free, but you just can't. Some behavioral economists argue that, in many cases, these addictions also represent a weakness of will. And with true addiction, your willpower can be completely obliterated; you're dependent on that extra cigarette, shot of alcohol, or hit of crack.

These possibilities are, at the very least, food for thought when making assumptions about whether people's choices represent their true preferences. Sometimes people's words don't reflect their true preferences — they say they don't want a Big Mac, but they really do. In other cases, people may require and want help to restrain themselves from buying products that they have trouble resisting.

Conventional assumption #9: People are capable of acting upon their preferences

A key assumption of conventional economics is that people have the ability to act upon their preferences — assuming that the price is right and they have the income to do so. This is yet another example of conventional economics assuming that people's choices reveal their true wants and desires.

However, as Nobel Laureate Amartya Sen and philosopher Martha Nussbaum point out, many individuals don't have the power or the knowledge to make choices that reflect their true preferences. A great example of this is women in oppressive circumstances who don't have a say on the number of children they bear or the types of goods and services that are purchased for the household.

If economists assume, without some investigation, that all people have the capacity to make choices that they actually want to make, we're ignoring the very real possibility that many choices *don't* reflect people's true wants and desires. It's important that economists understand whether the conditions are present for people to make the choices that they actually prefer.

Thinking about institutions

Conventional economics has paid little attention to *institutions* (the type of governance, laws, rules, and regulations that hold sway in a country). But institutions play an important role in much of behavioral economics. Conventional economics can easily dismiss the importance of understanding the rules of the game because it incorrectly assumes that the appropriate institutions are in place from the get-go or they'll come into play quickly. But we can't build rigorous models making this type of assumption. All too often, the right institutions simply aren't in place.

Because institutions affect incentives, they're very important to decision making. For this reason, determining the type of institutions that are in place is key when building economic models.

The right institutions may very well not be in place to allow people to act on their wants and desires or to contribute to growing and improving the state of their economies. Poor institutions can help explain poor economic and social outcomes.

Nobel Laureate Douglass North has long argued that a serious flaw in conventional economics is that it assumes "not only that institutions are designed to achieve efficient outcomes, but that they can be ignored in economic analysis because they play no independent role in economic performance." But the world doesn't have to be what conventional economics assumes it to be.

If you were an investor in a country where your property may be easily confiscated by the state, would you invest? If you were a woman whose life may be in danger if you revealed your preferences to your spouse, would you speak your mind? If you were rich and you could easily maintain your wealth and increase it by exploiting your political connections, would you invest in plants and equipment or take the easy way out? The latter is known as rent-seeking behavior.

These types of institutions wouldn't encourage most people to flourish as human beings or economies to prosper. Institutions matter in behavioral economics and can be ignored only at our peril.

Understanding Rational Economic Behavior

Conventional economics defines an individual who is engaging in rational behavior as a *maximizer*. A maximizer

- ✔ Is materially selfish, maximizing his or her own material wealth
- ✔ Focuses very much on himself or herself when making decisions
- ✔ Maximizes profits and productivity
- ✔ Is a prodigious and careful calculator

✔ Is forward looking

✔ Has stable and consistent wants and desires or preferences

✔ Has willpower

A more focused definition of rational behavior is provided by Gary Becker of the University of Chicago. According to Becker, rational individuals "make forward-looking, maximizing, and consistent choices." For Becker, you can be doing virtually anything and be regarded as perfectly rational, as long as you're maximizing something.

Behavioral economists have invested a lot of time and energy to uncover whether people actually behave as conventional economics expects them to behave and, if so, how much. The evidence suggests that people aren't conventional economics creatures. All too often, their behaviors are quite different from what conventional economics predicts.

Behavioral economics argues that these real-world behaviors need to be incorporated into the building of economic models. A big question is whether unconventional behaviors are smart or rational. Are people's choices laden with errors and biases, irrational, not so smart, and even dangerous to their health and welfare?

You can do no wrong: Errors and biases in decision making

Much of conventional economics assumes that people don't make mistakes in their decision making — or, at least, that economists can model people's behavior as if errors in decision-making don't take place. In other words, conventional economists assume that people typically behave in a fashion consistent with the behavioral and institutional assumptions of conventional wisdom.

Behavioral economists have found an abundance of evidence that suggests that most people, most of the time, behave in a fashion that falls far from the benchmark for correct behavior set by conventional economics. Most people use heuristics to make decisions. This is just a fact of life.

Behavioral economists of all stripes agree that the fact that people don't behave based on the behavioral norms of conventional economics should be incorporated in the building of economic models.

A big question for behavioral economics is whether such deviant behavior is error or bias prone, or actually smart or rational behavior. Here are the two schools of thought:

- **Those who believe that deviant behavior is actually smart and rational:** Some behavioral economists believe that smart people can make mistakes given the constraints they face. And in many other circumstances, heuristic-based behavior actually can be the best practice. Instead of representing biased behavior, heuristics actually improve upon the decision-making process.

  From this point of view, rationality is seen differently: Rational behavior is considered to be smart behavior that evolves over time. This type of behavior often isn't what's recommended by conventional economics. Rational and smart behavior is defined relative to the various constraints that people face as humans — neurological, psychological, and environmental — such as gaps in information and uncertainty about the future. Gerd Gigerenzer, Nobel Laureate Vernon Smith, and Herbert Simon all advocate this understanding of rational economic behavior. Psychologist Gerd Gigerenzer refers to this approach as *fast and frugal heuristics.*

- **Those who believe that deviant behavior is prone to error and bias:** For other behavioral economists, deviant behavior is substandard and may very well be wired in the brain. For these economists, human behavior, because it is deviant, is typically error prone and biased. It may even be irrational.

  This errors-and-biases approach to behavioral economics was pioneered by psychologist and Nobel Laureate Daniel Kahneman and psychologist Amos Tversky. It has become the public face of contemporary behavioral economics. However, the fast and frugal perspective carries considerable weight as well.

Both camps agree that behavioral and institutional assumptions matter big time and that conventional economics gets it wrong, also big time.

Selfishness and the smart society

One important assumption of conventional economics is that people are material maximizers. From this perspective, people are assumed to behave selfishly. But just as important, selfish behavior is often assumed to be smart and rational. In other words, one important component of being smart is maximizing your wealth.

A long-held argument in conventional economics, following Adam Smith and *The Wealth of Nations,* says that selfish behavior can result in improving not only the wealth of nations but also the well-being of individuals. Selfish motives driving the individual can have unintended positive consequences for society at large. People don't have to be saints in order for economies to flourish.

This is what Adam Smith wrote in *The Wealth of Nations* about selfish behavior:

> It is not from the benevolence of the butcher, the brewer, or the baker, that we expect our dinner, but from their regard to their own interest. We address ourselves, not to their humanity but to their self-love, and never talk to them of our necessities but of their advantages.

But Smith never considered selfish behavior as something to be celebrated, nor did he suggest that those of us who do good and make material sacrifices to benefit others are somehow not intelligent or rational.

In a lesser-known book, *The Theory of Moral Sentiments,* Adam Smith argues:

> How selfish soever man may be supposed, there are evidently some principles in his nature, which interest him in the fortune of others, and render their happiness necessary to him, though he derives nothing from it, except the pleasure of seeing it.

The fact is, there is a lot of evidence that suggests that most people engage in non-selfish behavior. And non-selfish behavior is not the exception to the rule. Behavioral economics integrates this reality into how it models the choices people make in the real world.

This is not to say that understanding selfish motives is unimportant when developing economic theories. It just means that caring for others and doing for others are also important. In both selfish and non-selfish aspects of your behavior, you may be smart and rational and contribute to growing the wealth of nations.

Getting to Know the Behavioral Economics Actor

The behavioral economics man or woman reflects, in simplified form, how people behave in the real world. Often, this individual can't even articulate why he or she made a particular decision. The best decisions are often experience based. The behavioral actor behaves in a boundedly rational fashion and can make mistakes that may persist over time. He or she may be selfless or selfish, depending on context. The behavioral actor is affected by the decision-making environment, by those around him or her, and by social norms, as well as by past behavior. The behavioral economics actor is influenced not only by institutions, but also by prices and incomes, as the conventional wisdom would have.

The simplifying assumptions that underlie our models should be relevant to the questions we ask. Overall, in behavioral economics, you need to get to know the behavioral economics actor if you want to build models that predict well and provide you with meaningful explanations of the world.

This isn't important just as an intellectual exercise — it also affects public policy and can have a huge impact on people's lives and the lives of future generations.

Chapter 3

Neuroeconomics: Exploring the Brain for Economic Analysis

. . . .

In This Chapter

▶ Understanding the role of neuroeconomics in behavioral economics

▶ Looking at how the brain affects economics

▶ Acknowledging the importance of emotion in decision making

▶ Recognizing what the brain can't do

▶ Looking at what brain science tells us about behavioral economics

. . . .

Conventional economics focuses on the choices people make. Behavioral economics is concerned with the decision-making process *and* the choices people make, paying special attention to the realism of *simplifying assumptions* (the bare-bones assumptions of economic models; see Chapter 2 for details).

In the past, neither approach has paid much attention to how the brain helps us understand decision making. The focus has mainly been on what researchers can see, on what's tangible. Increasingly, behavioral economists are examining not only how the brain is structured but also how the brain works as an additional tool to help understand people's economic behavior and improve the power of our economic models.

Neuroeconomics is one of the newest components of behavioral economics. It involves the study of the brain and how the brain impacts our understanding of economic behavior. So far, neuroeconomics has largely reiterated the empirical finding of behavioral economics that people typically don't behave according to conventional wisdom. It also suggests that some unconventional behavior is hardwired in the brain.

An important focus of neuroeconomics is the use of brain-imaging technology to measure people's physiological responses to economic stimuli. This technology helps map the chemistry of the brain from the perspective of economic issues, such as decision making, price changes, unfair economic treatment, trust, and cooperation. There remains considerable debate on how useful imaging studies are for mapping or explaining economic behavior.

Neuroeconomics also focuses on the study of brain-damaged individuals to figure out how the loss of functionality of certain parts of the brain affects decision-making capabilities. This area of study has been particularly important in determining the significance of the emotional side of the brain in day-to-day decision making.

Many scholars study the brain to determine if people behave in a manner inconsistent with the predictions of conventional economics. Scholars also are interested in whether brain research can help explain why people behave the way they do. Much of neuroeconomics provides a physiological face to many of the empirical findings that humans don't behave in a manner consistent with conventional economics.

One issue raised by the finding of neuroeconomics is whether policy should be designed to *counter* the behaviors produced by people's brains or to *accommodate* such behaviors. This issue relates to a long-standing question in behavioral economics, raised even before any sophisticated analysis of the brain: Are people's choices rational or not? Error-prone or not? And do they, therefore, require some repair?

In this chapter, I elaborate on the implications of neuroeconomics for economic analysis, focusing in particular on how the brain is structured. Then I explain how this structure results in emotions and other automatic, subconscious, more or less intuitive processes, as well as deliberative conscious processes — all of which have a role in affecting and even determining human behavior. I also cover what neuroeconomics has to say about cooperative behavior, as well as people's sense of fair play and reciprocity.

Overall, neuroeconomics reinforces the findings of behavioral economics that people's decision-making processes and choices often deviate — sometimes significantly — from what is expected and predicted by conventional economics. This finding is inconsistent with the worldview of conventional economics and has possible implications for economic analysis and public policy. However, not all behavioral economists find neuroeconomics enlightening, despite the fact that it casts light on the inner workings of the brain. For example, Richard Thaler of the University of Chicago, one of the leading behavioral economists, remarks that neuroeconomics hasn't produced many new insights on decision making. Nevertheless, it is possible that with more research, much more light may be cast on decision making down the road.

Where Neuroeconomics Fits in the Behavioral Economics Perspective

Behavioral economics has always challenged the long-held views of conventional economics about how people make choices and the choices people make. Experiments in economics and other more traditional empirical studies done by behavioral economists, economic psychologists, and more mainstream economists have found that most people don't behave as the conventional economics person, or *Homo economicus,* does.

Measuring brain activity

To measure responses, scholars from different fields, including economics, use brain-imaging technology. Individuals are asked to perform different specified tasks, with some economic content, to determine where brain activity takes place and the extent of that activity.

Different brain-scanning technology measures different things. The older electroencephalogram (EEG) technology measures electrical activity on the outside of the brain. The more modern positron emission topography (PET) technology measures blood flow in the brain. The newest brain-scanning technology, functional magnetic resonance imaging (fMRI), measures changes in blood oxygenation.

These different brain-scanning technologies all have their benefits and drawbacks, but they provide us with information that we can weave together to better describe and, some would say, understand how the brain functions in the decision-making process.

Very important to behavioral economics are studies on localized brain-damaged individuals. When the brain is damaged in specific regions, we can determine how this damage affects different aspects of a person's behavior, including economic decision making. We also can determine which part of the brain is key to different aspects of decision making.

This methodology allows us to make new guesses based on these new sources of brain-imaging data about, for example, the role that emotions play in decision making. It has emboldened some researchers to try testing the hypothesis that emotions can damage the decision-making process, although this is subject to ongoing debate. Still, this assumption is championed by some very influential behavioral economists.

Tests on individuals and histories of people with serious brain disorders can be used to better understand which part of the brain is responsible for specific activities. They also can help us to understand how the absence of certain brain functionalities will affect people's decision-making capabilities. We can learn a lot about decision-making processes and capabilities from individuals with serious developmental disorders, such as autism, critical mental illnesses (such as schizophrenia), and degenerative diseases of the nervous system (such as Alzheimer's and Parkinson's).

Behavioral economics has relied heavily on information derived from classroom experiments. The subjects of the experiments (mainly college or university students) are asked to respond to questions or participate in economic games to determine how they respond to different incentives or environments. In these experiments, the experimenter is able to control the environment of the experiment similar to what is done in chemistry or physics experiments.

Sometimes these experiments are conducted in the field, which is to say, outside the classroom and with people who aren't students. The results of these experiments provide us with some insight on how people might behave in the real world under different economic settings. These findings have had a big impact on economists' understanding of the process of decision making, economic outcomes, and factors that motivate the choices that people make under different economic and social settings.

The evidence from experiments suggests that people aren't calculating machines and that they're willing to make material sacrifices for reasons of fairness or fair play. Many people are more concerned about where they stand relative to others than about simply increasing their wealth or income. People often feel considerable distress when they experience losses, and these losses easily overwhelm equivalent gains. For example, a person may forfeit an uncertain gain of $2 (there may be a loss instead of a gain) for a *certain* gain of $1. Emotions and intuition drive many people's decisions and choices.

The empirical research of behavioral economics remains largely based on deriving information on human decision making from how people actually behave. It seeks to uncover insights on why people do what they do based on their own understanding of their own decisions.

Neuroeconomics examines the physiological basis of people's behaviors. Some scholars use neuroeconomic studies to determine physiological baselines for what conventional economics regards as rational or smart behavior. In many instances, neuroeconomics has confirmed the findings of traditional behavioral economics on decision making. Neuroeconomics also has located the division of labor within the brain that underlies the findings derived from experiments. It has provided scholars with some possible physiological reasons for why people typically don't behave like *Homo economicus*.

Neuroeconomics is an additional tool for behavioral analysis, and it has a lot of potential. But currently, the traditional empirical analyses based on experiments, field work, surveys, and the use of government data sets remain the main source of insight on decision-making processes and the choices people make in everyday life.

The Brain and Economics

The human brain is made up of various interacting parts. Figuring out the roles that the different parts of the brain play in decision making and how the parts of the brain respond to different economic stimuli is critically important to neuroeconomics.

In this section, I fill you in on how the brain evolved to be what it is today, the various parts of the brain, and what those parts are responsible for. Then I explain how the structure of the brain matters to behavioral economics.

The evolution of the human brain

The brain developed over thousands of years from the brain of the reptile (referred to as the *reptilian brain*) into the brain of the mammal (referred to as the *mammalian brain*) into the human brain. The human brain is much larger than the reptilian and mammalian brains. It developed in response to challenges faced by humans in a hostile world.

The mammalian brain controls basic bodily functions, including organs, body temperature, blood temperature, and the automatic nervous system. It's also responsible for filing and storing experience-based memories and for responding automatically based on past experience.

The development of the human brain involved the growth of a massive folded neocortex, which covers the mammalian brain. This "new brain" part, known as *gray matter,* makes up about 85 percent of the human brain. The neocortex is responsible for "higher" functions, such as language, longer-term planning, and conscious, deliberative acts, many of which are associated with conventional economics-type reasoning.

The neocortex is comprised of left and right hemispheres connected by nerve tissues, which allow the two sides to communicate. The left side of the brain typically controls the right side of the body, and the right side of the brain typically controls the left side of the body. But both sides of the brain have overlapping functions, and brain damage on one side of the brain that could disrupt vital capabilities and behaviors can sometimes be fixed by "rewiring" the other side of the brain.

The parts of the human brain

As mentioned earlier, the human brain is made up of various interacting parts (see Figure 3-1):

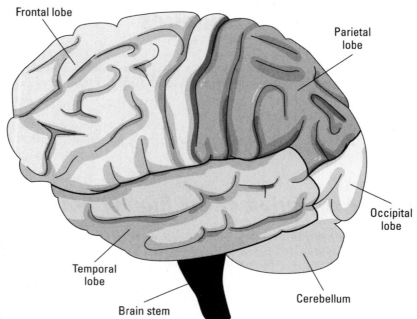

Frontal lobe

Parietal lobe

Occipital lobe

Temporal lobe

Brain stem

Cerebellum

Figure 3-1:
The parts of
the human
brain.

✔ **Frontal lobes:** The frontal lobes (one on each side of the brain) are responsible for conscious behavior, such as responding to environmental stimuli and executing judgments. These activities are crucial to economic decision making. The frontal lobes also deal with word association and help to regulate emotional responses triggered elsewhere in the brain.

✔ **Parietal lobes:** The parietal lobes (one on each side of the brain) are responsible for touch perception and visual attention. They also are responsible for movements that are goal directed (in other words, are a product of thoughts and deliberations). In addition, the parietal lobes allow people to manipulate objects and understand specific concepts.

✔ **Occipital lobes:** The occipital lobes (one on each side of the brain) are responsible for vision and aren't thought to play much of a role in the decision-making process. You can be deprived of your capability to see without being deprived of your capacity to engage in smart or rational decision making.

✔ **Temporal lobes:** The temporal lobes (one on each side of the brain) are responsible for hearing and memory acquisition. They're important for long-term memory, self-control, and the ability to categorize objects — all quite important to deliberative aspects of decision making.

 ✓ **Cerebellum:** The cerebellum is vital to the coordination of voluntary motor movements, balance, and muscle. But a person can still deliberate without the cerebellum being 100 percent.

 ✓ **Brain stem:** The brain stem is critical for basic bodily functions such as heart rate, breathing, swallowing, and automatic reflexes responding to sights and sounds. The brain stem also controls blood pressure, sweating, and body temperature. These functions are all critical to physiologically motivated decisions.

You may read about another part of the brain called the *caudate nucleus.* The caudate nucleus, which is located behind the frontal lobe and curves back toward the occipital lobe, is important to learning and memory. It's also important to feedback processes. As a result, the caudate nucleus plays an important role in decision making.

The amygdalae: Bridging the brain

The tiny amygdalae, located deep in the recesses of the temporal lobes (see Figure 3-2), help with memory-related activities in other parts of the brain. They also play a critical role in the emotional side of decision making and provide people with conscious feelings about events.

In the past few decades, it's become increasingly evident just how important the amygdalae are for efficient decision making. The amygdalae are responsible for emotional and instinctual behavior based on past experience.

This "non-human" (or, more precisely, pre-human) side of us plays an important role in making us human. The primitive self informs our "human" self, very often with positive results.

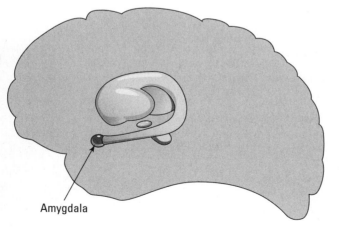

Figure 3-2:
The amygdalae are almond-shaped collections of neurons located in the temporal lobes.

Amygdala

The division of labor in the human brain

An important finding of brain science that is captured by neuroeconomics is the division of labor inside the brain. This division of labor has long been hypothesized by some behavioral economists, and modern brain imaging allows us to see it in action.

There is both communication and conflict among the key players in the brain. Some neuroeconomists argue that part of the brain is concerned with current well-being while another part of the brain is focused on future well-being, and these different roles can generate mixed messages, affecting decision making. For these behavioral economists, an important quest is to better understand how people resolve these conflicts and the implications of this resolution for the choices they make.

Some of what the brain does is automatic and some is more deliberate, requiring people to think things through. The automatic-processing components in the brain, especially the amygdalae, are fundamental to decision making. Prior to the rise of neuroeconomics, we knew that people developed *heuristics* (decision-making shortcuts) — not only for decisions that have to be made quickly, but also for decisions that they have some time to deliberate over. The brain provides people with a means to develop and implement these heuristics. And these heuristics, often mediated by emotion, fear, and intuition, are fundamental to how humans engage in decision making.

For many behavioral economists, the development and use of heuristics isn't a good thing, because it overrides people's deliberative capabilities. According to these economists, the overriding of deliberation causes errors in decision making. But at the end of the day, many decisions are a product of the interaction of different modules of the brain. Heuristics, which have clear neurological roots, often produce very effective results.

Related to the automatic actions that the brain engages in is the brain's incessant efforts at sense making. The brain is always trying to provide a fast and dirty understanding and picture of what you see and hear. Some behavioral economists argue that this can result in cognitive illusions or errors in perceptions.

The possibility of cognitive illusions in decision making, as well as the possible dominance of automatic processes, was raised long before the advent of neuroeconomics, by Daniel Kahneman and Amos Tversky.

Conventional economics, on the other hand, simply assumes away the automatic side of the brain — it assumes that people make decisions as if the amygdalae didn't exist. Of course, from the conventional economics perspective, it's the deliberate part of the brain that provides people with the best decisions and choices.

The brain paints a picture from incomplete information, filling in the gaps, which can result in distortions. What people see isn't always what is — and this can result in errors in decision making. But these errors often can be overcome by the deliberative part of the brain — where people think things through, when and if they have the time.

The brain is a costly resource, so adequate deliberation may not always be the most efficient course of action for nature to take.

The Emotional Brain

Emotive and intuitive factors are part of the complex decision-making toolbox of the evolved human brain. They help generate relatively intelligent and smart decisions efficiently and effectively. This type of analytical paradigm sits well with and is informed by ongoing pioneering brain research, which finds that optimal decision making *can't* be based primarily on rationality benchmarks.

Rationality benchmarks focus simply on calculating and logic-based behavior, in this framework. Emotions and intuition are treated as obstacles to rational decision making. This is the view adhered to in traditional economics, and it has adherents among leading behavioral economics thinkers as well.

Those who favor a neuroeconomics bent believe that emotion and intuition play a vital role in rational decision making. In fact, research has shown that people who suffer damage to the emotional part of the brain are no longer able to engage in rational decision making. After suffering damage to the emotional part of the brain, previously successful individuals become socially inept even at making such basic decisions as what to buy and what to do throughout the day.

Descartes' error: The somatic marker hypothesis

Antonio Damasio pioneered the research identifying the positive importance of emotions to rational decision making. Damasio's argument, set forth in the book *Descartes' Error: Emotion, Reason, and the Human Brain,* is referred to as the *somatic marker hypothesis.*

The somatic marker hypothesis suggests that a process exists whereby emotions help guide people's decision making. When decisions are complex or must take place in a high-pressure environment, emotions are an ever-greater help. But these emotive behaviors are based on past experiences that are stored in the brain and updated with new experiences. These past experiences fuel the emotions that impact, often positively, decision making and the choices people make.

Bonjour, Monsieur Descartes

René Descartes was a 17th-century French philosopher who argued that people are characterized by a rational, deliberative, calculating side on the one hand and the mind, which is driven by emotion, on the other hand. There is always a struggle between the two. The emotional side could override the rational side and create biases or distortions in decision making. The "animal" side has to be reined in if people are to make rational or smart (calculating) choices. Descartes paid special attention to how the physiology of the body motivates human behavior — a precursor to modern brain science.

According to the modeling framework put forth by Damasio, which is based on extensive brain research, emotions allow people to act smart without having to think smart, at least in many significant instances. Emotions help people make quick decisions when quick decisions have to be made. They also help people make smart business decisions that require quick calculation.

Emotions help people determine whether a decision makes sense. Damasio argues that people's gut feelings often keep them from making bad decisions and contribute to making smart decisions, especially when time is short. Emotions trigger decisions based on past experience. These experience-based decisions are ones people wouldn't make in the absence of this emotional side. This isn't to say that emotions can't lead people astray. Overall, emotions and deliberative behavior are partners in decision-making.

In some extreme cases, emotion can replace calculation in decision making. For example, when you're crossing the street and a car is about to hit you, you don't think about what to do. You jump out of the way, driven by your emotional side. You're all pumped, primed by fear. Your emotions can save your life — just as animals facing similar circumstances can be saved by their emotions. If you were to attempt to calculate the costs and benefits of jumping out of the way of an approaching vehicle, you'd be dead before you found your answer (because, no matter how good you are at calculations, you're not a rapid calculating machine).

Phineas Gage and the social and emotional side of rational decision making

Antonio Damasio tells the tale of Phineas Gage to illustrate key points of Damasio's argument, which are based on contemporary findings in brain science.

Thinking of Mr. Spock

The traditional view of decision making idolizes the type of behavior exhibited by the iconic Mr. Spock of *Star Trek*. Spock aspired to remove emotions from his decision-making process. He believed that only by suppressing his emotional side could he make the best possible decisions. His emotional side was there by virtue of his human mother. His "rational" side was courtesy of his Vulcan father.

In Spock's world, emotions were seen as a sign of weakness — just as they are in the conventional economics wisdom. Spock's "rational," Vulcan side was constantly trying to control his emotional side — something that Descartes and conventional economics (and many behavioral economists) would highly recommend.

Phineas Gage was a successful construction foreman working in Vermont in 1848. He was considered by peers and superiors to be highly efficient and capable. His deliberative skills were admired — Spock probably would have a positive thing or two to say about Gage.

Gage was responsible for supervising the blasting of stone to facilitate the laying of railway track. He supervised the laying of explosives, which involved drilling a hole in the rock, laying the explosive powder, inserting the fuse, covering the powder with sand, and carefully pounding the sand with an iron rod. Then the fuse was lit, and the explosion cleared the rock.

But one day in 1848, Gage was momentarily distracted before the sand was laid, and he inadvertently pounded the explosive powder directly, causing an unanticipated explosion. The explosion caused the rod to enter Gage's head from below. The iron rod was 3 feet 7 inches in length and $\frac{1}{4}$ inch in diameter. An illustration of Gage's injury is shown in Figure 3-3.

To everyone's surprise Gage not only survived but appeared to be okay — as okay as someone could be expected to be following such an accident. He spoke in a sensible, articulate, rational manner and looked well on the road to recovery. After two months, Gage appeared to be back to normal, as if he had just recovered from a minor cut or bruise.

But he wasn't back to normal. Although the reasoning part of Gage's brain was intact, the part of the brain responsible for the personal and social aspects of reasoning was damaged. He lost the ability to make smart and thoughtful decisions in social contexts and to plan for the future. He lost not only his capacity to interact with people in normal social settings, but also his sense of social and personal responsibility and pride in his work. Gage could reason and calculate, but he lost the ability to make decisions. The loss of this ability, in spite of his retaining the capacity to reason, transformed Gage from a respected successful man into a pauper.

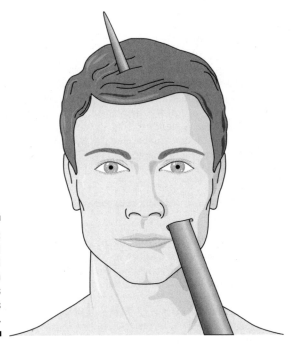

Figure 3-3: A metal rod was fired through Phineas Gage's brain.

Gage's injury went beyond emotions. He lost part of the "soft" side of the brain that was thought unimportant to smart decision making. This is why the fall of Phineas Gage was so surprising to so many experts.

Mr. Spock needs a human side

Brain research has demonstrated that effective decision making requires much more than careful deliberation. People need an emotional side to make good decisions. They also require social sensibility and pride of place to motivate their decisions and choices.

The hypothesis in conventional economics that emotions and the thinking of others may very well damage people's ability to think straight doesn't appear to be supported by the evidence. This doesn't mean that deliberative behavior is bad or that engineers and economists shouldn't calculate costs and benefits — they should, and errors should be corrected. But to explain everyday behavior, we need to introduce other neurologically based variables. Even as a norm for best-practice behavior, Mr. Spock shouldn't be the ideal.

How Emotions Affect Decision Making

Emotions play a vital role in day-to-day, effective, fast and dirty decision making. This is the principle message from the tale of Phineas Gage (see the preceding section). Fear and happiness are two important emotions that cause signals to be sent to the brain's decision-making nodes, spurring people into action in a fast and often effective manner. Without emotional capabilities, people would take forever to make decisions. They would do an abundance of computations and simulations, but to no practical end.

Fear and decision making

Fear is part and parcel of the brain's emotional control system. It affects the automatic decision-making process. Fear-based decisions are built on past experiences and can be modified over time.

Being afraid is critical to the survival of a species. If people didn't experience fear, they wouldn't know to jump out of the way of oncoming traffic or call a cab instead of walking home alone late at night.

In the conventional economics model, fear plays no role in the decision-making process. ***Remember:*** Conventional economics assumes that decision making is based on careful calculation and deliberation.

The role of intuition in decision making

Intuition is related to the emotive-type behavior that can be so important to actual decision making. Intuition involves non-calculating behavior.

If you have enough experience in the business world, you know a great business opportunity when you see it. You may even be better at identifying a great opportunity than a highly paid MBA with no practical business know-how would be.

A great hockey player knows where the puck is even without overtly processing information.

Consider the great Wayne Gretzky, considered by many to be the greatest ice-hockey player ever. Gretzky wasn't the most technically proficient player, but he was the best because he had a deeply intuitive sense of how to play the game.

In our world of uncertainty, people with experience can intuitively sense what may happen based on past experience and observations, all of which is stored deep in the recesses of their brains. Damage the part of the brain that facilitates intuitive behavior, and you damage your capacity to make reasonable decisions.

The emotional brain and dopamine

Dopamine is an important chemical in the prefrontal cortex. It plays an important role in controlling the brain's reward and pleasure centers by regulating people's emotional responses to what they experience. Dopamine is a neurotransmitter — it transmits signals between the brain's nerve cells or neurons. It serves as an important middleman in the brain's communication network.

One significant task executed by dopamine is predicting or anticipating, based on past experience, what should occur in various circumstances and how to respond. Dopamine allows the brain to determine, based on past experience, how best to behave in particular situations. With the assistance of dopamine, people react to stimuli, often without thinking.

When current events don't match what the brain has determined to be the norm, signals are fired indicating that something is off kilter — a type of mayday signal. This is registered as an error. Error signals, based on deviations from the norm, help people react quickly, without thinking, based on past experience, often saving their lives or helping them identify exceptional opportunities. The emotional brain, with the help of dopamine, helps people make effective decisions at a subconscious level.

The big question is whether the fear factor contributes to *good* decision making. The evidence suggests that it *does,* at least when we have to act quickly.

When you have more time, you can think more carefully about what to do. Some people would argue that even when you have some time to spare, overthinking a problem may result in poor choices.

Happiness and decision making

Happiness doesn't necessarily save your life the way fear does, but it facilitates effective decision making when people are under pressure. Employers and employees often make quick judgments on whom to hire and whom to work for based on gut feelings — something just feels right about this employee or employer. Consumers often do the same when purchasing big-ticket items based on how they *feel* about the salesperson.

The Limits of the Human Brain and Homo Economicus

The brain is not a natural calculating machine. That's why people use calculators, spreadsheets, and statistical programs, often without even understanding the nitty-gritty math that underlies their calculations. The limits of the brain apply to most decision-making problems, including the non-numerical ones that require cost-benefit calculations. The human brain has evolved over time to meet the requirement to make quick and effective decisions. And people have developed machines that assist them in making a variety of calculations. But nothing can replace the human gift for deliberation and contemplation in the decision-making process.

People can end up with decision-making errors when information is highly complex and presented in a manner not easily processed by the brain. But explicit learning and more experience often correct these errors. Nevertheless, the possibility of errors in decision making is part of the human condition.

The brain is not a calculating machine

There is no neurological evidence to support the argument that the brain is the calculating machine that conventional economics assumes it to be. This neurological research simply confirms the long-held arguments put forth by behavioral economists for decades. (This is what Herbert Simon's concept of bounded rationality is all about; see Chapter 2.)

Because the brain isn't a calculating machine, as it has evolved, it has developed decision-making heuristics (see "The division of labor in the human brain," earlier in this chapter). Without the appropriate heuristics in place, people can't be effective decision makers. On the other hand, using heuristics also can result in errors and biases in decision making. We all make mistakes, but we can correct them — and very often do — courtesy of the deliberative part of the brain. Correcting mistakes takes time, though, and it often requires education.

The brain is a scarce resource

The fact that people aren't blessed with unbounded computational capacities is exactly why the brain is a scarce resource — like fresh water in the midst of the vast expanses of a desert. People have evolved to accommodate this reality, so they use their brains very efficiently and effectively.

Given that the brain is a scarce resource, we can better understand the importance of innovations that improve people's computational capabilities. For example, computers and computer programs have contributed dramatically as aids to the brain's capacity to do necessary data processing. They give people more time to understand and deliberate, something that the computer just can't do.

The human brain versus the computer: Brain evolution and the chess master

The human brain evolves through learning and experience, within our own lifetimes, to meet the challenges of everyday life. Those of us who invest the time and effort in particular tasks end up being better at computation and reasoning.

Chess is considered by many people to be a game that demonstrates acute intelligence and even genius. In 1985, one of the world's greatest chess masters, Garry Kasparov, beat 32 different chess computers at the same time in a simultaneous chess exhibition.

Then, in 1996, IBM developed a super–chess computer, Deep Blue, to challenge Kasparov. Kasparov prevailed. In 1997, IBM challenged Kasparov with an upgraded Deep Blue, with double the processing capacity of the older version. The new and improved Deep Blue could compute more than 200 million moves per second, and it beat Kasparov two games to one, with three draws.

What's remarkable is how well Kasparov did in spite of the computational capabilities of Deep Blue. If Kasparov had employed preferred conventional computational methods to take on the computer, he would've been crushed. But Kasparov employed heuristics that drew upon the vast stores of experience stored in his brain to take on the vast computational capacity of the computer. Kasparov employed his stored experiences, which informed his intuition.

Deep Blue finally outdid Kasparov not only because of its massive computational capacity, but also because of its improved database on chess moves and past successful strategies. Deep Blue was increasingly designed to compute like a human using human-style heuristics.

When people fail to appreciate that computers can only *help* them calculate and that deliberation is just as important in order for effective decisions to be made, they can end up making very poor choices. Fancy computer software creates the illusion for many people that deliberation isn't required for effective decision making. But computers can only be an aid in decision making — one more tool in the decision-making toolbox.

The brain isn't a static resource. People have brains with different computational capacities and efficiencies. These differences, brain science suggests, are related to differences in learning and experience. Conventional economics assumes that people stay pretty much the same (and that they're great data processors).

What Brain Sciences Confirm for the Behavioral Economist

Some of the findings in the brain sciences — particularly those related to how the brain responds to different types of stimuli and behavior — reinforce many of the traditional arguments and findings in behavioral economics. The measured response of the brain is at least consistent with what many behavioral economists have been arguing for some time.

This empirical evidence doesn't provide any clear and unequivocal proof that the chemistry of brain is the cause of particular types of behavior. Also, bear in mind that behavioral economists' findings largely refer to "average behavior," but many people behave in a fashion quite different from the average.

Bottom line: The human brain is consistent with a variety of behaviors, some of which fit the arguments of many behavioral economists. In this section, I describe these arguments.

People prefer the present to the future

Long before neuroeconomics, behavioral economists and psychologists argued, based on a variety of pieces of evidence, that many people have a preference for present income over future income. In other words, a bird in the hand is worth two in the bush. We really don't know what will happen in the future — the future is uncertain. But we do know what's happening in the present. This situation often creates preferences that lean toward the present. In other words, if you're offered $100 today or $120 a year from now, you'll likely opt for the $100 today.

Related to this concept, but with some important differences, when they're young, most people won't save much for the future, even if they can afford it. Then when they're much older, many of those same people regret the saving decisions they made when they were young, and they would prefer that they had saved much more. When people get older, if they're offered $100 today or $120 a year from now, they'll likely opt for the $120 a year from now. In other words, many people's preferences flip from being present-oriented to being future-oriented as they get older.

Neuroeconomics provides some evidence that there is a neurological basis for this type of behavior.

Years ago, when life expectancy was short and saving for the future was even more difficult, present preferences easily dominated — and for good survival reasons. What neuroeconomics hasn't resolved is why, today, people still opt for the bird in the hand more often than not. Neuroeconomics also can't tell us which type of preferences are best for people and when.

People's aversion to loss affects their decision making

According to behavioral economics, people are averse to loss, and that aversion affects the decisions they make. Neurological research provides some support for these theories.

For example, there is now some evidence that the brain reacts more negatively to a given loss than positively to the same amount of gain. If you simultaneously win a dollar and lose a dollar, you are, according to the theory of loss aversion, worse off — your level of happiness falls, even though you're no worse off financially.

So it makes sense that many people sacrifice economic gains to avoid economic losses. According to some behavioral economists, the fear of loss also often produces an instinctual reaction against highly risky economic scenarios. So, fear of loss can result in people not accepting risky choices that produce higher incomes.

In conventional economics, a dollar is a dollar is a dollar. If there's a way to make more money, even if it involves winning and losing some money in the process (gain $40 and lose $30, for a net gain of $10, for example), no one should reject this option. There is no way you'd want to avoid taking advantage of the opportunity to increase your final state of income or wealth. Conventional economics assumes away loss aversion, sweeping it under the carpet.

What people feel isn't always what they experience

There is serious neurological evidence that what people say they feel about various stimuli (or *remembered utility*) is not always what they actually experience (or *experienced utility*). Contrary to what conventional economics says, there is often a disconnect between what people *say* they experience and what they actually experience.

Linking decision-making loss, aversion, and risk

Because there is a risk of loss when gambling for a higher income, many people prefer more certain but lower levels of income. For example, some people prefer investing in lower-yielding but safer bonds over higher-yielding but higher-risk stocks.

Conventional economics has long recognized the importance of many people being adverse to risks — nothing new here. But some behavioral economists go beyond this point, arguing that risk aversion, intertwined with loss aversion, results in behavior that produces unexpected income losses — unexpected from the perspective of conventional economics. Plus, even without introducing risks, many people are expected to sacrifice income, simply as a result of loss aversion.

Overall, many people are negatively affected, emotionally, by risky situations. This pushes people into avoiding risky situations, even if such behavior can be expected to increase their income or wealth. But then people are stimulated by gains, including monetary ones. So, there is an obvious trade-off between the negative vibes people get from taking on risks and the material gains that they may end up with if they endure the pain of risky behavior.

To make things a bit more complicated, some people are actually *stimulated* by risky behavior. Gamblers fall into this group.

Some behavioral economists consider loss aversion to be normal behavior, but not smart or rational. Other behavioral economists argue that loss aversion can be expected from many people, but it isn't irrational. Some people are characterized by loss aversion and others aren't. The evidence only suggests that people are, on average, characterized by loss aversion. And these people are actually happier when behaving in a fashion consistent with loss aversion, even if it means that their income or wealth is less than it would otherwise be.

Research pioneered by psychologist Daniel Kahneman suggests that people often do remember the totality of their experiences, but they tend to remember the endpoint of their experiences most. According to Kahneman, peaks and troughs are more important to decision making than total accumulated happiness or pain.

So, for example, if you had a painful operation that lasted four hours (with limited anesthesia), but the pain diminished markedly the last half-hour or so, you would remember the experience as not being all that bad. On the other hand, if the four-hour operation was largely painless, but the last half-hour was excruciatingly painful, you would remember the operation as being very painful — despite the fact that the total pain in the first scenario was much greater than the total pain of the second scenario.

In a number of interesting experiments, remembered utility or disutility appears to be much different from experienced utility or disutility. In one experiment, two groups of people are exposed to the same level of loud noise, but one group is exposed to much less noise at the end of the experiment. Individuals in this second group remember their experience as much less bothersome than the folks who were exposed to a constant level of noise.

The big questions are: Is the difference between remembered utility and experienced utility a problem, and if so, when? Many economists, including many behavioral economists, say that we should respect the subjective evaluations of people (or remembered utility). Others say that what should count most are the objective measurements of what people experience (or experienced utility).

This type of research raises the question of how to design policy that improves the level of happiness of different people. Of course, if experienced utility is respected as a benchmark for happiness, policy design becomes less important. There would be no need to determine experienced utility and impose or nudge choices based on what people experience as opposed to what they remember. In the operation example, it would make sense to configure operations such that *both* the total pain and the endpoint or last moments of pain are minimized.

On the other hand, this type of research also raises questions about possible errors in decision making. To the extent that people remember best what they experienced last, they may make choices that don't reflect what is objectively the best choice. Their endpoint memory doesn't necessarily reflect the total experience. This may be the case when someone has to make a decision under severe pressure.

For example, consider the hiring process. Often, a job candidate ruins his chances if he answers the last question poorly. When objectively looking at the interview as a whole, this person may be the best — but he may lose out to someone whose entire performance was less than stellar but who answered the last question better.

A person's well-being is improved if she hires the best possible person, so if the person doing the hiring places more emphasis on the last question the candidate answered, she may be missing out on the best person for the job. On the other hand, it's possible that people place a heavy weight on endpoint behavior for objective reasons — because it reveals critical characteristics of the job candidate. And so the debate continues. . . .

People care about keeping up with — and beating — the Joneses

Conventional economics assumes that people are material maximizers, so they make choices that will increase their wealth or income. The more people have and the more money they make, the happier they are — or so the conventional story goes.

From the conventional perspective, people don't think about where they stand relative to other people. Simply increasing their income is what matters, regardless of what's happening to the income of their friends or neighbors or people they read about in the newspaper.

Evidence from behavioral economics, especially derived from classroom experiments, suggests that what makes people happiest is increasing their income and wealth *relative to other people*. Behavioral economics says that if my income increases relative to yours, this should make me happier than simply increasing my income by the same percentage as your income. This is known as the *theory of relative positioning*.

Say you and I have the same income of $80,000 per year. If my income increases by $10,000 and yours increases by $6,000, this, according to the theory of relative positioning, can make me happier than if both our incomes increased by $10,000. Why? Because in the latter case, my income is increasing by a greater percentage than yours. I may even be happier if my income went up by $10,000 and yours went up by $6,000 than I would be if both of our incomes rose by $12,000! Improving my income relative to yours is what counts most.

Brain imaging studies support the relative income hypothesis put forth by behavioral economics. The brain's reward center lights up much more when participants improve their relative position than when everyone wins the same amount of money. This provides some physiological support to the experimental findings. According to neuroeconomics, thinking in relative terms as opposed to absolutes is natural.

People's brains evolve over their lifetimes

The traditional view of the brain is that it's fairly static over people's lifetimes, with important developments taking place when they're very, very young. Who people are in terms of their brains and what their brains allow them to do is locked in place. Genetics plays a vital role in determining what people can do, their decision-making capabilities, and the choices they make. This argument sits very nicely with the conventional economics perspective that people's decision-making capabilities are as fixed as their preferences.

But brain research is overthrowing this long-held view. Research on both humans and animals shows that brain functioning and the actual size of different parts of the brain can change throughout an individual's lifetime. This process of brain change, which includes the rewiring of the brain, is referred to as *neuroplacticity*.

Changes in the brain are often a product of challenges and experiences in day-to-day life. The changes can be positive (as when the brain repairs itself after a stroke) or negative (for example, as a product of depression or drug abuse). Not only has the human brain evolved over thousands of years, but it evolves throughout people's lifetimes.

The fact that the brain evolves during people's lifetimes has important implications for decision making. Learning, training, and experience all play a role in determining people's decision-making capabilities. They affect the efficiency and accuracy of the decision-making process and the choices people make.

In his popular book *Bounce,* Matthew Syed discusses how our brain transforms itself through deliberative practice and experience. For example, London cabbies, who have to memorize the streets of London, have a larger brain size in the area responsible for memory and spatial navigation than non-cabbies do. This allows cabbies to quickly determine where to go and how best to deal with traffic jams and sudden, unexpected detours. The area of the brain responsible for controlling movements in fingers of violinists increases with years of training. There is evidence that the quantity of *myelin* (the chemical in the brain responsible for the speed at which signals pass through the brain) increases with the number of hours that pianists practice. People can, at least to an important extent, reinvent their brains, just as they can reinvent their bodies with diet and exercise.

Overall, the human brain responds to challenges and experiences. People aren't who they were born or even who they are today. Their decision-making capabilities, which heavily rely on instinct and intuition built on evolved heuristics, are quite plastic. A person's individual decision-making capabilities and the quality of these capabilities are also highly contingent on experience. The quality of a person's decisions improves with experience.

People's brains differ based on the challenges that they face and how they deal with these challenges. A London taxi driver's brain is different from a chess master's is different from an economist's is different from a surgeon's. And, no doubt, the brains of economists differ depending on the type of economics they practice and the skills required to do their thing.

People value fairness

Behavioral economists have long argued that, based on various experiments, most people resent being treated unfairly and love being treated fairly. People also tend to reward those who treat them fairly and punish those who treat them unfairly, even if punishing comes at a cost to themselves. Basically, people tend to reciprocate: to pay back those who do well by them *and* those who do ill by them.

Brain science provides clear evidence that when people are treated fairly, it triggers the feel-good part of the brain. When people are treated poorly, it triggers the part of the brain that makes them feel disgusted. In other words, people's emotional reactions to fairness are rooted in brain architecture.

The feel-good part of the brain is also triggered, however, when people receive an offer of money, *even if this offer is believed to be unfair*. There appears to be a conflict in the human brain between accepting unfair offers (because what they're offered feels good) and rejecting unfair offers (because they're disgusted by the unfairness). The resolution to this conflict differs from one individual to the next, but a lot depends on people's understanding of fairness, the money they have to sacrifice to punish those who are unfair, and their level of disgust at being treated unfairly.

Valuing fairness tells us nothing about how different people *define* fairness. Hitler's and Stalin's views of fairness were quite different from Gandhi's or Martin Luther King's.

People like to trust and be trusted

People tend to be positively stimulated by knowing that they're trusted. They tend to feel good when interacting with others they like and even seeing trustworthy people. For this reason, they tend to reward those they trust and who they believe trust them. People also tend to feel good when they engage in positive social interaction and voluntary cooperation. This feeling is related to the positive stimuli they get from trusting engagements.

So, most people move toward more trusting and cooperative behavior whenever possible because of its positive neurological effects.

The neurological evidence is for the feel-good effect of *voluntary* cooperation. This isn't the same thing as slaves cooperating with a master or employees cooperating with a manager they don't like or trust. Forced or unavoidable interactions are not what generate positive stimuli in the brain.

People also tend to get high on punishing others, but they most enjoy punishing those who have betrayed them. They enjoy punishing individuals who have breached their trust or behaved unfairly. This feeling can be triggered by the emotional part of the brain, producing a reaction of anger against those who they believe have behaved in a fashion deserving of their retribution. This type of punishment, which behavioral economist Ernst Fehr refers to as *reciprocal punishment*, is payback for perceived bad behavior. It encourages people not to breach the norm of trust. Here, there is a trade-off between the pain that people incur by punishing others (often this involves a monetary cost) and the satisfaction they get in delivering the punishment.

Chapter 4

Why Incentives and Markets Matter, but Money Isn't Everything

● ●

In This Chapter

▶ Exploring how traditional economics views incentives

▶ Seeing how behavioral economics expands on opportunity costs

▶ Modifying supply and demand through behavioral economics

▶ Turning to psychology to make sense of people's decisions

● ●

*B*ehavioral economics tends to focus on non-economic factors, going beyond the traditional focus on prices and income, to explain the choices people make. It also pays much closer attention to actual human behavior when explaining economic phenomenon. It focuses on *anomalies* (observed behavior that is difficult to explain using standard economic theory), which is one reason why behavioral economics is often criticized as lacking theoretical substance.

The critics maintain that behavioral economics isn't much more than fluff — academically lightweight and not much more than a self-help narrative. Focusing on the descriptive side of behavioral economics, they claim that behavioral economists don't provide much explanation or analysis.

In economics, explanation traditionally lies on a narrow, well-made bed of economic incentives, with little or no room afforded to non-economic motivations. According to long-standing convention, established from the mid-20th century, economic and non-economic variables make strange bedfellows. This was not, however, the opinion of the venerable 18th-century thinker Adam Smith, author of *The Wealth of Nations* and *The Theory of Moral Sentiments,* whom most economists identify as the founder and spiritual fountainhead of contemporary economics. For Adam Smith, as for most people, economic factors matter to decision making, as do a host of other factors, including "soft" issues like moral sentiments.

Behavioral economics is not a new-age brand of wimpy social science that ignores the role of incentives to choice behavior. It isn't all about why money doesn't matter — instead, it's about why money isn't everything for most people who make decisions in the real world. Many examples of economic behavior can't be explained if you focus on economic (and, more specifically, monetary or financial) incentives alone. Introducing the non-economic side *enriches* the standard economic model.

This chapter discusses how, why, and when economic incentives matter to decision making and the important role played by other factors — such as morals, norms, reciprocity, moral sentiments, and trust — in choice decisions.

The Role of Economic Incentives for Economic Behavior

When you go shopping, you probably check for the price of the computer, car, or piece of fruit you're thinking of purchasing. You probably don't do a very careful and calculated investigation of price difference, but you consider *relative price,* where possible. For example, you check out the price of apples compared to the price of grapes when deciding what to buy. You also check for price of apples at, say, Costco compared to the price of apples at Walmart. And, more likely than not, you prefer what's less expensive to what's more expensive. Everybody does some price comparison if he or she has time. But behavioral economics clearly recognizes that people don't have the time or the know-how to do more than a small amount of it.

The concept of relative price is a core concept in economics. People are assumed to make decisions based on how the price of one product changes relative to the price of another. You're most interested in what happens when the price of apples increases or falls relative to the price of some worthy substitute, such as grapes. If the price of apples and the price of grapes increase or fall by the same percentage, there is no clear economic incentive for you to increase or reduce your demand for apples. Of, course when all prices change, this affects your purchasing power, which, in turn, affects demand (but that's another story).

You're also likely to purchase more of a good or service when the price falls and purchase less when the price increases. In addition, your income affects what and how much you can purchase. You may *want* to buy a Porsche, but if you earn $40,000 per year, you won't be able to afford one. You may *want* your child to attend a private school, but you may not be able to afford it if the annual tuition is $20,000.

These examples illustrate why economists place great weight upon the role that relative prices and income play in determining what and how much people purchase. Of course, if someone's income represents a bottomless pit, these economic considerations would be of little consequence — but very few people have that kind of money. In fact, even the super-rich think about relative prices and what's affordable (however, their benchmark for what's affordable is quite different).

In the following sections, I discuss the role of relative prices and income in decision making. I also elaborate on the concept of opportunity cost — people can't have everything they want given their income, so they have to make choices and, therefore, sacrifices in what they consume and what they do. These concepts are not only key to conventional economics, but also important to most behavioral economists.

Why money is all that matters in conventional economics

Conventional economics considers economic factors to be the best way to explain how people behave and why economic outcomes are what they are. Traditional economists believe that introducing non-economic factors simply adds unnecessary tools to the economic toolbox, without providing a means for improving our understanding of the workings of the economy. They claim that considering non-economic factors would be like using a sewing machine to sew on a button or a Ginsu knife to cut your peanut butter and jelly sandwich in half.

Conventional economists maintain that all these fancy tools may look impressive, but they argue that little practical substance is being added to the toolbox. Moral sentiments, trust, and fairness don't need to be added into the story because, conventional economists argue, they don't add much of anything to an economic analysis. The focus of much economic analysis is on how much and what is purchased on the market — from apples and oranges, to plants and equipment, to labor. This type of analysis, the conventional wisdom would have us believe, doesn't require non-economic add-ons.

In a nutshell, conventional economists assert that when engaging in economic decisions, people are most concerned with the following:

> ✔ **Income:** Information on income tells people what economic resources are available to them and what constraints they face when making economic choices. People's choices are constrained by their limited or scarce resources.

✔ **Relative prices:** Relative prices provide people with information on how much income they must sacrifice to purchase one commodity as compared to some other, preferred commodity. If someone spends $5 on soup, he or she has $5 less to spend on cheese, tofu, or fish. When the price of one desired commodity increases relative to the price of another, people tend to search for less-expensive substitutes to minimize the sacrifice they must make.

When price goes up, the quantity demanded goes down. When price goes down, the quantity demanded goes up. When income goes up, the quantity demanded goes up. When income goes down, the quantity demanded goes down. This is how economists expect you and society to behave, on average. In fact, this expectation is pretty much what occurs in the real world. Economists even refer to regularities as laws, such as the *law of demand* (which specifies the expected negative relationship between price and the quantity of a commodity demanded at alternative prices given income).

Figure 4-1 illustrates the law of demand using the demand curve, for the individual, which is standard fare in the economics toolbox. The *demand curve* tells how much of a good or service a person is willing to purchase at alternative prices. This assumes that the prices of all other goods and services are held constant. So, if the demand curve is for apples, it illustrates the demand for apples as the price for apples increases or falls relative to the price of other products, such as oranges.

Figure 4-1:
The demand curve illustrates the relationship between price and the quantity of a commodity that you would purchase at alternative prices given your income.

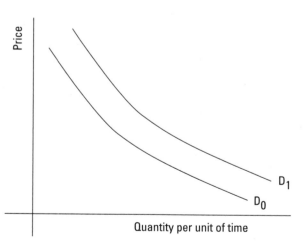

The demand curve is generally assumed to slope downward, to reflect the fact that, for the most part, as relative price goes up, people buy smaller quantities. Increasing income and holding prices constant tends to shift the demand curve outward (in Figure 4-1, from D_0 to D_1, for example), and decreasing income tends to shift the demand curve inward. The curve shifts inward because, at every price, most people are willing to purchase more apples, as their income increases; with less income, most people are willing to purchase fewer apples.

Market demand is a product of adding up all the individual demand curves in particular markets. So, for example, we have the demand curve for automobiles, the demand curve for different makes of automobiles, the demand curve for apples, and the demand curve for different types of apples. Each market has its own specific demand curve, each derived from the demand curves of the individuals who partake in each market.

Here's the Golden Rule for economic behavior, according to the conventional economic toolkit:

> Thou shall behave in a manner consistent with maximizing material welfare and in a fashion consistent with economic incentives. Be selfish, and thou shall prosper and maximize thy happiness.

Opportunity costs for Homo economicus

Because you have limited or scarce resources and your wants exceed them, you must make sacrifices when you choose to purchase one commodity over another or when you choose to work at one task as opposed to another. Economists call these sacrifices *opportunity costs*. Opportunity costs are typically measured in monetary terms; they measure these sacrifices in terms of your next best alternative in use. For example, if you spend $200 to go to a Rolling Stones concert, you'll have to sacrifice or forfeit all those DVDs you were hoping to purchase, up to the value of your concert ticket.

If you choose to purchase a coffee, your opportunity cost may be a fancy pastry that you really wanted. Or your purchase of a pack of cigarettes may come at the cost of a set of school books that your kids really need. If cigarettes cost $11, the opportunity cost of purchasing your smokes may be one textbook for your child. In this case, opportunity cost is measured as the number of textbooks that could have been purchased for the money used to buy the cigarettes.

Consumers aren't the only people who confront opportunity costs when making choices. Business owners and managers must do the same. Given resources, if you were the owner of a garment factory and you wanted to purchase new sewing machines for your factory, you may have to postpone the purchase of the new cutting tables that you've been eyeing. If you were the CEO of Ford, you would have to decide whether to produce more truck or cars — more of one means less of another. If you were the superintendent of a school district, and you needed to hire a math teacher and a gym teacher, but you had the budget for only one, hiring a math teacher may mean the elimination of your athletics program.

Opportunity cost is also important when considering the alternative use of time. Time is a scarce resource, and if you choose one task, you must sacrifice engaging in some other preferred task. If you choose to work overtime, you must sacrifice time that you would've otherwise spent with your children. If you choose not to work for paid employment, your economic sacrifice can be measured by the income you forgo.

Most people can't do everything they want in the time available to them in a day, a week, a month, a year, or a lifetime. Death is a powerful binding constraint that everybody faces. People must make choices — often hard choices — on how to allocate their time, what to do, and what to leave undone.

Opportunity cost is typically illustrated by an *opportunity cost curve* (see Figure 4-2). If the opportunity cost curve is given by a straight line, the opportunity cost increases with increases in item B as the line becomes steeper. The opportunity cost is greater along opportunity cost curve *CF* than it is along curve *CD*. Increasing the consumption of item B by a small amount (*JM*) involves more of a sacrifice in terms of item A (*SN*) along opportunity cost curve *CF* than along curve *CD* (*VT*). The opportunity cost curve shifts outward to *RE*, for example, when income increases. With more income, you can purchase more of both commodities. But given your new and improved state of income and purchasing power, you're still faced with opportunity costs and trade-offs along the new opportunity cost curve *RE*. When your new purchasing habits are established, to purchase one more of item B involves purchasing less of item A.

In the realm of production, the opportunity cost curve represents the maximum that can be produced with given levels of inputs, such as labor, plants, equipment (capital), efficiency, and technology. This curve shifts outward with technological change or as the firm becomes more efficient. With improved technology or efficiency, you can produce more of item A and item B with available labor and capital. As with consumption, there is a trade-off between producing item A and producing item B.

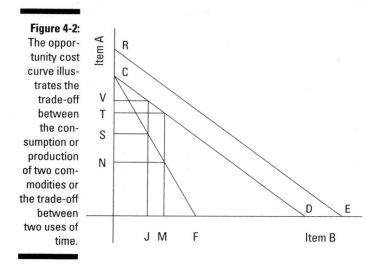

Figure 4-2: The opportunity cost curve illustrates the trade-off between the consumption or production of two commodities or the trade-off between two uses of time.

Decision Making and Opportunity Costs

Opportunity cost tells us that life is characterized by choices and that these choices involve sacrifice. This important insight doesn't conflict with behavioral economics at all. Neither does the conventional view that sacrifice, or opportunity cost, is often measured in money terms using market prices. But in conventional thinking, sacrifice largely involves time and money, with a hard focus on monetary sacrifice.

In behavioral economics, there are important additional ways of thinking about and analyzing opportunity costs, besides money — including psychological factors and the time and energy that you must invest in decision making. In this section, I explore the concepts that enrich the notion of opportunity cost, making it even more relevant for an understanding of the sacrifices that people must endure when making choices.

Using up your mind: Bounded rationality

The concept of opportunity cost easily incorporates an important behavioral consideration introduced by Nobel Laureate in Economics Herbert Simon, one of the founding fathers of behavioral economics. Simon argues that brain-processing capacity is a scarce resource because people are endowed with limited cognitive capacity or brain power. People face limits on how much information they can process during a particular block of time, and how well they can process this information. Some people are more efficient than others, but at the end of the day, no one has unlimited processing capabilities. Processing information involves both time and energy, of which everybody has a limited amount.

The mind is a scarce resource and its use involves opportunity costs. People must make choices about what information they'll process and assess. This important reality-based assumption is part and parcel of Simon's concept of *bounded rationality* (see Chapter 6 for more on this subject).

The concept of bounded rationality is in contrast to the conventional view, which assumes that the mind is *not* a scarce resource. With bounded rationality, your decision-making capabilities are bounded by your *computational capabilities* (the limits of the human brain in processing and understanding information). These limits are, in turn, affected by technology, such as computers and related software, and your ability to make use of these types of technologies. For example, something as simple as a calculator can improve your computational capacity, but only if you know how to use it properly. The same holds true for computers: The web can be a wonderful time-saving tool, but only if you know how to use it efficiently.

Considering costs other than money: Psychological costs

The opportunity cost of purchasing a product or taking on some project involves much more than sacrificing the consumption of some other product or project. If you want to purchase a car, you must sacrifice more than a bedroom set. Acquiring and processing all relevant price and quality information necessary to making your purchasing decision also can be taxing in terms of your time and energy — and even your emotions. All these are also opportunity costs. However, these particular opportunity costs are not taken into consideration by conventional economics because they aren't monetary costs. Instead, they're psychological costs.

When you engage in an economic decision, psychological considerations are almost always critically important. The fact that it takes time and energy to think through your decisions affects the decisions you make. You may buy the first or second car you see because it makes sense, given your understanding of what you want. You may send your kids to the college you attended (even if you weren't too pleased with your experience), because, as the expression goes, better the devil you know than the devil you don't. Most people won't search all over the place for the "best buy" — it's just not worth the time and effort. You may simply postpone purchasing a car because of such time costs (for more on this subject, check out the next section).

Adam Smith and altruism

Adam Smith was definitely a fan of markets and recognized that people are motivated by self-interest. But he also argued that people aren't entirely narrowly self-interested — they're also motivated by concern for others. As Smith puts it in his *Theory of Moral Sentiments:*

> How selfish soever man may be supposed, there are evidently some principles in his nature, which interest him in the fortune of others, and render their happiness necessary to him, though he derives nothing from it, except the pleasure of seeing it.

It is this concern for others that contributes to making the economy more effective and more efficient. If you show some concern for the well-being of your employees, they'll be more productive, and the size of the economic pie — the wealth of nations — will increase.

Shopping also can be an emotional experience. For some people, it can be fun; for others, it can be stressful. The desire to minimize stress can affect where you shop and how you shop. Replacing old products with new products also can be stressful — you may decide not to replace your parents' old dining room set with a more stylish one because of the emotional opportunity costs involved. You may resist closing your restaurant even though you may have an easier time making a living as a lawyer or a fashion designer because you're emotionally attached to your restaurant, into which you've invested so much love and attention.

Reducing opportunity costs in the real world: Satisficing behavior

When searching for a car, people don't check for all information; they often end up checking out one or two dealerships and making a decision based on limited information, intuition, and trust. This process is referred to as *satisficing behavior.*

Satisficing behavior is another of Herbert Simon's concepts. People typically set a minimum criterion or standard for what would be a satisfying result of their choices and go for the option that meets that benchmark. This process serves to reduce the opportunity cost of decision making, because people don't have to engage in a detailed and time-consuming search for the best — they just have to find something that'll satisfy.

This minimum standard is often a product of individual circumstance, of who you are — your wants, needs, and desires. This is especially true for consumers and workers, when choosing which products to purchase or which job offers to accept. Everyone has his or her own standards. An environmentalist searching for a new car will have different minimum standards than a person who's less concerned with environmental issues. If you're already employed, you may have much more demanding standards for a new job than someone who's been out of work for a year and has mortgage payments due.

Behavioral economists also argue that businesses often don't maximize profits or minimize costs, which is contrary to what conventional economics says. Business owners or managers engage in satisficing behavior. They shoot for target profits and costs that can pass the test of the market without incurring significant *cognitive costs* (the costs of locating, assessing, and processing information). In this case, profits aren't maximized and costs aren't minimized, but owners and managers are still satisfied by their decisions. Owners and managers end up with solutions that are good enough given the constraints they face.

 According to many behavioral economists, satisficing behavior represents an improvement in decision making in the real world of bounded rationality, over and above what is recommended by conventional economics. Satisficing results in making decisions more efficiently, leaving you with more time and energy to be productive.

Tipping because it's the right thing to do (or because it impresses your friends)

Billions of dollars are spent on tips around the world. Tipping plays an important role in compensating employees for their work, especially in the often poorly paid service industry. But conventional economics would suggest that tipping may not be rational and isn't something that we should expect smart people to do. Tipping often represents, after all, an unnecessary sacrifice of income. Tippers aren't income or wealth maximizers.

For conventional economics, tipping can be rational in two situations:

✔ **You frequent a particular restaurant and there is a good chance of getting the same server again.** In this case, if you don't tip or you tip below the norm, you may face some retaliation down the road. Tipping at least guarantees that you won't be retaliated against and possibly ensures good service in the future.

✔ **You're with friends or acquaintances who would look down on you for not tipping.** In this case, tipping to preserve your reputation makes sense.

But how can we explain the fact that most people tip even if they know that they'll never return to that restaurant again and even if they're alone? Even conventional economists who subscribe to the notion that tipping is irrational, tip. In this case, tipping is not an economic imperative, but even conventional economists choose not to maximize their incomes.

People tip for a variety of non-economic reasons — for the warm glow, to assuage their sense of guilt, and, with others present, to preserve their identity. People tend to tip based on prevailing social norms, and tips tend to be scaled up or down based on the quality of service delivered. Your budget for other things is reduced by the tip amount, but your level of happiness is enhanced.

Weighing the opportunity cost of altruism

The concept of opportunity cost also can be applied to altruistic behavior, which many economists (excluding the venerable Adam Smith) consider to be irrational or not-too-smart behavior. Although *Homo economicus* wouldn't engage in it, altruistic or self-sacrificing behavior takes place all the time: People donate money to charities, volunteer their time, and donate blood. The economic cost of being good can be measured using the concept of opportunity cost. This measured cost reveals what material sacrifice you're willing to endure to do what you believe to be right. In behavioral economics, such materially costly behavior can be quite smart and rational.

When you engage in materially self-sacrificing behavior because it makes you feel better, it increases your level of happiness, of overall well-being. It generates what American economist James Andreoni, who researches on charitable giving, refers to as a *warm glow effect,* more than compensating for the opportunity cost of your altruistic behavior (see Chapter 13).

Supply and Demand and Behavioral Economics

Alfred Marshall, the late 19th- and early 20th-century Cambridge University economist and one of the founders of contemporary economics, invented contemporary supply-and-demand analysis. He made the salient point that, in order to understand how prices are determined, you must model the economy with both blades of a pair of economic scissors. You need both the supply curve and the demand curve to cut an intelligent pattern through the cloth of how market prices are determined — why housing prices or the price of gas rise and fall, for example.

A foundational economic model states that the market price and the quantity sold at that price are determined by the intersection of both blades of the economics scissors: supply and demand. At this price, consumers are willing to purchase what businesses are willing to supply. This price and quantity combination is referred to as the *equilibrium price and quantity*. Prices increase when demand goes up or when supply goes down.

These basic results are illustrated in Figure 4-3. Points *a, b,* and *f* represent different equilibrium points established by different combinations of supply and demand curves. At point *a,* supply and demand are equal. At point *b,* supply and demand are equal, but at a lower price; this lower price is caused by a fall in demand, which can be caused by a drop in consumer income. At point *f,* supply and demand also are equal at a lower price; this lower price coincides with more of the product being demanded and can be caused by an increase in supply, which may be a product of improved technology or an increased number of businesses in an industry.

Having a point such as *c* is also important. In this case, the economy is out of equilibrium, or in *disequilibrium*, if we take supply curve S_0 and demand curve D_0 as our points of reference. At the relatively high price of P_1, firms are willing to supply more than consumers are willing to buy. There is a surplus on the market — too many mountain bikes for sale at the relatively high price. Eventually, something has to give. The price must drop to P_0, where supply and demand will be equalized.

Figure 4-3:
Demand and supply analysis models how the interaction between the forces of supply and demand determine market price and the quantity sold at this price.

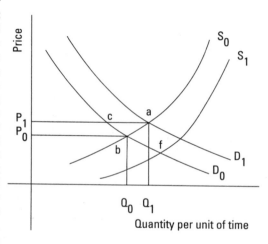

Behavioral economics doesn't do away with supply and demand. Instead, it expands on the concept much in the same way that behavioral economics enriches the idea of opportunity costs. The economic scissors in the hands of a behavioral economist, every so often, cut a different and more insightful pattern from the fabric of economic life than they do in the hands of a conventional economist. Behavioral economics introduces variables in addition to the traditional product price and income variables to help explain the steepness of the supply and demand curves and positions and shifts to these curves.

Introducing the bandwagon effect

In conventional economics, you alone are the master of your demand curve. Your needs and wants are never influenced by what friends, neighbors, enemies, and even strangers may think about your choices. But as anyone who's ever bought a hula hoop, a Pet Rock, or a Cabbage Patch Kid can tell you, sometimes economic decisions are affected by what everyone else is doing. This point can be illustrated by outward shifts of the individual demand curve. When other people buy more, so do you. The iconoclastic early 20th-century economist Thorstein Veblen referred to this as the *bandwagon effect*. His narrative was developed and enriched by Harvard University economist Harvey Leibenstein.

In conventional economics, there is no bandwagon effect. Individuals are assumed to make decisions in isolation.

According to the theory of the bandwagon effect, if your demand for a Susan Boyle CD is related to your knowledge that other people are buying her CD, your demand curve and the market demand curve are higher than they would otherwise be. If your friends and neighbors are buying their kids some strange new toy for Christmas, you may buy it as well — even if you would never have dreamed of purchasing this toy had you made your decision in isolation.

As mundane as these observations may be, they aren't part of the traditional economic model, which consequently can't explain fads. Bringing human behavior into the equation better enables economists to understand why people will drive up the demand for something en masse.

Investigating the snob effect

Traditional economists say that the lower the price of a good, the higher the quantity demanded will be. But sometimes, people pay for a good precisely because it's pricey — being seen with that expensive product means that they've "made it" or hit the big time. Paying more produces a feel-good effect. This makes sense to anyone who's bought a flashy car or designer clothes. At least up to some price, demand will increase as price goes up. Of course, this is the opposite of what the law of demand predicts. Veblen refers to the appeal of high-priced goods as the *snob effect*.

Most scholars refer to the commodities that are in demand because of the snob effect as *Veblen goods, status goods,* or *positional goods.*

The snob effect can explain the demand for status goods such as automobiles and jewelry; certain people wear their purchases to signal to themselves and to others their self-perceived high status in society. Some people purchase works of art, cars, or houses as status goods as well. The higher the price, the more status these individuals believe the goods signal.

As long as people are willing to pay for the social boost they derive from the purchase of status goods, a snob effect will exist.

Explaining high prices for moral goods

In theory, according to conventional economics, businesses that sell high-priced products that are identical to relatively low-priced products should be driven out of the market by consumers, who are all wealth maximizers, searching for the best bargain in town. Isn't this exemplified by Walmart's aggressive expansion?

But the market isn't that simple. People *do* search for bargains, but they're also willing to pay higher prices for products that they believe have been produced or are being sold according to higher moral standards. Some people would be willing to pay more for fair-trade coffee and tea. Others may be willing to pay more for union-produced goods and services or to support a local business. Still others may be willing to pay more for free-range chicken.

Higher-income people may be willing to pay more than poor people, because they can afford to. But individuals across the income range are willing to sacrifice some income to pay for the unique moral characteristics of particular goods and services. This allows for the existence of sustainable markets for relatively high-priced moral products. Not even Walmart can drive businesses producing and selling these products into economic oblivion.

People who are willing to pay more for moral goods aren't income or wealth maximizers, but they *are* doing what makes them happier. And this type of non-economic behavior helps determine what and how much is produced in the marketplace.

Interjecting morals and ethics

Ethical and moral considerations also affect supply and demand. Even though moral and ethical benefits are intangible, they have a real value for many people, causing them to select one product over another (often at a premium) or to offer up their time and labor at a reduced cost (or even for free).

For example, if you get a warm glow or satisfaction from buying products that have been ethically produced, such as free-range chickens or union-made clothing, you may be willing to pay an ethical premium for such commodities. You may give up your Saturday mornings to build houses with Habitat for Humanity because it's just the right thing to do. You may work as a lawyer or accountant for a "green" company, offering your professional services at well below your going rate. In these cases, you're sacrificing money or time — and a materially maximizing individual (which conventional economics assumes we all are) wouldn't do that.

These ethical and moral considerations can be illustrated by a demand curve that is situated farther to the right than it would be otherwise. Your demand would be characterized by demand D_1 as opposed to D_0 in Figure 4-3. Given supply curve S_0, this yields a higher price. In other words, you're willing to pay a higher price for an "ethical" product, and this can be expected to result in a higher market price for that product. On the other hand, you may be willing to pay less for a product that has unethical characteristics. This shifts the demand curve to the left, yielding a lower market price for the unethical product. The equilibrium price for the "ethical" product would be higher than for the "unethical" product.

Because people are willing to pay more for "ethical" products, even if these products can be produced only at a relatively higher cost, businesses producing higher-priced ethical products can make it on the marketplace. As long as there is a market for higher-priced ethical products, they'll be sold profitably on the market.

Firms selling the same product, with no ethical dimension, at a lower price won't drive the higher-priced ethical firms out of the market, as long as the higher-priced product has recognizable ethical characteristics. So, for example, fair-trade coffee can be sold at a higher price than the standard fare. But, as you can guess using conventional economics, a $20 package of fair-trade coffee can be driven out of the market by a $15 package of fair-trade coffee.

Introducing sociology to supply and demand

Economists tend to make the simplifying assumption that social factors other than prices and incomes are uninteresting and possibly unimportant to understanding how people make choices and the choices they make. When defending their view that sociology is of little or no consequence to economic analysis, economists often refer to a statement made by economist James Duesenberry in 1960: "Economics is all about how people make choices. Sociology is all about why they don't have any choices to make."

Economics is, without a doubt, highly concerned with how people make choices. But explaining the choices people make often is informed by social factors.

Behavioral economics is very interested in introducing social considerations to economic analysis. Overall, behavioral economics recognizes that people make decisions in the context of the society in which they live. It understands that people are influenced by what their friends and neighbors think and say and by what they think strangers may think and say about their decisions. People also are influenced by how they're raised, by their past decisions, and by the culture(s) of their society.

This doesn't mean that people's choices are predetermined by society. They still make choices, but these choices are rooted in a broader social context.

Understanding how your past affects your present

When you decide what to do today — whether buying a meal at a restaurant or deciding to accept a job offer — you're often influenced by decisions made in the past. Decisions are often what some scholars refer to as *path dependent.* Path dependence exists when history matters to decision making. What you did last year or even ten years ago influences what you buy today. Economists can't understand current choices without understanding and having knowledge about past choices. American economists Paul David and Brian Arthur played an important role in developing the concept of path dependence.

Gary Becker of the University of Chicago discusses the importance of past consumption choices for future consumption choices. One extreme but highly revealing example is the past consumption of addictive substances at an early age. If you're convinced by your peers to smoke a cigarette just for a bit of fun, you may not think twice about it. This is especially true if you don't want to disappoint your friends or, even worse, a girlfriend or boyfriend. But having some fun while you're young may lead to an addiction. This results in your consuming products today that you prefer not to consume. But kicking the habit is too painful — the psychological costs are too high, so you're stuck!

Conventional economics would say that you're in *equilibrium* (you're in a state of rest and nothing is pushing you to change your choice), and many behavioral economists would add that you may be in equilibrium but not in a happy or preferred equilibrium. Had you never gotten involved with your group of friends in the good old days, you may not have been addicted to cigarettes in your 30s or 40s. History — your past behavior — matters big time when it comes to your future choices and your future level of happiness.

Because history matters, your current demand curve for the Scottish delicacy *haggis* (comprised of sheep's heart, liver, and lungs, mixed with oatmeal, onion, suet, various spices, salt, and stock, and traditionally cooked in the animal's stomach) will be much higher today if you were raised on haggis as a child. So, history is also important for non-addictive substances as well.

Also, your demand for such products would be much less sensitive to price increases. If the price of cigarettes increases, your demand may not drop by very much if you're addicted. The same goes for haggis. Economists refer to your sensitivity to price changes as the *price elasticity of demand.* History can both increase demand and make your demand less sensitive or elastic to price changes.

Introducing identity to decision making

An individual's *identity* is his understanding of who he is and with whom and with what he chooses to identify. And people's identity can affect their economic choices. Differences in identity among people can help explain different economic decisions that simply can't be explained by relative prices and income. This goes well beyond helping to explain the different amounts of commodities different people choose to buy. Individuals' identities also help explain their different life choices, such as whether they choose to study hard or the job they think of pursuing.

Being part of a group with whom you identify informs and affects your preferences. If you're part of a community that values charitable giving, you're more prone to donate some of your income than someone who was raised in a community where charitable giving is frowned upon or not celebrated. If your identity is tied with a community where eating pork is forbidden, such as in Jewish or Muslim communities, your demand for pork may be zero, no matter how low the price of pork happens to be and no matter how hungry you may be.

American economists George Akerlof and Rachel Kranton have pioneered economics research on the importance of identity to economic decision making. Their basic argument is a simple one: Your level of happiness is enhanced when you or others do things that enhance your self-image or identity. Also, your level of happiness decreases if you or others engage in behavior that diminishes your identity or self-image. Your identity also is linked to the groups that you identify with.

So, it isn't a far stretch to argue that your choices will be influenced not only by relative prices and income, but also by how your choices affect your identity and, therefore your level of happiness. Contrary to what conventional economics says, identity *can* play an important role explaining why people behave the way they do.

The U.S. military attracts people with a multitude of backgrounds and a host of identities. As Akerlof and Kranton point out, a critical objective of the elite West Point military academy is to forge a common identity among its cadets. You may initially identify as being an African American, a Latino, a Native American, a Southern Baptist, a Muslim, a Jew, a feminist, or gay, or you may even have multiple identities. But to get through West Point, your primary identity must be closely tied with being part of the American military family for whom you'll risk your life. Your preferences are changed so that your self-image is largely enhanced by how well you do by your new family and how well they do by you. With your new preferences, your other identities (for example, as a Jewish feminist) play second fiddle to your new one. Your revised preferences produce different choices on the market and in your personal life.

Explaining gendered choice

More often than not, conventional economics pays little heed to the fact that in many important situations, men and women have different preferences.

Conventional economics assumes that males and females are identical in terms of their wants and desires, at least with respect to their economic behavior. The household is assumed to make decisions as if all members of the household are one — there is no conflict in the household and no one person dominates the other. Plus, after a decision is made, everyone is as happy as can be.

But in the real world (and in behavioral economics), gender matters. Men and women frequently have different preferences, often influenced by their perspective on identity. Whose preferences rule the roost very much depends on who has more bargaining power, and this, in turn, often depends on laws and social customs.

Traditionally, male preferences have dominated, although this has changed in many countries. Kids, especially girls, have typically had little say in terms of which preferences set the household's decision-making agenda, but this, too, is changing, especially in more democratic societies.

The fact remains that there are often losers and winners in household decision making. Who wins impacts the economic choices made by the household, from what is purchased to how much is saved. When men and women make choices independent from one another, these choices are often gender specific and color the landscape of what is produced and consumed.

Examples of gendered preferences and choices abound. In general, women are more risk averse than men; they're less apt to engage in risky activities. Women also typically have a stronger preference for certain outcomes, so many women would sacrifice a higher income in exchange for more economic security. In some situations, women are more altruistic than men. They also tend to reciprocate more than men do. Women tend to be more tax-compliant than men are. And they also tend to be more concerned about their families' well-being, especially that of their kids (which has important implications on how income is allocated). For example, when in control, women tend to ban the consumption of alcohol and use family income to buy groceries and pay the rent instead. On the other hand, men tend to save more money than women do; the more savings you have, the better the family is in the longer run.

There is some evidence that such differences between men and women are learned. In a different environment, some of these gender differences may very well disappear. For example, there is some good evidence that girls attending all-girls schools tend to be characterized by the same level of risky economic behavior and behave as competitively as boys do. Girls no longer feel compelled to behave in a manner that reflects boys' image of how girls should behave.

But in real-world environments with men and women, these gender differences exist. There is a lot that we can't explain in the world if we assume these differences away, as conventional economics does.

Conventional economics tends to argue that giving birth to a large number of children reveals the preference of both partners in a relationship for a large number of children. It also argues that the number of children desired is largely a function of the cost of raising the kids. Increase the cost of raising a child, and there will be fewer children. But women often prefer fewer children than men do, especially in societies where women traditionally give birth to a large number of children. Yet, women still have a large number of children in these societies. If you're a women in a society where you have no power and no say on the number of children you'll have, and if you have little information on or access to birth control, you may very well have as many kids as your husband and his family desire. There is strong evidence that increasing female education on birth control and empowering women decreases the number of children born. Female education and empowerment helps to explain a reduction in births and population growth — they reduce the actual demand for children, regardless of the cost of children.

Exploring how education affects decision making

Economists pay considerable attention to education, especially how it may affect productivity and the wealth of nations. But education can have other effects as well. For example, education can influence how cooperative, trustworthy, and trusting you'll be in the economy. Education also can affect your ability to make effective decisions in the economic realm.

Individuals aren't identical in terms of how they interact and treat others in the economics sphere. Nor are they naturally predisposed to narrowly selfish or cooperative behavior.

There is some evidence suggesting that traditional economics education — celebrating narrowly selfish behavior as the standard for rationality and intelligence — influences how those trained in contemporary economics behave as compared to people educated in other fields of study, ranging from philosophy to accounting. Economist Robert Frank and his colleagues, among others, show that the more you're trained in conventional economics the more self-interested you become. This should come as no surprise. If you think being narrowly self-interested and uncooperative is the smart thing to do and this is how other smart people will behave, then you, too, will probably behave in a narrowly self-interested way.

Education can influence how you behave in the marketplace. It helps determine whether businesses and households are trusting, trustworthy, and cooperative. To the extent that such behavior is better for economic growth, the type of economic education you receive may have implications well beyond influencing how productive you are in the future.

Education also improves your ability to make quality decisions. Conventional economics tends to assume that everyone is a pretty good calculating machine and a highly efficient information processor. But this isn't case (except for a very select few individuals).

Financial literacy is a clear case in point: Throughout the world, most people have difficulty answering questions about compound interest, inflation, or risk diversification when investing, and they don't understand budgeting and saving programs and financial information in general. Getting education about financial matters can reduce the chances that people will make mistakes in their finances or be duped into making costly decisions. This can influence their demand for various financial products and services, which in turn impacts the price of those products and services. Experts hope that financial education will help kill the market for poor financial products.

Economic Psychology: How Thoughts and Feelings Impact Decisions

Economic psychology is very much about how people think and feel about particular economic events and scenarios and how this impacts their decisions. Economic psychology focuses on how emotion and perception (and feelings in general) affect our decisions and how these factors can overwhelm material or wealth considerations.

For example, you may decide not to maximize your income or wealth because hitting the maximum reduces your level of happiness. For some people, income maximization may involve behaving unethically. For others, it may incur some economic losses along the way, which many people prefer to avoid, even if it ends up generating more income. More money isn't everything. Although this runs contrary to mainstream economic thinking, recognizing the importance of psychological factors for economic decision making helps us to better describe and explain economic behavior and price determination.

This approach to understanding decision making was largely pioneered by psychologists Daniel Kahneman and Amos Tversky and has become a key pillar underlying contemporary behavioral economics. In the following sections, I delve into economic psychology in greater detail.

Loss aversion: How framing, ownership, and control affect economic behavior

Most people have a serious aversion to losses — they really hate to lose, and losses hit their level of satisfaction big time. Gaining $100 will give you a certain level of satisfaction. But if you lose $100, this not only pains you but, according to some evidence, reduces your level of satisfaction by more than two times the satisfaction gained from the receipt of $100. Losses are, therefore, often regarded as more than *twice* as powerful as gains. For this reason, most people are willing to sacrifice some gains in income in order to avoid possible losses. Conventional economics says that losses and gains should be given the same weights, but behavioral economics disagrees, because this isn't how people behave in the real world.

In the marketplace, loss aversion helps to explain why you're more apt to purchase a product whose price is framed to suggest that by buying this product now you are avoiding a loss. So, for many people, avoiding a surcharge (or a loss) is more attractive than getting a discount (gaining some money).

In financial markets, one reason that average returns to stocks are so much higher than average returns to bonds are is because of the fear of loss that most people have when investing in the relatively risky stocks. Many people overpay for insurance because of the fear of loss, so they're willing to pay for the feeling of additional security.

Related to loss aversion is something called *status quo bias* and the *endowment effect,* two closely related concepts. People show a preference for the status quo (which is *status quo bias*) and for what they currently have or are endowed with (the *endowment effect*), even if doing so doesn't yield higher levels of material welfare. For example, many people value an asset by more than its purchase price, even when its market value is not expected to increase compared to some other asset. In various economic experiments, after offering a price for an item, such as a coffee mug, and gaining possession over it, subjects in the experiments asked for more money to sell this same mug. In the eyes of the individual endowed with an asset, possession, in itself, increases the value of the item possessed. Your satisfaction is increased for psychological — not for evidently economic — reasons.

How the fear of uncertainty influences decisions

Uncertainty generates a real fear of loss. Many people fear the unknown — outcomes that are uncertain, where there are no guarantees. And in the real world, most economic outcomes are characterized by uncertainty.

On average, many people have a preference for certain options (such as a 100 percent guarantee) even if the monetary value of that option is less than the monetary value of the uncertain option. Most conventional economists would accept this proposition because people are risk averse — they don't like uncertain outcomes. But behavioral economists argue that many people are willing to make a much larger sacrifice for certain and less-risky options than conventional economists would ever expect. This point is made by psychologists Daniel Kahneman and Amos Tversky.

Conventional economics expects that smart people are willing to make some sacrifice in the name of certainty, but not much. And this makes sense if emotional factors are unimportant. But emotional factors *are* important, at least to most people. The fear of uncertainty and the related fear of loss motivate many decisions. How much would you be willing to pay for certainty? It all depends on how strong your aversion to uncertain outcomes is. The answer very much depends on how much of an emotional aversion you have to uncertainty and the possible losses associated with uncertainty.

Following from a Kahneman-Tversky type of example, a person prefers a guaranteed $100 payoff to a payoff where there is only an 80 percent chance of obtaining $140. In this case, there is a 20 percent chance of ending up with nothing. The latter option yields what is referred to as an *expected return* of $112. So, according to the certainty effect, people would be willing to sacrifice $112 – $100 = $12 in expected value to gain a certain outcome. But when you change the probability of the $100 payoff from 100 percent to 25 percent and the $140 payoff from 80 percent to 20 percent — both probabilities are scaled back by the same percentage — people prefer the former option. Notice that the $100 option still has a higher probability of success than the $140 option. But now the $100 option has an expected return of $25 and the $140 option has an expected return of $28. The $140 option still has a higher expected return. When both options are uncertain, people tend to prefer the higher-return option. This type of reversal or flipping of preferences, which is inconsistent with conventional economics, suggests the overriding importance of certain monetary outcomes to many people.

Expected value is a very important concept in economics. The expected value of an option is a probability-weighted average based on attaching probabilities to outcomes and multiplying the outcome by the probabilities. If you're offered an option of $1,000 with a 100 percent probability of getting this money and a 0 percent probability of getting some other outcome, the expected value of this option is $1,000. If the probability of winning $1 million is 1 out of 100,000 and the probability of winning nothing is 0, then the expected value here is as follows:

Expected value = (outcome A) × (probability A) + (outcome B) × (probability B)

In this example, we get:

Expected value = (1,000,000) × (1/100,000) + (0) × (99,999/100,000)

So,

Expected value = 10 + 0 = 10

Conventional economics expects that if they're offered $5 for certain, many people would choose the uncertain $10 expected value. In the real world, most people don't even know what expected value is or how to calculate it. But even if they did, some people would pick the $5 option because, as the saying goes, "A bird in the hand is worth two in the bush."

The warm glow: Why people sacrifice money for fairness or justice

People often make charitable donations, donate time to help victims of a disaster, or accept a job offer at a lower rate of pay because they believe in their new employer's goals. Many companies won't increase their prices on essential goods and services to take advantage of short-term shortages due to a disaster.

Most people get a warm glow from doing the right thing, or doing the right thing grows their identity and self-image. People are willing to pay something to be fair or just — each person has a different price that he or she is willing to pay based on a variety of non-economic factors, including identity.

Conventional economics says that people shouldn't be willing to sacrifice income for doing the right thing. There is no such thing as a warm glow in conventional economics — people are all assumed to be cold fish. Succumbing to emotion (the warm glow) would be irrational according to conventional economics. But in behavioral economics, doing the right thing, even if it's at a material cost, can make a lot of sense, increasing people's level of satisfaction or happiness and helping coordinate economic activity to boot.

Following the devastating earthquake in Christchurch, New Zealand, many people were without paid employment and were desperate for cash. A woman, accompanied by her kids, was in line to pay for her food. Her stock of food and other essentials was destroyed in the earthquake. The bill was totaled, and it exceeded her ability to pay. But a man waiting in line behind her — no relation, not even an acquaintance — offered to pay for her entire bill. Is this person a fool, or is he just a nice guy? Well, from the perspective of behavioral economics, he was no fool. He was increasing his level of happiness by doing what he believed to be the right thing — being a Good Samaritan. These types of good deeds effectively represent a voluntary redistribution of income that increases the level of happiness for all parties involved.

Robert Frank of Cornell University provides numerous examples of individuals taking lower-paying jobs to do the right thing. Many Harvard-trained lawyers, for example, have sacrificed tens of thousands of dollars to work for environmental and social justice organizations, turning down lucrative offers from traditional corporate law firms.

Forfeiting money for status

Some people are willing to accept less monetary compensation when taking jobs at prestigious or high-status companies or organizations. They're willing to sacrifice income to gain the prestige or status of being employed by that company or organization. They may not be maximizing their income, but they're maximizing their level of happiness.

Low-prestige organizations, on the other hand, can still hire top-notch individuals if they can compensate them for their loss of status.

Donating blood: Supply and demand without money changing hands

In the developed world, blood is largely donated. (The selling of blood was banned in the United States in the 1970s.) There is a tremendous demand for blood that is largely met by donors who are effectively engaging in self-sacrifice, most evidently in terms of pain and time.

The conventional economics model doesn't predict such good deeds. But people will make such donations when it makes them feel good, when it strengthens their sense of identity, and when they think it's fair (because it helps other people).

The blood supply tends to increase during times of crisis, when the demand for blood goes up. Market prices aren't always necessary for supply to meet demand. Psychological and social factors can sometimes substitute for economic incentives to bring supply in line with demand.

Part II
Understanding Choice

The 5th Wave   By Rich Tennant

"So, what do you want to hear?"

In this part . . .

Free to choose is a mantra in conventional economics. Freedom of choice is thought to be the goose that lays the golden eggs of happiness and wealth.

In this part, I examine the role and limits of free choice in real-world economic decision making in both the conventional economics narrative and from the behavioral economics perspective.

I also fill you in on the unconventional tools people have developed to make decisions and tell you when these tools produce efficient and effective decisions and under what conditions they're prone to generate errors and biases.

How people's choices are framed plays an important role in determining their decisions, and I discuss this subject in some detail in this part, paying particular attention to the importance of negative and positive frames for decision making.

I cover the important influences that history, culture, norms, peers, and family have on people's choices. People don't make choices in a vacuum, contrary to what conventional economics would have you believe.

Finally, I elaborate on the roles that gender, children, and age play in decision making.

Chapter 5

Exploring the Limits to Free Choice

onventional economics says that people engage in free choice based on free will, given the constraints they face. The focus is on income and relative price — the budget constraint. According to conventional economics, as long as people don't cause harm to others, their free choices and preferences should be respected; this idea is often referred to as *consumer sovereignty.*

In addition, according to conventional economics, people's choices reveal what they believe to be and what is in their own best interest. Freedom of choice produces the best results for the economy and society, maximizing their welfare or well-being (which is Adam Smith's notion of the *invisible hand*).

People's economic choices expressed in the market for goods and services are what ends up generating output that best reflects their wants and desires or preferences. This view is strongly advocated, for example, by Nobel Laureates Milton Friedman and Friedrich Hayek, both of whom make the case that no one can know better than you what's in your best interest. Certainly, no bureaucrat or expert has the ability to accurately determine your preferences.

A growing argument in behavioral economics says that people are *not* free to choose — instead, choices are imposed upon them and they simply live under the illusion of free choice. Tied to this approach is the idea that people are easily manipulated and deceived; for this reason, contrary to what conventional economics says, the choices people make often don't reflect the choices that they most *prefer* to make. If individuals' choices don't reflect their preferred choices, these choices can't be used as a measure of their economic well-being.

According to this behavioral economic perspective, government should intervene to produce choices that are in people's best interest. (This worldview was actually expressed decades ago by economist John Kenneth Galbraith.)

This chapter examines both perspectives on decision making and the choices we make. It examines alternative behavioral perspectives that focus on the environmental factors that affect people's choices, such as labeling, education, and the power to choose.

Free Choice in Economic Decision Making

Both conventional economics and behavioral economics agree that free choice should be ideal, but they differ in some key ways. In this section, I fill you in on what both schools of thought have to say about free choice in economic decision making.

What conventional economics says

Freedom of choice has always been a big deal for contemporary economics. It's closely linked to the idea that free markets are best in order for people to improve their economic and social welfare — make better lives for themselves, their families and friends, and even strangers.

The basic idea of conventional economics is that free markets allow people to express their wants or desires on the market. And markets — through the middleman of supply and demand and prices — will then invariably translate those preferences into goods and services. People end up with what they want.

Of course, people's preferences are constrained and affected by relative prices and income. They can't buy what they can't afford, and they won't buy what's too expensive.

A key assumption that conventional economics makes is that you know best what's best for you. Only you can know what's in your best interest. Only if you're free to choose do you have the ability to act upon what you know to be in your best interest. Conventional economics also assumes that all people are created equal — no one person is better than another and no one person's preferences are better than another's. For this reason alone, no one person has a right to impose his or her preferences on another person.

The exception to this rule would be if a person's choices cause harm to others. Just because someone *prefers* to sell faulty goods doesn't mean he or she should be allowed to do so — the intervention of others is necessary in this case.

The free market is the mechanism that gives voice to people's wants and desires. This perspective has been advocated by economic scholars across the political spectrum. And this worldview has a solid footing in the classical liberal thinking (I'm talking about philosophy not political parties here) that has developed over the past centuries, where the freedom of the individual to pursue his or her preferences and aspirations, in all domains, including the market, is sacrosanct.

Under communist-type regimes, where economies are planned by a bureaucracy, a person's preferences are rarely met. Rather, the bureaucrats set the pace, sometimes with the best of intentions.

What behavioral economics says

Many behavioral economists say that people's decisions tend to be biased because decisions are based on *heuristics* (decision-making shortcuts). Heuristics, along with emotions, result in preferences and choices that simply don't serve people well. The problem isn't so much that people's choices don't reveal their wants and desires, but that their wants and desires are often biased and error prone.

Some of these biased preferences and choices have, according to some behavioral economists, a neurological foundation. It's how people are hard-wired to behave. On other occasions, people simply don't have the power of will to translate their preferences into choices. So, they end up making choices that they regret — choices, that in retrospect, they would prefer not to have made.

The most well-known behavioral economics understanding of decision making and individual choice is presented by economist Richard Thaler and legal scholar Cass Sustein, both of the University of Chicago. Thaler and Sustein argue that because of people's biases and error-prone behavior, it would be best for experts and governments to, at a minimum, nudge people to do what they understand to be in their best interest:

Almost all people, almost all the time, make choices that are in their best interest or at the very least are better than the choices that would be made by someone else. We claim that this assumption is false. In fact, we do not think that anyone believes this on reflection.

In this case, freedom of choice is significantly undermined. But the market and market forces still determine what's bought and sold after experts and governments reconfigure people's choices, at least up to a point.

But behavioral economists, including Thaler and Sustein, don't simply emphasize biased behavior; they also pay considerable attention to decision-making errors based on false or misleading information. Also of importance is people's lack of power to make the choices they most prefer. In this case, an individual's freedom to choose remains of fundamental importance. Factors outside a person's control are identified as impeding him from making decisions that are in his best interest.

Revealed Preferences: When Choices Reveal Your Inner Self

Revealed preference theory in economics is pretty simple: Your choices reveal your preferences — in other words, what you actually want. You wouldn't buy what you don't want. And what you buy is what you want. Otherwise, why would you spend your hard-earned cash? According to this perspective, what you choose is always what you want.

Revealed preference theory was pioneered by Paul Samuelson of the Massachusetts Institute of Technology (MIT). It was an attempt to provide meat to a very abstract theory of consumer behavior. But it's definitely rooted in the assumption that people's choices express their preferences and that their preferences, when translated into choices, reflect what's in their own best interest. Their choices, which reveal their preferences, reflect their efforts to maximize their well-being given their income and relative prices.

If these assumptions hold true, then it follows that you can make use of the revealed preferences to measure the well-being achieved by all members of society. When income and relative prices change, people respond to these changes by adjusting their choices given their established preferences for goods and services. These adjusted choices still represent their revealed preferences — and these choices still serve to maximize their well-being.

The narrative about preferences

The standard way in which the narrative about preferences is told takes the form of indifference curve analysis, with an interplay between budget constraints and relative price curves (see Figure 5-1). The budget line tells how much people can purchase with their income. The slope of the budget line reveals the relative price of two products, such as apples and pears. The indifference curve is an imaginary construct (part of the economics theoretical toolkit) that indicates a given level of well-being or *utility* (happiness or satisfaction) for alternative combinations of apples and pears. Apples and pears simply represent alternative baskets of products that people may consume.

Figure 5-1:
The indifference curve indicates a given level of well-being, satisfaction, or utility for alternative baskets of products.

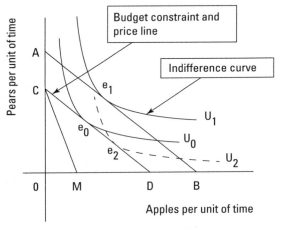

Along indifference curve U_0, people experience the same level of well-being or satisfaction. If the indifference curve shifts outward — to U_1, for example — people's utility goes up. If the indifference curve shifts downward — from U_1 to U_0 — people's utility falls.

But indifferences gain substance and meaning from the point of view of economic analysis only when combined with information on income and relative price. As the Rolling Stones song goes: "You can't always get what you want." You can get only what you can afford. Given your income, you'll then want what you get.

The income or budget lines *AB* and *CD* reveal how much people can purchase. When their income increases, the budget line shifts up, from *CD* to *AB*, and people can purchase more. When their income falls, the budget curve shifts inward, and people can buy less.

The slope of the budget line tells us the price of pears relative to the price of apples. The slope is given by dividing $0C$ by $0B$. If you increase the price of apples, for example, the budget line pivots from CD to CM. The slope increases here. Apples have increased in price relative to pears. Your current income can now purchases fewer apples.

Bring these three bits of information and you end up with a bit of a story of what people would buy given their preferences, income, and relative prices. If their preferences for apples and pears is given by indifference curve U_0, they would purchase a combination of apples and pears given by e_0. Only at e_0 are people maximizing their level of well-being. Increase income, and they would purchase at e_1.

What many behavioral economists would say is that people do their best to get to e_0 or e_1 using the various heuristics at their disposal. But all too often, even when their preferences are given by indifference curve U_0, they end up with choices based on U_2.

So, their revealed preferences are given by e_0, but their preferred preferences are given by e_2. It's even possible that their preferred preferences are given by e_0. But this is a biased choice — it's a choice that isn't in their best interest, according to the experts. And, they should, perhaps, be nudged from e_0 to e_2.

False preferences versus true preferences

Conventional economics makes the assumption, pretty much automatically, without much thought (almost as if a heuristic were being used), that people's revealed preferences are their true preferences. But this assumption holds up only under very specific circumstances. And these necessary circumstances are not always in place in the real world.

If your preferences are based on false or misleading information, you don't have the opportunity to carefully assess all relevant information, so your revealed preferences won't be the same as your true preferences. And if you're forced to form your preferences under duress, your revealed preferences won't be the same as your true preferences.

In these situations, your revealed preferences can't reflect what's in your best interest, unless by some fluke. Instead of forming true preferences, your preferences are, in a sense, "false preferences." They aren't the preferences you would form under ideal but reasonable circumstances.

A brain science interlude

Brain science (see Chapter 3) suggests that quick decisions made under stress can be efficient and effective when based on quality information stored in memory. So, making decisions under duress doesn't have to keep people from expressing their true preferences. If sometime in the past, careful thought went into forming those preferences, people can rely on that memory of the past to make decisions, and it would generate true preferences and choices today. This is the case even if the choices are based intuition.

When a person's preferences are based on false or misleading information, her revealed preferences can't tell us anything about her level of well-being or whether her choices are in her best interest. False information results in preferences and choices that may differ immensely from what they would be if the person had access to more accurate, more unbiased information. This is the case even if that person assesses the false information carefully.

Economists can't simply assume that revealed preferences reveal what makes people happiest (what economists refer to as *welfare maximizing* or *utility maximizing*). First, we need to know the circumstances under which preferences are created and choices are made.

Another precondition for revealed preferences to reflect people's true preferences is that people must be able to translate their wants and desires into choice. People also must be able to express their opinions about their preferences and discuss their opinions with their peers. Otherwise, people's preferences are not what they could be — they aren't enriched by a give and take or rational conversation.

If these conditions aren't present, people end up making errors in their decisions. They would have made better decisions under better circumstances.

For example, if you want to buy a punk rock CD, but it's banned by the government, you may purchase a Rolling Stones CD instead. Your *revealed preference* (for the Rolling Stones) reveals absolutely nothing about your *true preference* (for punk rock). At best, your purchase reveals your second-best preference for the Rolling Stones.

Comparing capabilities deficiencies to decision-making biases

From the perspective of the capabilities approach, pioneered by Nobel Laureate Amartya Sen and philosopher Martha Nussbaum, people typically engage in rational or smart decision making, and they can even make mistakes. But the type of "errors" in decision making that are the focus of the capabilities approach are related to the conditions under which preferences are formed and choices are made. They aren't related to cognitive errors and biases that are so important to many behavioral economists.

From the capabilities perspective, you can make wrong choices even if you aren't suffering from any cognitive biases. Just not having access to proper information can produce errors in decision making. This focus sits well with the emphasis of some behavioral economists on the importance of information and social and political power in generating welfare-improving or welfare-maximizing choices.

For example, if a woman doesn't want to give birth to another child, she can't act on this preference without adequate and appropriate information. She also can't act on this preference if she doesn't have the power to do so. This is one reason why improvement in the quantity and quality of birth control information given to women has a large effect on birth rates, as does the extent to which women have enforced legal rights to have a say on the number of children they have.

Another example: If your revealed preference is to oppose a government, but speaking your mind may result in a prison sentence or other forms of legal sanction, you may cease and desist. Under these circumstances, your revealed preferences would be false, with only the *appearance* of being true. Your true preferences remain hidden. And you would certainly not be maximizing your well-being or utility.

The limits of revealed preferences and free choice

Free choice can do wonders for a person's well-being when it actually exists. The point made by behavioral economics is that we can't simply assume that free choice exists, if free choice is supposed to reflect a person's true wants and desires. Plus, your *revealed* preferences can't be read as a mirror of your *true* preferences.

Certain conditions must be met in order for your choices to reflect your true wants and desires or preferences. By recognizing that these conditions aren't necessarily present, we open the door to the possibility that a person's choices aren't necessarily welfare maximizing. It also allows economists to build models that may provide an understanding of why this may be the case.

The Illusion of Free Choice

Behavioral economics suggests various reasons for why people's choices may be less than free. For many behavioral economists, of critical importance is the way many people appear to be easily swayed or even manipulated. They end up making voluntary choices that they'll later regret. Even worse, people may make voluntary choices that they believe to be in their best interest but that may very well be damaging to their well-being. People may not even know what's in their own best interest. Even when they're free to choose, their choices may not be their own.

If this is the case, then experts and governments should, according to many behavioral economists, play a substantial role in determining the choices that people make in the present and into the future. Highly critical to the discussion of whether experts and governments should play a key role in determining people's choices is whether you believe that people's preferences should be respected. The belief that people's preferences should be respected is fundamental not only to conventional economics, but also to much of Western society.

However, respecting people's preferences doesn't imply that experts and governments shouldn't intervene to improve the environment in which preferences are formed and choices are made.

In the following sections, I discuss how choices can be affected and even distorted by various factors.

Advertising and preference distortions

Over $1.5 trillion is spent on marketing in the world, with over $2,000 spent per person in the United States alone. Some conventional economists argue that advertising is simply a means of providing information to consumers.

More recently, Gary Becker of the University of Chicago has argued that when someone purchases a product, one of the things he or she looks for is how the product is packaged or advertised; this is one of the characteristics of the product that gives consumers satisfaction. This important point is not always incorporated into conventional economics. The fact that consumers are interested in packaging doesn't make them irrational. People are motivated in their choices by a variety of factors, including how a product is presented to them.

Many other scholars believe that advertising manipulates and changes people's preferences, getting them to buy what they wouldn't otherwise buy. People's preferences are flipped when they're presented with trivial or irrelevant information. They end up with the *illusion* of free choice. They buy a car because of the scantily clad woman stretched out on the car, not because of any special features of the car — or so the story goes.

However, following from Gary Becker's perspective, if how a product is presented serves to enhance a person's utility, then this type of advertisement isn't actually manipulating the person's taste. Also, snazzy advertisements didn't help U.S. automobile giants in their competition with their Japanese, European, and South Korean counterparts. Obviously, most consumers were looking at the quality of the automobiles, as well as the way the automobiles were presented.

This idea fits into what Daniel Kahneman and Amos Tversky refer to as the *framing effect*. Any decision problem, such as whether to purchase a car, can be framed in different ways. Kahneman and Tversky argue that even if the frame provides no substantive information, it can change people's preferences and choices. This is especially true if the frame is positive. Because of loss aversion, simply framing a choice option in a positive light will increase the chances of something being chosen. The package is more important than substance.

Other behavioral economists point out that in a world of bounded rationality, advertisements provide information and signals to consumers that help them decide what to purchase.

Still, advertisements can provide false information. This can easily result in rational or smart consumers making choices that they'll later regret. This is not the same thing as people being manipulated by advertisements. Basically, you can make choices that you wouldn't regret if you had the correct information at hand.

When information is misleading, people's preferences won't be their true preferences and their choices won't be welfare maximizing. In the world of bounded rationality and imperfect information, it's impossible to say beforehand if someone's choices made freely, not subject to coercion, are his best choices, from his own perspective.

Self-control and free choice

Conventional economics assumes that people have self-control — so, if people smoke, it's because they want to, not because they have no self-control. And yet we all know that nobody has perfect self-control. So, sometimes people do things that they later regret, making choices that don't maximize their welfare or satisfaction. If people prefer not to smoke but they smoke, if they prefer not to eat potato chips but they eat potato chips, if they prefer not to watch too much TV but they watch too much TV, if they prefer not to gamble but they gamble, they're showing signs of lack of self-control or the absence of adequate willpower.

Self-control problems are important because they clearly result in many people making choices that they prefer not to make, choices that they eventually regret. Some issues regarding self-control are rooted in addictions. Some behavioral economists call for experts to intervene on the marketplace to restrict the sale of items that many people may prefer not to purchase but purchase anyway. Some economists would argue that these sought-after items should be made more difficult to purchase.

But limiting the purchase of, say, cigarettes or alcohol would interfere with the choices of people who actually desire those goods. Straightening out one group's choices can very well create problems for others.

Other economists argue that mechanisms should be put in place to assist people in overcoming their weakness of will. For example, governments may provide accessible drug rehabilitation facilities for those who want them. This type of intervention respects the preferences of all while helping those who have problems with self-control.

Addiction and the illusion of choice

Addiction is a subset of the self-control problem. If you become an addict because of earlier consumption choices or because of prior medical treatment, you have a limited capacity to stop smoking, stop drinking too much, stop gambling too much, or stop taking drugs. Of course, some addicts prefer to do what they're doing. They're maximizing their own well-being, no matter how others may frown upon their behavior.

The revealed preferences of an addict, who genuinely wants to kick the habit, don't reflect his or her true preferences. An addict may appear to be engaging in free choice, but this is often an illusion. This person is a puppet to his or her addiction. Economists can't predict or analyze choice behavior without integrating addiction into their economic analyses.

The bottom line is that when self-control issues are genuine, people's free choices aren't welfare maximizing, and this should be recognized in economic theory. The big question is how best to address self-control issues, especially if people's true preferences are to be respected.

Defaults as a determinant of choice

Behavioral economists have introduced the notion that *defaults for choice* (the options for choice presented to you and how they're presented) can play a large role in determining your choices. They argue that people are fairly easily manipulated by defaults for choice — people may think that they're engaging in free choice, but it's the defaults that are doing the choosing.

This idea relates directly to the framing effect (see "Advertising and preference distortions," earlier). What appears to be a trivial change in a default option determines your choices — as opposed to something meaningful, like the quality of the product, the rate of return on an asset, or the size of your pension fund at the time of retirement.

If the default in investing in a pension fund is *not* to invest, most people won't. If the default is not to donate organs upon death, most people won't. If the default is to purchase a cable and satellite package with 30 channels as opposed to the 12 basic channels, most people will choose the default option of 30 channels. Defaults matter, contrary to the expectations of conventional economics (which says that people make the choices that are right for them, regardless of what the defaults are).

Some behavioral economists argue that because defaults matter and because defaults are pervasive (they're almost everywhere we look), governments and experts should intervene to establish defaults that will improve everyone's welfare. For example, if society would benefit from higher rates of organ donation, government may intervene so that the default is that everybody's organs are donated upon death; if a person wanted to opt out of organ donation, she could, but opting out would not be the default.

Critics of this perspective point out that we would just end up with the preferences of the few being imposed on the many. In addition, this perspective assumes that the experts know better what's in people's best interests than the people do themselves. There is a significant debate on the extent to which governments should intervene in establishing defaults and whose defaults should be designated.

This debate is particularly important because, as some behavioral economists have argued, defaults send signals to people on what the right choice is. When the default is to invest in pension funds, shouldn't government provide some assurance that the pension is a relatively safe one? On the other hand, if cable companies set defaults that are clearly designed to hook people on more channels than they want, should this be regulated? If so, to what extent?

Herding, the bandwagon effect, and free choice: Are followers irrational?

Many people follow the crowd when forming their preferences and making choices. This is just another example of how social context matters for decision making. When share prices are increasing in the stock market and when people of good or even great repute are investing, other people tend to follow. In other words, people often behave as a herd. There is a bandwagon effect from the leader to the follower. This type of behavior is not consistent with conventional economics, but it is, nevertheless, quite important.

TECHNICAL STUFF

The choice architect

Behavioral economists Richard Thaler and Cass Sustein popularized the concept of the *choice architect,* a type of expert on the best choices people can make. A choice architect is responsible for framing choices, setting defaults for choices, and the like. A choice architect sets defaults for saving plans, designs menus to establish the ordering of the food, and designs the food displays in supermarkets (determining which foods are displayed more or less predominantly).

Remember: Frames and defaults are never neutral and they're pervasive. So, why not have choice architects design environments to encourage choices that some experts deem to be in people's best interest?

But many behavioral economists agree with conventional economics that no one should necessarily be forced to make any specific choices. Instead, frames and defaults should be designed to nudge or encourage people to make choices that the experts believe to be in people's best interest. This idea is referred to as *soft paternalism.* Potato chips, candy, cigarettes, soft drinks, beer, wine, designer jeans,

hot dogs, and corn beef sandwiches wouldn't be banned. Instead, the choice architects would design a choice environment in which people would be discouraged from choosing particular goods and services and encouraged to choose others.

The question is, would private- and public-sector firms be legislated to accept the planning directives of these architects of choice? Or would choice architects largely be design advisors? Some behavioral economists believe that choice architects should be employed by firms to help them design a choice environment that will encourage people to make proper choices — proper choices from the perspective of the choice architect.

Many other behavioral economists argue that, regardless of whether we have choice architects, people's free choices would be improved if they had more accurate, trustworthy, accessible, and understandable information. In this case, people aren't nudged to choose one thing or another. Instead, better information would result in better choices.

To some extent, people's choices are affected by the choices of other people. Obviously, those in the know or imbued with considerable self-confidence end up leading the herd. And some people end up making a pretty penny following the leaders. Others who follow the leader end up jumping off the cliff instead of stopping short, and they suffer considerable material and psychological damage in the process.

Some behavioral economists consider this sometimes pervasive behavior to be irrational, resulting in serious errors in decision making. Others argue that this behavior is sensible in a world of bounded rationality.

Constraining Choice versus Freedom of Choice

Most economists agree that all choices are constrained, but just because choices are constrained doesn't mean that they aren't free. Conventional economics focuses on relative prices and income as the major determinants and constraints on choice. But even given these constraints, people can choose what they want if they can afford it.

In behavioral economics, constraints are broadened to include information and deliberation constraints (the brain is a scarce resource), social constraints, as well as constraints imposed by the environment. Some behavioral economists maintain that choices are highly constrained and plagued by cognitive errors and biases such that freedom of choice is more of an illusion than anything else. Others argue that constraints still leave a lot space for freedom of choice, and this space can be increased by improving the environment in which choices are made (known as the *choice environment*).

In the following sections, I discuss various factors affecting people's ability to make their most preferred choices — choices that they won't end up regretting.

Information

Critically important to behavioral economics is recognizing not only that the brain is a scarce resource but also that quality information is costly to come by and to process. Without appropriate information, it's very difficult for people to develop their true preferences and make choices that they would make under ideal circumstances. This absence of information can lead to errors in decision making and choices that people will later regret.

Improving the information environment is critical in order for people to construct their true preferences and make welfare-improving choices. Many revealed preferences may be damaging to people's well-being because they lack the knowledge to make appropriate choices — choices that they'll come to regret down the road.

Education

Information, even quality information, must be processed and understood. In order for people to make choices that they would make under ideal circumstances, they need the education necessary to process and understand relevant information. At the very least, they should have access to experts who are trustworthy and can help them make quality choices.

If people can't understand the information provided to them, they may very well make choices that they'll later regret. Ignorance is not bliss when it comes to having correct information about risks and having a proper understanding of this information.

Consumer rights

Because of the importance of quality information for welfare-improving choice, proper and trustworthy product labeling can play an important role in improving the choice environment. So can rules and regulations that minimize the extent of false or misleading advertising. People rely on information to construct their preferences and make their choices.

Well-enforced and well-articulated consumer rights can help improve the choice environment by improving the quality of information available to people.

If people are led to believe that a product will make them more intelligent within two weeks, many of them will buy the product. Many people would also buy high-yield financial instruments that they're told would be safe bets. People may be naïve or they may be engaging in wishful thinking. But they aren't behaving irrationally — they're acting on information that they believe to be true. The better the information, the better the choices that rational or smart people will make. Strong consumer-protection laws can contribute to creating that kind of conducive environment.

Chapter 6

Quick and Simple Heuristics and Real-World Decision Making

. . . .

In This Chapter

▶ Looking at what conventional economics says about decision making

▶ Delving into bounded rationality and satisficing

▶ Understanding unconventional human behavior

▶ Looking at loss aversion and the pain of loss

▶ Thinking about errors and biases in decision making

▶ Introducing fast and frugal heuristics

. . . .

*T*he populist perspective on behavioral economics — what makes it so sexy to many people — is that behavioral economists say that people are irrational and even just plain dumb. Although this interpretation of one important perspective in behavioral economics is a bit extreme, it does hit home.

This chapter examines this mainstream "errors and biases" perspective of behavioral economics, a view that holds that people tend to make decisions that are persistently error prone and biased. According to both conventional economics and many behavioral economists, *heuristics* (decision-making shortcuts) and emotions aren't much help when it comes to making smart or optimal choices and producing the best possible outcomes. However, behavioral economics identifies heuristics as a fundamental feature of real-world decision making.

In this chapter, I also discuss the side of behavioral economics that argues that people typically make smart choices given the psychological and environmental constraints that they face. Smart choices are choices that are rational — they do the job well, given the constraints people face.

These choices often appear to be dumb on the surface, especially if you use conventional economic assumptions as the baseline for what the world looks like and for best possible or optimal decisions and choices.

However, when people make intuitive or emotionally based choices, these are often smart and better choices — as opposed to the "calculating choices" of conventional wisdom. Indeed, often, taking the calculating route can be disastrous. Just think about deciding when to jump out of the way of a speeding car or making a snap investment decision given serious time constraints. This perspective in behavioral economics also argues that if we change environmental factors (the environment or framework within which choices are made), we improve people's choices.

A Bird's-Eye View of Smart Decision Making in Conventional Economics

In conventional economics, there isn't much interest in how people make decisions. Conventional economics assumes that people make rational decisions — decisions that are thoughtful, deliberative, cold (not affected by emotions), carefully calculated, materially maximizing, and forward looking. It makes no difference if people don't actually behave in this way. What actually happens in the real world of decision making is beside the point for conventional economics.

Conventional economics assumes that all decisions are in some sense maximizing — people are always maximizing their *utility* (happiness or satisfaction) or welfare. In a sense, conventional economics is all about demonstrating that people's choices are ideal.

But lurking deep in the background of this worldview is the idea that conventional economic models can be scientific. In other words, these models can explain economic phenomenon without going into the gory details of decision making.

But more than that, many conventional economists add a normative twist to their argument. They maintain that people actually should behave in a manner consistent with the rationality of assumptions of conventional economics.

But the fact of the matter is that most people don't behave according to the conventional economics definition of *rationality*. Most people aren't the super-calculating beings that inhabit the world of conventional economics. This reality is an important shortcoming of conventional economics, often dramatically weakening its explanatory and predictive powers.

Decision-making norms in conventional economics: The human calculating machine

Conventional economics doesn't pay much attention to real-world decision making, but its idea of how people should behave is vested in its "as if" assumptions of behavior. Conventional economics assumes that people behave in a cost-minimizing, profit-maximizing, and utility-maximizing manner.

Implicit in this argument is that only a specific set of behaviors is consistent with optimal outcomes, such as cost minimization and profit maximization. Other behaviors couldn't survive the test of the market, nor could they easily generate cost-minimizing, profit-maximizing, and utility-maximizing outcomes. Conventional norms are said to be the ideal norms for rational or smart decision making.

Being able and willing to coldly and deliberatively calculate the costs and benefits of a decision — for the present and into the future — is a critical behavioral norm in conventional economics.

Conventional economics also assumes that we can best predict or explain economic events if we assume that people are, on average, materially and even spiritually selfish. In other words, people don't give a damn about each other. Selfishness is an important behavioral norm in conventional economics.

In conventional economics, the reality of assumptions doesn't matter. However, the specific simplifying assumption of the cold, calculating, consistent, and selfish person remains important to conventional economics. If the predictions of conventional economics don't hold water, economists often argue that there must be something wrong with the data or that people aren't behaving as they should. In other words, people should behave in accordance with conventional behavioral norms.

Conventional economics also assumes that, in the long run, people will end up behaving as expected. But how long is "the long run"? If the long run is too long, this time frame may not be relevant for the analysis at hand.

During many classroom experiments testing various propositions of conventional and behavioral economics, the subjects of the experiments don't behave in the selfish manner predicted by conventional economics. Subjects also don't always maximize their material well-being. The punch line of many conventional economists is that the wealth-sacrificing subjects are irrational or not smart — they should've taken a course (or a better course) in economics.

But the prediction of conventional economics is wrong — people often aren't wealth or income maximizers — because people don't follow the conventional rules for rational behavior.

The optimizing decision-making machine in conventional economics

A key assumption in conventional economics is that people make choices that generate optimal results. They make choices that make them the happiest, make average costs the lowest, and make the rate of profits the highest. Conventional economics also argues that non-optimizing behavior is not rational or smart. Because people are assumed to be rational or smart, they aren't expected to behave in a non-optimizing manner.

Conventional economics also assumes, sometimes implicitly and quite often explicitly, that there is pretty much only one way to optimize. And this is marked by the standard tale of comparing marginal benefits to marginal costs in a cold, deliberative manner — people are assumed to be Mr. Spock–type optimizing machines. Deviating from conventional ways — deviating from the well-marked conventional route — will result in choices that are suboptimal for the decision maker.

Painting a bull's-eye after the fact

Harvey Leibenstein of Harvard University liked to tell the following story, helping expose some problems with the conventional optimizing assumption: During the Russo-Japanese War, the Russians weren't doing well at all. The Russian army needed some serious help in the form of sharpshooters. So, a Russian general scoured the countryside for a legendary sharpshooter who was rumored to live and practice his art deep in the forest. As good fortune would have it, the general heard some shots and located the peasant marksman who was digging out his bullet from a bull's-eye target marked off on one of the very large trees. The general asked the peasant for a demonstration of his skills. The peasant fired at the trees. He then took a bucket of paint and marked a bull's-eye where one of his bullets managed to strike a tree. "There," remarked the peasant with great pride. "See how I've hit the bull's-eye."

Well, if you assume that people are all optimizing machines and their choices reflect optimizing behavior, then whatever the outcome, economists may very well assume it to be optimizing. And they may end up painting a bull's-eye no matter where the bullet strikes. This situation prevents economists from determining if particular choices did, in fact, result from a process of optimization and from more deeply understanding the actual processes by which those decisions were made.

Because conventional economics assumes that people are always optimizing, and doing so in a prescribed manner, what economists see is often assumed to be an optimized result. Economic problems are thought to be a product of outside forces (such as government) interfering with people's efforts to make optimizing decisions and choices.

Sometimes markets can fail, when people don't bear the costs of their choices — for example, when they pollute the environment at no cost to themselves. People can and should deal with market failures. Still, most outcomes are regarded to be optimal, by definition, given that people are assumed to be optimizing decision-making machines.

Conventional economics tends to lead to arguments that all financial markets are efficient (known as the *efficient market hypothesis*). Scholars devote boundless amounts of time and energy trying to demonstrate that prices of financial assets, no matter how bubbly, are efficient — all prices reflect the underlying economic fundamentals.

Core conventional benchmarks for rational choice: To dream an impossible dream

The conventional benchmark for rational choice is the type of unemotional, forward-looking, narrowly self-interested, materially maximizing, deliberative, and calculating behavior (not affected by others), with no weakness of will, which I discuss throughout this book. Such behavior is expected to generate optimal economic results, including maximizing people's level of well-being or happiness. Many conventional economists believe that this is how people should behave if they're rational or smart.

Behavioral economists, on the other hand, argue that such behavior is not possible given how people are wired physiologically and given the information environment they face when engaged in decision making. People also are affected by institutions that constrain or facilitate certain behaviors and choices.

For the most part, people just can't behave in the manner prescribed by conventional economics. They can only be boundedly rational, as Herbert Simon would argue. *Bounded rationality* refers to decision making that makes sense given the constraints people face not only in terms of the limited processing and computational capacity of the brain, but also in terms of the relevant information they possess. Also, people don't maximize — they just can't do it. So, they satisfice instead — doing something that works well enough given the constraints people face (see "Rethinking Bounded Rationality and the Limits of the Mind," later in this chapter).

This is not to say that people can't follow some of the normative rules of conventional economics. Many people choose not to. But they actually *can't* engage in the deliberative detailed calculation demanded by conventional economics. Hence, bounded rationality and satisficing.

Behavioral economics isn't methodologically or ideologically opposed to optimizing. Nor do behavioral economists argue that people don't *try* to maximize their well-being or that firms don't *try* to minimize costs or maximize profits. Many do try — and this is what satisficing is all about.

The limits of conventional rationality

Behavioral economics has provided a mountain of evidence that people don't always behave in accordance with conventional economic norms. Even if they *can* (for example, by acting selfishly and unfairly), they often don't. Many people make decisions that they regret. They often don't have decision-making power to make the choices they prefer.

A large number of firms also get away with not performing optimally. Some firms persistently under-perform. And many markets, including financial markets, appear to be hopelessly inefficient, at least in the short run — give or take a few years.

Very often, when people do behave "optimally," they do so while violating the decision-making norms of conventional economics. This caused Nobel Laureate Vernon Smith to remark that we have a choice between conventional theory, which provides us with behavioral norms that don't work, or modifying our theory based on behavioral norms, which appear to generate not only good but optimal or efficient economics results.

In conventional economics, *rationality* implies that people behave in accordance with very specific behavioral norms. Basically, smart behavior implies that people behave in a particular manner and achieve particular results. Conventional rationality is often tied to the assumption that there is only one path to maximizing happiness and the wealth of nations. But behavioral economics suggests that this doesn't have to be the case — other paths may exist. And we shouldn't exclude these other paths by assuming that alternatives aren't available.

Conventional norms for rational behavior may not be the be all and end all to achieve optimal results for ourselves, our community, or our society. Conventional norms often aren't even a possibility. People often behave in ways that appear to be irrational from the perspective of conventional economics.

James March and human rationality

In 1975, James March, a pioneer of behavioral economics, wrote that engineers of artificial intelligence and organizational decision making modify their models based on their study of actual real-world behavior:

> Modern students of human choice behavior frequently assume, at least implicitly, that actual human choice behavior in some way or other is likely to make sense. It can be understood as being the behavior of an intelligent being or group of intelligent beings. Much theoretical work searches for intelligence in apparently anomalous human behavior. . . . It preserves the idea of rationality; and it preserves the idea that human behavior is intelligent, even when it

is not obviously so . . . if there is sense in the choice behavior of individuals acting contrary to standard engineering procedures of rationality, then it seems reasonable to suspect that there maybe something inadequate about our normative theory of choice or the procedures by which it is implemented.

Many behavioral economists, however, argue that conventional economic norms often make sense in determining the benchmark for rational, smart, and optimal behavior. All too often, people just don't conform to these behavioral norms. Other behavior economists reject, for the most part, conventional behavioral norms as a benchmark for rational or smart behavior.

Rethinking Bounded Rationality and the Limits of the Mind

Bounded rationality refers to decision making that make sense given the constraints people face not only in terms of *physiology* (how the human brain works) but also in terms of information (see Chapter 2). These constraints often don't conform with conventional economic behavioral norms. We can't use normative behavioral benchmarks that aren't reasonable, given our human decision-making capabilities and the environmental constraints we face.

Over time, people develop decision-making processes and decision-making shortcuts (known as *heuristics*) that are rational, based on physiological and environmental constraints. These deviant decision-making shortcuts often get the job done effectively and efficiently.

This type of behavior is referred to as *satisficing* (doing the best they can given the constraints they face; see Chapter 2). People don't have to live up to the strict behavioral norms of conventional economics to get the job done.

Sometimes people make mistakes. These mistakes often are corrected over time — people tend to learn from their mistakes (although there are always exceptions to the rule). Some behavioral economists argue that learning *doesn't* take place or takes place much too slowly to make a difference, so some people may end up with persistent decision-making errors.

Bounded rationality and satisficing: Rationality within reason

Bounded rationality defines real-world smart behavior. It's based on the decision-making capabilities of the human brain and the decision-making environment within which people develop their preferences and make choices. Bounded rationality is part of what Herbert Simon refers to as *procedural rationality*.

What is of significance to our understanding of real-world decision making is not that people consciously follow certain maximizing rules of conventional economics. They don't. Rather, what matters is that people adopt decision-making procedures that work to achieve ends that they aspire to. These procedures may even be intuitive in nature. And those ends may include improving material well-being or minimizing production costs.

Satisficing is simply the label assigned to decision-making behavior that doesn't abide by the particular decision-making norms of conventional economics. Instead of maximizing or minimizing, people satisfice, producing decisions that are good enough given the constraints they face.

People develop procedures to effectively achieve their goals given the constraints they face. These constraints are typically assumed away in the conventional economics approach to rationality and decision making.

Satisficing behavior is a form of procedural rationality. It's a type of rationality that is reasonable given the multifaceted constraints that people face when forming their preferences and making decisions.

The two blades of the decision-making scissors: Ecological rationality

Bounded rationality assumes that people are procedurally rational given the constraints they face, even if they violate the norms of conventional economics. Violating norms that just don't work in the real world can't make people irrational.

If you have to make a spot decision to buy or sell a stock, you can't carefully calculate the costs or benefits of different decisions. You have to act quickly. You have no choice but to satisfice. If you're a professional, your rapid-fire decisions are based on experience. The more experience you have, the more effective your intuitive decisions may be.

The decision-making environment affects the decision-making process you adopt. If you have a lot of time, you may choose a different decision-making process than if you have no time at all. There is no one-size-fits-all decision-making norm or procedure. What's rational in one set of circumstances may be silly in another. Also, smart decision-making rules or procedures evolve over time as circumstances change and as the human brain evolves.

Herbert Simon discusses how people's decision-making norms are affected by the two blades of the decision-making structure:

- ✔ Physiological constraints, or the reality of neurologically based decision-making capabilities
- ✔ The decision-making environment

The two blades combined cut the fabric of the decision-making norms that people choose. They also determine which norms generate the best results or choices given people's preferences.

One approach to bounded rationality combines the two blades of the decision-making structure, producing what Gerd Gigerenzer, a leading psychologist from Berlin, refers to as *ecological rationality*. People are ecologically rational when they choose decision-making heuristics or abide by decision-making norms that make sense, that work, that are relatively efficient, given the capabilities of the human brain and the decision-making environment. These heuristics evolve relative to what is required by the choice before us. They evolve from below — they're bottom up.

Heuristics differ for different environments and change as environmental conditions change. They can be summed up by the expert. But typically there is no one-size-fits-all set of optimal norms that can or should be imposed from above. Gigerenzer refers to these decision-making procedures as *fast and frugal heuristics*.

Both Gigerenzer and Nobel Laureate Vernon Smith champion the idea of decision-making rationality as something that evolves based on circumstance. Often, people can't even articulate why they do what they do in any great detail — it just works!

The concept of ecological rationality is not inconsistent with errors in decision making. But it recognizes that conventional economic behavioral benchmarks for optimal behavior and for predicting optimal economic outcomes often can be highly misleading and without empirical foundation.

Not all behavioral economists would agree with some basic premises of ecological rationality. Indeed, the mainstream within behavioral economics supports the assumption that conventional economics benchmarks or norms for rational behavior are often quite appropriate.

Prospect Theory: Describing Average Decision-Making Behavior

The mainstream of behavioral economics argues that people are all too often subject to *cognitive illusions* (errors in understanding reality based on how information is presented or framed and how our brain processes information) causing errors and biases in decision making. Moreover, these events are typically not one-time occurrences: People fail to learn appropriately from their mistakes, which is a product of not abiding by conventional economics behavioral norms. This approach to behavioral economics, pioneered by Daniel Kahneman and Amos Tversky, is often referred to as the *errors and biases approach*.

If people somehow were able to conform to the conventional behavioral rules, we would end up with a more efficient economy and people would be better off. People often fail to maximize their satisfaction because of the heuristics they persistently choose.

The errors and biases approach doesn't abandon the norms of conventional economics.

According to the error and biases approach, people make persistent mistakes and often end up regretting their choices. Very often, when people *don't* regret their choices, it's because they don't appreciate what's in their own best interest because they suffer from those pesky cognitive illusions.

In contrast, the bounded rationality approach to behavioral economics (see the preceding section) often finds good sense underlying the decision-making norms people choose. Bounded rationality doesn't close the door to the reality of errors in decision making. But when decision-making errors occur, the bounded rationality approach says that it's often a product of things like poor information or lack of empowerment. In the errors and biases approach, errors are the product of people's minds, not of their choice of inappropriate heuristics.

Important aspects of the errors and biases approach are captured by *prospect theory,* which was put forth by Daniel Kahneman and Amos Tversky as an alternative to conventional economic modeling of decision making under uncertainty. Prospect theory also was seen as an alternative to the bounded rationality approach.

Both approaches to behavioral economics — bounded rationality and the errors and biases approach that includes prospect theory — forcefully argue that the conventional economics approach is largely without empirical basis. In contrast, these alternative approaches are built upon a much richer understanding of the human condition.

Introducing prospect theory: Real-world decision making under uncertainty

For many behavioral economists, what clearly distinguishes conventional economics from behavioral economics is that behavioral economics integrates emotions and the possibility of cognitive illusions into the modeling of decision making. Some behavioral economists argue that this is critical because emotions and cognitive illusions are embedded in brain architecture and can produce errors and biases in decisions. In this errors and biases perspective, even if people had the cognitive skills assumed by conventional economics, they would still fall far short of the behavioral norms of conventional economics because of cognitive illusions and emotions.

Emotional factors play a particularly important role in decision making that involves losses and gains. Also, both emotions and cognitive illusions come to the fore when we deal with economic prospects that involve uncertainty — where we have to estimate or guess the probability of gains and losses.

In contrast to the errors and biases approach to behavioral economics, the bounded rationality approach focuses on physiological constraints on behavior. Emotions, for example, don't have to produce errors and biases in decision making. Indeed, they often contribute to a more effective and efficient decision-making process.

Prospect theory was developed as a descriptive theory of certain aspects of average decision-making behavior. Conventional economics can't describe, explain, or even predict choice behavior. But conventional behavioral norms — how people should behave — is not under fire here. Prospect theory often paints a more accurate picture of average decision-making behavior than conventional economics does.

Thinking about prospect theory and conventional norms

Daniel Kahneman, Amos Tversky, and other behavioral economists argue that, in conventional economics, what matters — and what should matter to people — is the final state of wealth or level of income. How much income you have, how much you end up with, and whether it increases or falls over time is what you should value most. Moreover, you should be most concerned with maximizing your long-term levels of wealth or income. The present shouldn't take precedence over the future.

The higher your income, the better you should feel and the higher your level of well-being — so you should take action to increase your income if you're rational. Conventional norms are, therefore, pretty much spot on, at least in this instance, from the Kahneman and Tversky perspective on behavioral economics.

Exploring emotions as a hot bed of irrationality

A key aspect of prospect theory is the introduction of emotions as key determinants of people's choices. Also of importance in prospect theory is the notion that people are much more concerned by their relative standing in terms of income or wealth — what they have relative to what others have — in contrast to their total amount of income or wealth.

In prospect theory, emotions — how a person feels about loss and gain, his feelings of regret and sorrow when he makes mistakes — are an important driver of that person's behavior. Emotions affect a person's level of well-being.

Emotions, because they affect a person's well-being, can push a person to make economic decisions that are not objectively in her best interest, at least according to the conventional economic norms of utility maximization. Emotions can fuel the flames of irrational choice behavior.

This perspective is certainly not accepted by all behavioral economists. For many behavioral economists, emotions and, related to this, intuition often play a positive role in determining people's choices.

The fundamentals of prospect theory: Understanding the value function

Daniel Kahneman and Amos Tversky developed the graph shown in Figure 6-1, to illustrate prospect theory. The S-shaped value function is drawn from data and represents average behavior. For this reason, by definition, you would expect many people not to fit the value function — many people would be located above or below this function.

A key characteristic of this value function is that it has both a positive dimension and a negative dimension. The shapes of the positive and negative parts of the curve differ in slope, and the value function has a reference point.

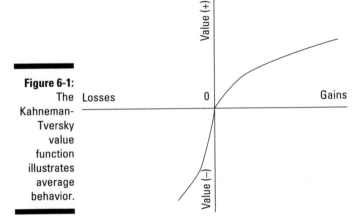

Figure 6-1:
The Kahneman-Tversky value function illustrates average behavior.

Gains versus losses: Which matter more?

Prospect theory argues that, more often than not, people value gains differently from the way they value losses. Prospect theory places a greater weight on losses than it does on gains — a dollar lost more than outweighs a dollar gained. To illustrate this, we need the positive and negative components to the value function. In conventional economics, gains and losses are treated equally — a dollar lost simply cancels out a dollar gained.

The values measured along the vertical axis represent the level of utility derived from a gain or loss. In prospect theory, people are expected to maximize their level of utility as opposed to maximizing their income or wealth. Income or wealth maximization (subject to the risks involved in the economic outcomes and where gains and losses are equally weighted) is, of course, the be all and end all of conventional economics. So, given the risks involved in economic outcomes, conventional economics expects that people will try to maximize their income or wealth. If people are risk averse, they're willing to sacrifice possible increases in future income or wealth for less risky or safer economic prospects.

Because gains are weighted or valued more than losses, in prospect theory the positive part of the S-shaped value function has a lesser slope than the negative part, producing a kink in the function. A $10 gain generates a smaller increase in value or satisfaction than the loss in value produced by an equivalent $10 loss. Moreover, based on some evidence, proponents of prospect theory argue that the loss in value is between 2 and 2½ times the increased value from an equivalent change in income or wealth. Therefore, gains and losses are assigned different weights. I'll put it another way: If you lose $1, you'll need to gain about $2.50 to keep your level of satisfaction from falling. In conventional economics, $1 gained is assigned the same weight as $1 lost. But behavioral economists argue that many people have a more negative reaction to losses than they have a positive reaction to gains.

When people weight losses more than gains, they may very well reject opportunities that increase their net income if possible losses are involved. The gains must be large enough to overwhelm the pain they incur from suffering possible losses.

For this reason, behavioral economists don't expect people to be conventional utility maximizers on all occasions, in contrast to the predictions of conventional economics. People's emotional reaction to losses keeps them from maximizing their wealth or income.

Weighting losses more than gains gives rise to the concept of loss aversion (see "Unveiling Some Implications of Loss Aversion," later in this chapter). Bottom line: People tend to be averse to losses. They try to avoid losses when possible. If people were designed like Mr. Spock from *Star Trek,* they wouldn't allow their emotions to interfere with the "rational" imperative to maximize their wealth or income.

Sometimes, in behavioral economics, it appears as if people try to avoid losses at all costs, but this isn't the case. Many people attempt to avoid losses, within reason. Very often, gains are such that they overwhelm the pain of loss.

> # Resurrecting James Duesenberry and the relative income hypothesis
>
> As a historical footnote, I want to out James Stemble Duesenberry of Harvard University who, in 1949, developed the relative income hypothesis. Duesenberry clearly situated people's level of satisfaction or utility with the relative positioning of their income. But his contributions have been ignored for decades, only to find new life in the behavioral economics of Kahneman and Tversky. Unlike Kahneman and Tversky, however, Duesenberry did not consider conventional behavioral norms to be superior to the norms most people actually use to evaluate their well-being and drive aspects of their decision-making.

It's all relative

Many people pay special attention to reference points when income or wealth increases or decreases. What counts isn't total income or wealth but the relative changes in income and wealth. This is why the negative and positive dimensions of the value function are drawn from a reference point. In conventional economics, what people are most concerned about is the endpoint or total amount of income or wealth. But from the perspective of prospect theory, many people are happier if their income increases by 10 percent from a lower level of income than by 2 percent from a much higher level of income. If my income goes up by 10 percent from $1,000 to $1,100, I'll be happier than if my income goes up by 2 percent from $10,000 to $10,200. Of course, in conventional economics, you'd be happier with $10,200. But in conventional economics, your emotions don't introduce concerns about reference points that may override your desire to increase your absolute level of income.

Many behavioral economists argue that most people would be happier with an income of $10,000 than an income of $1,000. However, people's behavior is also influenced by the relative changes to their income or wealth. So, given your level of income, your level of well-being or happiness increases most with the greatest increases in your relative income. Relative increases to your income as well as relative increases in your income compared to your neighbor's income are important to increasing your happiness and, therefore, to motivating your behavior.

How people see probability

A final important point about the value function is that it maintains that people filter the objective probability of a gain or loss taking place. According to prospect theory, many people use heuristics when evaluating uncertain events, such as gains and losses. And these heuristics distort the actual probabilities of the events occurring.

People tend to underweight extremely low-probability events, giving them a weight of zero. Extremely high-probability events receive a weight of 1. So, very low-probability events are assumed to be impossible and extremely high-probability events are assumed to be certain. But low-probability events are overweighted, while moderate- and high-probability events are underweighted.

Unveiling Some Implications of Loss Aversion

Loss aversion is an important behavioral trait unearthed in the development of prospect theory. Wealth maximization and income maximization aren't everybody's unequivocal objective, contrary to what conventional economics says. Many people need to be heavily compensated to take on tasks or projects where there is a probability of loss involved. This type of compensation goes beyond what conventional economics predicts.

In one example, a particular prospect will increase your net income by $200, through the combination of a loss of $1,000 and a gain of $1,200. Many people will reject this prospect because the psychological pain of losing $1,000 exceeds the pleasure of gaining $1,200.

In another example, we introduce uncertain outcomes. If the probability of winning an additional $1,000 is 90 percent and the probability of not winning is 10 percent, the expected value or income of this type of gamble or prospect is ($1,000 × 0.90) + ($0 × 0.10) = $900 + $0 = $900. If given a choice between this prospect and a sure win of $800, a large number of people would opt for the certain win of $800 — even though they may be sacrificing some expected income in the process.

Loss aversion and the certainty effect

Conventional economics says that people are interested only in the satisfaction they get from income and wealth. They wouldn't attach any value to the certainty of an outcome. But in prospect theory, people are introduced to the certainty effect: A certain outcome is preferred over a gamble (an uncertain outcome) with an equal or greater expected value.

For example, if the sure thing is $700 (option one) and the expected value of the gamble is $(0.90 \times \$1,000) + (0.10 \times \$0) = \$900$ (option two), the loss-averse individual may choose the sure thing even though it yields a lower monetary value.

The satisfaction of the sure thing (no gamble) exceeds the satisfaction of the uncertain but higher monetary value. To accept a gamble requires an even higher return to offset the *disutility* (psychological pain or discomfort) of engaging in the risky prospect.

The fact of the matter is that even when the expected value of the gamble is higher than the certain outcome, a gamble is a gamble. You actually do stand to gain absolutely nothing, even if the probability of doing so is small. Only if you win do you end up with an outcome that surpasses the certain outcome. And the certain outcome, by definition, is certain.

By choosing the certain outcome, you're sacrificing only a *potentially* higher outcome. This type of behavior — although deemed irrational by some economists — doesn't have to be irrational from the point of view of those who value certainty. Of course, gamblers choose the higher-value but more uncertain outcome. For some economists, the gambler represents the rational individual.

One of the points made by some behavioral economists is that if you reduce the probability of gain *equally* across the certain option (option one) and the uncertain option (option two), people shouldn't change their choice of prospects. But they do. Their choice shifts from the lower-value option one (now no longer a sure thing) to the higher expected value, option two. Moving marginally from certainty to uncertainty has a big effect, given how much people like certainty. When both outcomes become uncertain, many people choose the option that generates the higher expected monetary value. The lower-valued option is no longer worth it, when there is some uncertainty, even a small amount, attached to it.

Risk seeking in losses

Because many people are loss averse, these same people would be risk seeking in losses. Risk-seeking behavior here refers to a situation where a certain outcome is rejected in favor of a gamble yielding an equal or lower monetary expected value. If there is a choice between a sure loss of $700 or a gamble of $(0.90 \times -\$1,000) + (0.10 \times \$0) = -\$900$, you may choose the latter option because there is a possibility that the result will be no loss. So, you keep taking risks to avoid a certain loss. This explains why some people hold on to losing investments for too long in the hope of recovering their losses.

This situation violates an important conventional economics rule for rational behavior: Thou shall avoid sunk costs. In other words, don't cry over spilled milk. *Sunk costs* are unavoidable costs — you've already built a factory, you've already purchased a concert ticket, you've already purchased an iPad. These are sunk costs and shouldn't affect your decision making. But they often do affect people's decision making, given that so many people are loss averse.

Many behavioral economists (as well as conventional economists) consider this behavior to be irrational: You're chasing after a gamble that may generate more losses than necessary. But it doesn't have to be irrational from the perspective of the utility-maximizing or satisficing individual and if you take into consideration the emotional cost of incurring potential losses.

On the other hand, many people dump bad debt when others do the same. This is what is referred to as *herding.* So, not everyone is always risk seeking in losses. But both herding behavior and risk seeking in losses are inconsistent with conventional economics.

The endowment effect: Explaining attachment to possessions

Tied to the concept of loss aversion is the endowment effect, which says that many people value a product more after they gain possession of it. For example, you pay $30 for a sweater. After you gain possession of the sweater, you would typically want more than $30 — say, $40 — to sell the sweater.

Some behavioral economists argue that this type of behavior — which suggests that people change their preferences for a reason as innocuous as possessing or owning an object — is inconsistent with conventional economics. Some economists would even argue that this type of preference reversal may be irrational (using conventional economic benchmarks).

Obviously, many people's level of utility derived from a product changes with possession and time. And people suffer the pain of loss if they give up a possession. This is why people often ask a price in excess of their purchase price to give up a possession (at least in experimental settings).

Of course, this isn't the case for shopkeepers or CEOs of major corporations — sellers of products from pots and pans to cars, trucks, and computers. If the owners of firms were to feel affectionate toward their stock and display loss aversion in their pricing policies, it's unlikely that they would stay in business for very long. Vendors mark up prices based on profit targets, not on the basis of loss aversion.

Uncovering Errors and Biases in Decision Making

Behavioral economists have identified a large number of behaviors that are inconsistent with conventional economics. Some behavioral economists consider these behaviors error prone and biased (using conventional economics benchmarks), even irrational. Other behavioral economists view at least some of these unconventional behaviors to be *boundedly rational* (smart behavior given people's brain-processing capabilities and their environmental constraints).

Overconfidence

People tend to overestimate their decision-making capabilities, which often results in their making risky choices — choices in which their chances of success are well below what they think.

You may think that the new restaurant you've opened will be stupendous, that your stock portfolio selection will produce yields well above the average market return, that your new software firm will exceed all expectations. This expectation persists in the face of odds that are stacked against your success. Experiments suggest that most people think that they'll do better than most others — which isn't possible statistically.

But people make these optimistic claims based on a highly uncertain future. Predicting the course of future events is very difficult. Clearly, people aren't using probability theory to determine how confident they should be. Most people don't have a clue about probability theory, and their intuition doesn't easily adhere to probability-driven behavior.

This reality raises an important question: How should economists regard such objectively risk-taking behavior? Some economists see this behavior as very much in tune with the spirit of entrepreneurship — entrepreneurs often view the glass as half-full. But other economists regard overconfidence as a prelude to disastrous economic decisions.

Herd behavior

People tend to mimic the behavior of others, especially when they're dealing with highly uncertain outcomes. They tend to follow the crowd, hoping that the crowd knows more than they do. Or, when possible, they follow people they believe to be experts or people the media celebrates as all-knowing and all-seeing. This behavior is known as *herding*.

Herding causes cascades in particular choices, such as investments in particular assets on the stock market. (Cascades result in choices made by a few individuals giving rise to a multitude of similar choices made by others.) We end up with a wave effect that surfers love. This is exemplified by bubbles and busts in asset prices. Herding also can result in errors in decision making or in great fortunes being made.

Herding is obviously not deliberative and calculating behavior. When people herd, they're breaking conventional decision-making rules. But whether herding is irrational or silly is another question. People often engage in herding when they don't have adequate information to make an "optimal" decision on their own. There is so much uncertainty that following the crowd makes boundedly rational sense to many people.

Confirmation bias

People overweight evidence that supports their views and underweight evidence that runs contrary to their views — all without objectively assessing the evidence. If someone believes that the world is flat, he seeks out evidence to affirm that position. If he believes that government spending is bad, he seeks out experts who confirm his opinion. This tendency is known as *confirmation bias*.

Confirmation bias can lead to serious errors in decision making. But the big issue for debate and discussion is: How, when, and why do people open their eyes to information that challenges their prior beliefs? This issue is especially important when so much information by the experts is conflicting. One side says the market will go up for many years to come. The other side swears that a crash is imminent. Whom should people believe?

Anchoring

People tend to *anchor* their choices to reference points that aren't objectively relevant to the decision at hand. The reference point may be a piece of information that is suggested to them or something they're already familiar with.

For example, let's say you aren't from New Zealand and you're asked to guess New Zealand's population. If you're told that New Zealand has a population smaller or greater than 2 million people, your guess will approach the 2 million anchor. If, instead, you're told that the size of New Zealand is smaller or greater than 20 million, your answer will approach 20 million. (By the way, the correct answer is about 4.5 million.)

Anchoring can result in incorrect results. But it's a heuristic that people use when they don't have accurate information. If your anchor is wrong (20 million people, in the preceding example), you end up with the wrong answer. If you had the chance to check your facts online, you wouldn't use an anchor.

People can be misled by false anchors when they don't have the facts at their fingertips. So, they end up using heuristics to make boundedly rational decisions that can be off the mark.

Generalizing

People often generalize from facts derived from a small sample to the entire universe. In the same light, they often treat facts from a small sample with the same level of trust as they do facts from a larger sample.

Overall, statistical theory suggests that the larger the sample size, the more likely facts are to be representative of what's happening in the larger population.

The media may focus on a small town's massive poverty to illustrate the horrors and extent of poverty nationwide. The small town's plight is no doubt real and heartbreaking. But this small sample size doesn't necessarily say much about poverty in the larger community. A problem arises when some people believe that the small town is representative of something happening nationwide, even when they're presented with information about the larger community that contradicts the portrait of poverty painted by the small town.

Some people accept the facts about the small town in the absence of further and conflicting information. This type of behavior could be a boundedly rational decision in a world of imperfect and incomplete information.

Less Is Best in Decision-Making: Fast and Frugal Heuristics

Many behavioral economists argue that people shouldn't always use conventional economics behavioral norms as the benchmark for optimal decision making. In some instances, breaking with conventional norms may even produce superior results.

In other cases, unconventional heuristics make sense based on workable decision-making shortcuts that humans have developed over the past few thousand years, even when they generate errors in decision making. These errors can be corrected over time through learning. But the improved heuristics still may seriously deviate from conventional norms.

This approach has been spearheaded by Gerd Gigerenzer. Gigerenzer's perspective on heuristics, often referred to as *fast and frugal decision making,* is consistent with Herbert Simon and James March's view that people often find rationality in decision making, even where they appear irrational from the perspective of conventional norms.

Exploring the superiority of heuristics

A key proposition of the fast and frugal approach is that less calculation and information often results in better results than the prescribed behavior of conventional economics does. People often develop heuristics that make the most of the brain's limited resources in order to deal with the question at hand.

The take the best heuristic

People typically don't check everything out, carefully weighing the costs and benefits, when deciding what to buy or what to do. Instead, they *satisfice* (make decisions that work well enough given the constraints they face). The take the best rule is one such satisficing heuristic.

When comparison-shopping, people typically search for selected information — certain key product characteristics. They typically stop searching when they find one attribute that clearly makes a particular product superior to another; this is referred to as the *stopping rule.* For example, price, weight, gears, and brakes may be key attributes when you're shopping for a mountain bike. If two bikes are pretty much the same, but one bike is lighter than the other, you may stop your search and make your purchase. Sweet and simple. This is how people typically behave.

The take the best heuristic not only is a pretty good description of how most people behave much of the time, but it also appears that this heuristic ends up producing the best possible results.

The recognition heuristic

The *recognition heuristic* (in which people choose what they recognize) can produce superior results when people have inferior information. Your instinct is to go for what you recognize.

In one experiment, introduced by Gigerenzer, when a group of Americans was asked if San Diego or San Antonio had a larger population, the majority responded that San Diego was larger. When a group of Germans was asked the same question, everyone said San Diego. The Germans got it right because they didn't recognize San Antonio — they chose the city they recognized. And it happened to be the correct answer. Many Americans, however, recognized both cities. Given that not everyone knew the correct answer, there was some guessing involved and only 66 percent chose San Diego. Apparently, the Americans knew too much or recognized too much, causing the recognition heuristic to fail. When you recognize both cities, you can't use the recognition heuristic.

Another example of the recognition heuristic is relying on brands to make choices. Many people go to McDonald's when they're in a strange town. They recognize the brand and can trust in the product — even if they don't love McDonald's burgers, they know what the burgers taste like, so McDonald's is a sure thing (whereas unknown restaurants are riskier).

When more information is available, people may make another choice — for example, if they get a restaurant recommendation from someone they trust who's been to that town before. But choosing by brand is a cost-saving recognition heuristic that often delivers the goods in a world of imperfect and costly information.

The gaze heuristic: When humans beat the machine

Many experts argue that people should behave as if they're calculating a massive number of equations to get the correct answer. Of course, this is how a computer typically gets the job done.

In a neat example of how humans can do better when they break with conventional norms, Gigerenzer introduces us to the *gaze heuristic*. People take immediate action by fixing their eyes on their objective as opposed to any sort of careful calculation. Their eyes remain locked on the object as the object moves and as they move in the direction of the object. This is how a baseball or cricket player catches a ball. Most players can't explain how they get the job done efficiently. They just do it! And they get the job done intuitively after a lot of hard practice.

Some coaches would like their players to behave as if they were calculating a bunch of equations — figure out where the ball will end up after being hit, and run to that spot — but the best players don't abide by such recommendations. They actually fix their gaze on the ball, lock in on the angle, and run toward where the gaze leads them. The speed and direction of the player adjusts in real time for how the elements affect the movement of the ball. More often than not, the player ends up getting the job done.

The gaze heuristic circumvents any type of calculations, implicit or otherwise, that people find almost impossible to do quickly and efficiently. And the gaze heuristic actually works.

Understanding human rationality: New benchmarks built on human capabilities

People often don't make decisions in conformity with conventional economic behavior norms — that much is clear. And this includes allowing emotions to affect decision making and using heuristics that don't involve any careful calculation and processing of information.

An important point made by behavioral economists is that human beings appear to break with conventional norms — left, right, and center. Economists disagree on whether this implies that people tend to be biased, error prone, or even irrational in their decisions.

Certainly, the heuristics they use can result in choices that aren't wealth or income maximizing. And sometimes heuristics can result in errors in decision making.

But there is now serious debate and research on whether people should always use conventional economics behavioral norms as the default benchmark for best-practice behavior. For many behavioral economists, in many instances, the default should be changed to be more consistent with human capabilities, human wants, and the decision-making environment.

The debate rages on. But there is no dispute that people are breaking conventional rules. And economists are trying to better understand not only why this is the case, but also the implications of this reality for economic analysis and public policy.

Chapter 7

How the Framing of Choices Affects Decision Making

Framing is how options and opportunities are presented. According to conventional economics, how options and opportunities are presented shouldn't affect people's choices — people are expected to look beyond the frame, at what's really important.

This chapter discusses how the framing of options impacts choices. I provide a variety of examples, including the impact of defaults on choices, the effect of relative positioning on choices, and the role of negative versus positive frames in motivating choice. I elaborate upon some public policy implications of framing, which is particularly important when frames can distort the choices people make, thereby producing market failure.

The Framing Effect

According to conventional economics, the frame should have no effect on the decisions people make. In conventional economics, people's opinion of their options should not be affected by how those options are framed. Their choice of what is best shouldn't be at all sensitive to how their options are framed.

But behavioral economists argue that very few decisions are *not* affected by how the choices are framed. In fact, behavioral economists would say that just about all choices are framed in one way or another.

Framing and the economic schools of thought

Conventional economists maintain that framing should not — and does not — affect people's behavior. So, even if context matters in the real world, people's choices should be consistent with a hypothetical world where framing plays no role in decision making.

Decision making that is independent of context or the framing of options is the benchmark for objective, rational, unbiased decisions. Because people are rational (or so conventional economics maintains), they should be making context-free decisions.

Behavioral economics has found that people are affected by how choice options are framed. The context within which people make decisions affects how they view their choices. Change the frame or context, and you can change the choices people make. And the power of framing holds up even when the frame isn't of any substantive importance.

Some behavioral economists argue that because framing affects choice, people's choices easily can be manipulated — and very often are. Many of these economists argue that the fact that people are affected by frames demonstrates that many people are irrational, producing errors and biases in decision making.

Other behavioral economists maintain that seemingly trivial frames contain important information that, in turn, impacts people's choices. In a world of imperfect information and where the brain is a scarce resource — in other words, in a world of bounded rationality — frames can influence the rational or boundedly rational choices of decision makers.

Bounded rationality makes reference to the type of decision making that makes sense given the constraints people face not only in terms of the limited processing and computational capacity of the brain, but also in terms of the pertinent information they possess. This is in contrast to the rationality of conventional economics, which ignores these very real constraints faced by real-world human decision makers and focuses on the detailed calculation of the costs and benefits of making various alternative decisions.

The effect of framing on preferences and choices

Behavioral economists — and even some conventional economists — would agree that changing a frame can change the choices people make. But there is an important distinction between changing choices and changing preferences. Preferences are a person's wants and desires at a given point in time. You *want* a hot sports car. You may or may not end up buying what you really want, though, given relative prices and your income.

Conventional economics doesn't pay much attention to frames influencing either choices or preferences. Many behavioral economists, on the other hand, suggest that frames can change *both* your preferences and your choices.

Obviously, if your preferences changes, so will your choices. But your choices can change, even as your preferences remain the same. Your preference for a hot sports car may remain quite stable over many years, completely unaffected by framing. In other words, your preferences — your wants and desires — can remain stable over time.

But frames can influence your choices. A frame can provide misleading information, and you may end up buying what you actually would not have purchased had better information been available.

A product may be framed in such a way that you would choose the less preferred product. For example, if your choices are between two hot sports cars, and one car is marketed with a frame that you find more attractive (driving fast through the streets of Monte Carlo with a sexy woman), you may flip your choice from the car you initially wanted, to the one that is now being marketed with a preferred frame. Nothing's changed with respect to the two sports cars. All that's changed is how the sports cars are being framed.

Appreciating the objective unimportance of frames: The errors and biases approach

Many behavioral economists argue that frames shouldn't influence the choices people make when the frames aren't important, when they don't add anything of substance to the information about the choice options before you. What should count for the decision-making process and outcomes, according to many behavioral economists, is what's inside the frame. People should judge the *Mona Lisa* by the painting itself, and they shouldn't be at all influenced by the frame around the painting. They also shouldn't be influenced by what others think about their decisions, choices, or opinions, with or without a frame. In this case, if frames affect choices, we end up with errors and biases in decision making.

Objectively speaking, according to some behavioral economists, people's choices *should* be frame independent — but they aren't. These economists acknowledge that frames actually do affect people's choices by biasing their preferences or by distorting their perspectives. So, people should better understand this reality of choice behavior, especially if they end up making choices that are error prone, biased, or even irrational.

This is a dominant view of framing in behavioral economics, advanced by Daniel Kahneman and Amos Tversky.

Understanding frames as heuristics

Not all behavioral economists subscribe to the view that frames produce errors and biases in decision making. In a world of imperfect information, frames provide signals that help people make optimal or at least best possible decisions. This doesn't always work out — frames can be misleading and can send false signals. But people often learn from their mistakes.

Given that just about all choices are context dependent, an important issue raised by behavioral economists is how to construct frames that facilitate choices that help people perform well. These would be choices that people prefer to make under conditions of reasonably accurate information — choices that people typically won't regret.

Framing in Pictures: The Possibility of Cognitive Illusions

The human brain processes information and fills in the missing pieces based on past experiences and context. When people are presented with identical pictures in different frames, their brains often paint different images of what appears to be the same thing.

In other words, framing can affect what people see. It affects the images the brain constructs, given the information presented (what is seen visually) and the relevant information already stored in the brain. Framing plays a role in determining the choices people make.

Framing the Mona Lisa

The *Mona Lisa* was painted by Leonardo da Vinci in the early 16th century and now hangs in the Musée du Louvre in Paris. You've likely been told how beautiful and important this painting is. You're also used to seeing the *Mona Lisa* without a frame or framed as it actually is, in a way that doesn't at all distract from the portrait.

Imagine that you knew nothing about the *Mona Lisa,* and you saw it for the first time decked out in a frame celebrating the swastika (see Figure 7-1). This "frame" would no doubt affect your opinion of this work of art. If you were shown the *Mona Lisa* without any framing embellishment, your opinion would no doubt be different. Your decision on whether the *Mona Lisa* was beautiful would be influenced, in this case, only by the portrait itself.

Your opinion of the intrinsic value of a painting is partially contingent on how it's framed. Even if the *Mona Lisa* is "objectively" beautiful, it may appear otherwise, depending on its frame. This is one reason why people spend so much money on framing artwork.

Of course, an expert wouldn't be fooled by the frame, according to some behavioral economists. The expert wouldn't necessarily pay more or less for a classic painting simply because of a frame.

But a person who knew nothing about the work of art, and knew about what the symbols on the frame represented, may not pay a penny for the *Mona Lisa.* The frame would dominate that person's decision making, not the intrinsic value of the work of art. This is why people often judge others, at least initially, by how they dress — in other words, by how they frame themselves.

Distorting the line illusion

People's perception of the length of a line can be distorted by how the line is framed. Even if all lines are the same length, one line may appear longer than the other. This illusion is illustrated in Figure 7-2. All three lines are the same length, but the middle one looks longer because of how it's framed.

If you were shopping for the longest line, you wouldn't be indifferent. You would select the middle line from both sets. However, objectively, you should be indifferent because all lines are the same. Your choice would be especially problematic if you were willing to pay a higher price for the longer line — you would be duped by a cognitive illusion.

Figure 7-1:
The *Mona Lisa* without a frame (left) and with a frame that may influence a person's opinion of the work of art (right).

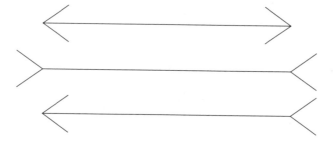

Figure 7-2:
The three lines are all the same length, but the middle one looks longer because of how it's framed.

Framing faces

A classic cognitive illusion is illustrated in Figure 7-3. Here you see either two faces or a vase. How your brain interprets the information that it processes is very much a function of context. For example, if you were discussing a bouquet of flowers prior to seeing this image, your brain might very well see a vase. On the other hand, if you were discussing identical twins, you might identify two faces staring at each other.

What you see in Figure 7-3 is a product of context — and immediate context at that. Context can trick people into seeing what's not there.

Figure 7-3:
The vase illusion was developed by Danish psycholo-gist Edgar Rubin. The brain can interpret this image to be either a vase or two faces.

Framing automobiles: Surface beauty versus substance

Automobile advertisements have framed the automobile with pretty women right from the beginning. Buy the car and you purchase the frame — or at least the potential of the frame.

Often, the ads make no mention of the product itself, except that it goes fast and attracts or is driven by pretty women in an attractive environment. The idea here is that the brain processes information in such a manner that people are influenced more by the frame or context within which the car is presented in the advertisement than by the substance of the vehicle itself.

The argument would be that people are willing to buy the car with the best frame or pay more for the car with the best frame. This suggests that the mechanics of the car matter less than the pretty woman and the environment that frame the car.

This would be a serious problem if your objective was to purchase the best car from an operational perspective. It would also be a serious problem if you ended up buying a substandard vehicle, from your perspective, simply because this poor excuse for a quality automobile was framed by a pretty woman.

But what the framing literature often suggests is that if you have two fairly similar vehicles, and one has a better frame than another, you'll go for the car that is framed better. Your choices are affected by the frame, but the frame doesn't induce you to purchase a vehicle that you wouldn't otherwise want to buy. You probably wouldn't actually purchase a substandard car simply because of how it was framed.

The letter illusion

The letter illusion is drawn from an example presented by Daniel Kahneman. In Figure 7-4, you see two lines, both of which contain the number 13. In the first line, the number 13 is framed by letters. In the second line, the number 13 is framed by numbers. All letters and numbers are handwritten. The number 13 is handwritten in such a way that it might be identified with a handwritten version of the letter *B*.

As Kahneman points out, the brain identifies the number 13 as *B* when it's framed by the letters *A* and *C*. But when the number 13 is framed by the numbers 12 and 14, the brain tends to identify the number 13 as the number 13. A lot depends on how the object is framed.

Gary Becker and Kevin Murphy: Betwixt and between behavioral economics

Gary Becker and Kevin Murphy aren't behavioral economists, but they present a theory of advertising that goes well beyond conventional economics perspective on how smart people make decisions. They make the simple point that many people purchase a product not only on the basis of the intrinsic value of the product, but also on how it's packaged. Framing can easily influence people's choices even if it provides them with no useful information — nothing of "objective" or "scientific" substance. If you have two products that aren't really very different from an operational point of view, many people may very well choose the better-framed product because it makes them feel better about what they buy or because they believe that the producer is taking better care in marketing the product. Either way, framing can affect choices. Even if this effect appears to induce irrational patterns of behavior, it may have quite discernable rational affects. But this type of rationality or smart behavior incorporates objectives or goals usually sidelined by contemporary economics.

In this instance, a particular frame can mislead people into identifying a number as a letter, resulting in an error in decision making.

Figure 7-4:
In the letter illusion, you're presented with a number that is first framed by letters and then by numbers. The brain tends to identify the number only if it's framed by other numbers.

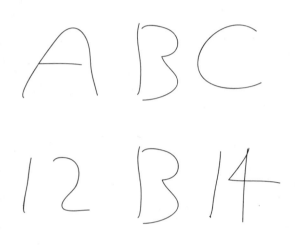

We're All Framed: Framing and Decision Making

Behavioral economists have produced an abundance of evidence that frames have an important impact on choice, contrary to the expectations of conventional economics. What makes this finding critically important is that frames are just about everywhere. And to the extent that frames affect choice, we need to better understand how people are influenced by frames in their everyday decision making.

Of particular importance when it comes to framing is whether people are presented with a negative or positive frame. People tend to shift their choices toward positively framed options.

Many behavioral economists believe that the framing effect is evidence of serious errors and biases in decision making. Other behavioral economists believe that the framing effect suggests how people make use of the information provided by frames to make good decisions in a world of bounded rationality. Some of these decisions may be error prone when frames are biased and perverse.

Framing and loss aversion: The classic Asian disease experiment

A classic case of framing — one that gave birth to a revolution in our under-standing on framing and decision making — was presented by Amos Tversky and Daniel Kahneman in 1981. This case was based on an experiment in which subjects were asked to imagine different scenarios and provide choices based on these scenarios.

The experiment was designed to determine the impact that negative and positive framing have on decision making. Specifically, it investigated how *loss aversion* (the strong aversion that many people have toward loss) affects people's choices.

Participants were asked to imagine that the United States was preparing for the outbreak of an Asian disease that was expected to kill 600 people. The first group of subjects was presented with a choice between two programs to deal with the hypothetical Asian disease. The two programs are framed in the following fashion:

Six hundred people will be struck by the Asian disease.

Program A: Two hundred people will be saved.

Program B: There is a one-third probability that 600 people will be saved and a two-thirds probability that no one will be saved.

Given this frame, 72 percent of subjects preferred Program A. The rest of the subjects of the experiment (28 percent) chose Program B.

The second group of subjects in the experiment was presented with two pro-grams aimed at fighting the Asian disease, framed in the following way.

Six hundred people will be struck by the Asian disease.

Program C: Four hundred people will die.

Program D: There is a one-third probability that nobody will die and a two-thirds probability that 600 people will die.

Given this alternative frame, 78 percent of the subjects of the experiment chose Program D. Only 22 percent chose Program C.

Kahneman and Tversky stipulate that programs A and C have identical expected values, as do programs B and D. In both Program A and Program C, 200 people are saved and 400 die. So, subjects of the experiment change their preferences as a consequence of changing the decision frame, not on the basis of changing the substance of treatment programs.

In the first group, the majority of subjects chose Program A because it's positively framed. In the second group, the majority chose Program D, because Program C is negatively framed and Program D is positively framed.

Only programs A and C offer an assurance that 200 people will be saved. But by changing the frames, the majority of people flip or reverse their preferences from a certain outcome of lives saved to an uncertain one. For the uncertain outcomes, the expected value of lives saved is 200 lives. So, for all programs, the expected value of lives saved is 200 lives. However, for only two of the programs is there certainty about lives being saved. And when it comes to saving lives, for most people, certainty ranks high in their choice agenda.

Remember the concept of expected value? In this example, the expected value of lives saved is given by the following equation:

$$(\tfrac{1}{3} \times 600) + (\tfrac{2}{3} \times 0) = 200 + 0 = 200 \text{ lives saved}$$

This type of experiment raises the question of how and the extent to which framing an option negatively affects people's choices. It also raises that question of the extent to which most people understand probabilistically framed options. Most people don't have a clue how to calculate expected value.

For example, economist Nathan Berg and psychologist Gerd Gigerenzer found that doctors who do mammograms every day are, for the most part, statistically illiterate and routinely overestimate the conditional probability of breast cancer given a positive mammogram. Even economists who are well trained in probability and statistics don't follow statistical rules when asked for their beliefs about the risks of prostate cancer.

For many behavioral economists, the type of behavior exposed by this experiment suggests that people are irrational — or at least that their preferences are easily manipulated. For other behavioral economists, people are rational even when they're influenced by frames. An important example of this is when all outcomes have the same expected value. In the Asian disease experiment, all choices had the same expected value in terms of lives saved. But choices were affected by negative and positive frames. People preferred choices that were positively framed given the positive signal this sends about the efficacy of the treatment.

In a world of bounded rationality, where information is imperfect and most people aren't good with probabilistic calculations, people tend to use frames as a way of gathering information. This is a smart move — people are *satisficing* (doing the best they can with what they have).

But frames don't have to change preferences. The participants all appear to have a preference to save as many lives as possible — framing doesn't appear to change preferences. But choices are influenced by frames. People end up making choices that they believe have a good chance of making their preferences come true.

Of course, using signals that are misleading can result in people making choices that don't reflect their true preferences. This raises the important question of whether a person would choose a program that would actually result in an easily identifiable number of fewer lives being saved if the program that saved the most lives was negatively framed. There is no clear evidence from this type of experiment that this is the case. Framing influences many people's choices with respect to programs that generate the same expected value in terms of lives saved.

When money isn't everything

Another classic framing experiment takes the form of the decision to purchase a ticket for a highly sought-after event, an event that you really want to attend.

In one scenario, you end up purchasing a ticket to the desired event, but you lose the ticket. Let's say the ticket cost you $50. In another scenario, you're presented with the same desired event and, once again, the ticket costs $50. In this scenario, you lose $50 *prior* to purchasing the ticket.

When people are asked if they would try to purchase the ticket if they actually lost the ticket, most would say no. However, if it was the $50 that was lost, most would still want to purchase the ticket.

According to conventional economics, if you really want to go to the event, and you have the economic resources available, you should choose to purchase the ticket regardless of whether you lose the ticket or the cash. You should be indifferent to the two instances of loss.

But real-world decision making is often overwhelmed by loss aversion or, related to this, people's adherence to sunk costs. *Sunk costs* are expenditures that have already been made and that can't be reversed. Conventional economists and many behavioral economists argue that sunk costs are and should be ignored in decision making. Behavioral economists argue that often, this is not the case, and the result is irrational choices.

Some behavioral economists regard the decision not to replace the lost ticket, while being willing to purchase a ticket after losing its value in cash, as possibly quite rational (even though this runs contrary to the conventional economics benchmark for rationality). You may have gone to a lot of time and trouble when purchasing your ticket. You may not be willing to go through the same hassle to get the ticket again. Replacing the cash to get a ticket is no big deal, if you have the money on hand. What may appear to be irrational from the perspective of conventional economics may be quite sensible if you delve a little bit below the surface into what motivates people's behavior.

Saving a penny to lose a bundle: Framing prices through relative positioning

According to experimental evidence, once again pioneered by Daniel Kahneman and Amos Tversky, some people would be willing to sacrifice considerable sums of money and time to make a relative saving on the purchase price of a product. A lot depends on how their options are framed.

If they're told that they can save $1 on a $5 purchase or $10 on a $200 purchase, many people would hunt down the 20 percent saving on the $5 purchase. This, in spite of the fact that they would save only $1 on the 20 percent savings compared to $10 on the 10 percent savings.

In the original experiment, participants were asked to imagine a salesman informing them that they could save $5 on a $15 calculator in another branch of the store located a 20-minute drive away. Most participants responded that they would make the drive to save the $5.

Another group of participants was asked to imagine that they were about to purchase a calculator for $125. They could save $10 on the calculator if they drove 20 minutes to another branch of the store. Most participants responded that they would not be willing to make the drive.

Conventional economics says that people shouldn't respond in this way — not if they strictly follow cost-benefit thinking. Many behavioral economists don't see this type of non-materially-maximizing behavior in a positive light, but they recognize it as a fact of life and figure that it's a product of how the sales discounts are framed.

Many people are concerned by relative savings as opposed to absolute savings. Some people's level of satisfaction will increase by quite a lot if they hunt down the big-percentage savings, even if it's only pocket change. At the same time, some people won't go out of their way to make significant savings if it doesn't constitute a large percentage of the original sale price.

For people whose level of satisfaction is influenced by reference points or relative positioning, this type of behavior is quite rational even if it isn't income or wealth maximizing. It isn't clear, however, how big a material sacrifice most people would be willing to make simply to get a larger relative saving.

Frames as Defaults: How Anchors Sway the Course of Decision Making

Not only are people surrounded by frames, but they're surrounded by frames that are defaults. According to many behavioral economists, these defaults serve as anchors or starting points for decision making. And defaults can result in choices that many people end up regretting.

But even if people don't regret their anchored-based choices, these choices may not be in their best interest, according to many behavioral economists. People may end up making bad choices simply because people tend to choose the option that's the default. On the other hand, for the same reason, people may inadvertently make good choices because of how the defaults are set.

If defaults are pervasive and have an overwhelming impact on people's choices, this raises the question of whether choices are easily manipulated. It also raises the question of whether the free market should be allowed to set defaults without any form of regulation.

Many behavioral economists argue that defaults should be set by experts, or at least regulated through government agencies — influencing or nudging the choices people make toward those that are in their best interest or that they won't end up regretting.

Changing default options and choices

The discussion of framing has garnered considerable hype in academia, in political circles, and in the media because of the way it contextualizes framing in terms of defaults. Defaults, many behavioral economists argue, flip both preferences and choices. More important, defaults can swing choices in directions that often have huge consequences for the decision maker and society at large.

This particular take on framing and defaults has been forcefully articulated by Richard Thaler and Cass Sustein of the University of Chicago. (Their arguments are introduced in Chapter 4.) In line with the errors and biases perspective in behavioral economics, Thaler and Sustein argue that our choices are fairly easily manipulated by defaults.

Many behavioral economists argue that people's choices often end up being inconsistent with their preferences. They end up making choices, as a consequence of defaults, that they would rather not have made — at least in retrospect. These behavioral economists, such as Thaler and Sustein, maintain that, all too often, people are unable to appreciate what's in their own best interest, which makes it much easier for their choices to be nudged in the wrong direction. This, in turn, opens the door for positive intervention in the decision-making process, to motivate people to make choices that the expert believes to be in the individual's best interest. According to some behavioral economists, the expert's role is to nudge people's choices in the direction that the expert considers to be correct.

Even if you don't buy the argument that people's choices are easily manipulated, that they're easily deceived by defaults and frames, people *are* influenced by defaults. People often are affected by whether the default is to donate their organs at death, to invest in a pension fund, to donate to a charity, to accept a higher limit on their credit card, to commit to a larger number of channels from their cable or satellite provider, and so on.

There can be good, rational reasons for going for the default in a world of imperfect information and where the brain is a scarce resource. People often defer to defaults as providing a signal of what's the sensible thing to do. Defaults are set by some type of expert — or so people are made to believe — and people often follow expert advice.

Sometimes people don't realize what the defaults are. Often, this is because the default choice is not made very explicit — it lingers in the shadows in small font or far deep in the dark forest of a multi-page document. The consequences of choices may not be immediately evident. If the default option is to donate your organs at death, people actually don't ever discover that they're donating their organs before it's too late — they're already dead. When the default is not to invest in pensions, which is often the case, people don't realize that they've underinvested in their retirement until it's too late — they're too old to build up their retirement income.

But often defaults are unavoidable — they must be set one way or another. Some behavioral economists argue for more government involvement and expert participation in the determination of defaults. At a minimum, defaults should be transparent — they shouldn't mislead people. Providing some assurance that defaults are clear and transparent requires some regulatory intervention. Only with the proper regulations is it more likely that the choices people make are the choices they prefer to make.

Revisiting choice architecture

Many behavioral economists argue that we need experts to construct choice environments so that people are nudged toward the choices that are best for them (according to the experts). At a minimum, they argue, the choice environment should somehow nudge people toward the choices that people prefer. This line of argument is referred to by many as *soft paternalism* (see Chapter 5).

These economists tend to refer to nudging vendors of goods and service to display products or lists of products (on a menu) in a manner that induces people to buy, for example, healthier foods. They also suggest that taxes could be imposed to induce people to not buy what the experts deem not to be in people's own best interest.

Taxes on goods and services aren't the same thing as a simple frame — they aren't as innocuous as framing cars with pretty women. Taxes have real effects. They alter the relative costs of what's out there in the marketplace.

Soft paternalism hypothesizes that people's choices and preferences can be manipulated easily. It also assumes that the choice architect necessarily knows more than the consumer about what's in the consumer's own best interest. As discussed in Chapter 5, the *choice architect* is an expert on the best choices people can make and is responsible for framing choices and for setting defaults for choices.

But for the most part, soft paternalism doesn't necessarily imply the use of coercion in the decision-making process — it's all about *nudging* choice behavior.

Not all behavioral economists necessarily agree with the general idea of taste and choice manipulation. But they pretty much agree that choice architecture is a fact of life: There are experts everywhere trying to induce people to choose what they want them to choose.

It isn't clear, however, that all people are easily manipulated. Instead, their choices are affected by how those choices are framed, the information provided by frames and defaults, and the perceived signals contained in frames and defaults. For these reasons, we should appreciate how context affects the choices people make.

Jamie Oliver and school lunches

Jamie Oliver, a celebrity cook with a serious social conscience, promotes healthy school lunches. He and others also advocate bans on unhealthy foods served in school cafeterias — these are serious nudges with a strong dose of hard paternalism. Oliver's efforts may have no effect in households where families don't have the money and time to eat healthy or when school meals come at a significant cost to lower-income families. But when school meals are provided through the public purse, children can be made to eat healthy, especially if the healthy foods taste good — healthy food that tastes awful won't have much reach. Being exposed to good-tasting healthy foods also has the effect of changing the preferences of children and their parents in favor of healthy foods.

Getting kids to eat healthier is especially important because studies show that healthy eating has a large effect on academic performance.

However, strict bans on unhealthy food sold in schools have resulted in a large black market for fast foods, candy, soda, and the like, supported by students as well as teachers. Hard paternalism causes serious backlashes. Also, the health-food programs have been most successful among middle-income and wealthier kids.

Income, price, information, and preferences are all important in influencing people's choices. Nudges — soft or hard — often don't work, especially on their own.

Framing is important, but so are income and prices

Although framing is quite important when thinking about what and how we choose, it's important not to forget the significance of relative prices and income, and gaps in information and knowledge as additional determinants of the choices people make.

When many people aren't eating healthy, it's often because they don't have the time or money to put together a healthy meal. If healthier food costs too much given a person's budget, he or she may simply be priced out of the market for healthy foods. If you're a mom running a single-parent household, changing the choice architecture of food placement may not get you to eat healthier.

Also, many people don't have the know-how to eat healthier. Some people form preferences for certain foods and ways of cooking that aren't the best for them, at least healthwise. Simply changing frames won't get those people eating healthier. But as some behavioral economists point out, getting them better information may do the trick. Soft paternalism can involve providing people with high-quality, well-presented, and easy-to-understand information on healthy eating.

The Inescapable Frame and Rational Decision Making

Because framing is so pervasive, it's important to appreciate framing as an instrument that goes well beyond wrapping on a package that may sway people's choices.

For many behavioral economists, frames (including defaults and, more generally, choice architecture) are exploited by humans as a type of heuristic, a fast and frugal tool to make decisions. Using frames to make choices is seen by these economists as a smart move in a world of bounded rationality, where information is imperfect and the brain is a scarce resource.

Understanding frames as an information-generating machine

A number of behavioral economists regard frames as providers of information in a world of imperfect information. The imperfect creatures that humans are, we take advantage of whatever information is at hand to make decisions, for better or worse.

A particular default suggests to many people that the default is the best option. The default serves as a fast and frugal heuristic. Sometimes defaults and the implications of choosing the default option aren't well understood, and that can lead to decisions that people later regret. But the same can be said of any choice environment.

Repairing frames and rational decision making

There is considerable evidence that frames not only can influence our choices, but also produce choices that people later regret — in other words, errors in decision making. These errors aren't necessarily evidence of irrationality, as some behavioral economists argue. But no matter how rational the errors may be, errors are errors.

When smart people make mistakes, they can be corrected. If a negative frame induces you not to buy a particular product and that frame was misleading, you could and would fix the problem when you had better information.

To the extent that frames generate errors in decision making because they're misleading, send false signals, and so on, those frames can be repaired. With improved frames, people stand a better chance of making the choices they would most prefer to make.

Introducing product labels into the framing arsenal

Incomplete, misleading, and false information produces choices that often are in direct conflict with the intent of the decision maker. In this case, people's revealed preferences — their choices — would tell us little about what their true preferences are. Their choices would reveal little about what their choices would've been had they been better informed.

As Yale University behavioral economist Robert Shiller has argued, trustworthy product labels provide people with the information necessary to make informed decisions. For example, if you don't know what's in that can of soup you're about to buy, you may end up buying the soup that's framed most to your liking.

If you don't have good information on the breakdown of the financial assets you're thinking of purchasing, you may end up buying the one that's framed in a way that appeals to you or from a broker you think you can trust. You use frames and related signals in the absence of anything better. Hopefully, the frame is a good reflection of the fundamental value of the asset and the broker you trust is trustworthy.

Product labeling becomes critically important in a world of imperfect information. But product labels are even *more* significant in a world of asymmetric information: When the seller has better information than you do, you can be deceived easily. And this isn't because you're a fool — it's because you're a human being, dealing as best you can with imperfect and flawed information.

Improving product labeling can improve the quality of decision making by improving the quality of the frame. And it does so without infringing on free choice.

Market Failure and the Framing Effect

Behavioral economists agree that in a world of bounded rationality, people can end up making decisions that they later regret. This can be a product of a choice environment that induces them to make choices that they would eventually consider to be an error in judgment.

Market forces often fail to repair the frame or fix the default option. The choice environment becomes distorted, producing choices that aren't always in line with people's preferences. Such choices are inefficient, suboptimal, below par in regards to people's own benchmark of what's the best choice. This situation represents some sort of market failure — but market failures can be corrected.

Market failure is a situation in which the free-market solution to an economic problem can be improved upon. The invisible hand of the market can't do it all. A classic example of a market failure is pollution. Pollution is, in part, a product of individuals who are out to maximize profits, acting on the incentives provided by market forces. People pollute because market prices don't force them to internalize the pollution costs that they're imposing on others.

Frames generate market failures when they provide false or misleading signals to people, inducing them to make choices that they wouldn't otherwise make. Frames can distort people's choices.

To use a term coined by American economist David George, people's preferences become *polluted* — we end up with preference pollution. More precisely, in this case, we end up with choice pollution.

Economists of all stripes recommend some form of government intervention to fix market failures. Conventional economists have been at the forefront when it comes to articulating public-policy questions dealing with market failure. But the possibility that the framing aspects of the choice environment can contribute to market failure hasn't been part of the economics toolbox.

Although there are differences of opinion among behavioral economists on the extent to which framing distorts choices and causes errors in decision making, there is agreement that framing affects the choices people make. But there is disagreement on the extent of intervention that should take place to correct for market failure.

Many behavioral economists call for more pervasive government and expert intervention because they assume that people are easily misled by the choice environment in general and frames in particular and don't have a strong sense of what's in their own best interest. They argue that choice architects should help correct people's error-prone behavior by nudging them (and sometimes driving them) to do what the experts think is right.

Other behavioral economists argue that, for the most part, people are smart decision makers who make the best possible use of their choice environment (including frames and defaults) to make smart decisions and to correct identifiable errors in decision making. Sometimes, what appears to be a dumb decision is a product of smart choices being priced out of the market. Other times, people lack the economic literacy needed to make the best possible decisions. But errors in decision-making can take place because of distortions in the choice environment, which can include false and misleading advertising, as well as defaults that are misleading, hidden, or poorly thought out.

Governments and experts can help fix this problem by ensuring that the information that people use to make choices is up to the task. Defaults need to be designed so that they don't mislead and deceive and meet, at a minimum, the preferences of most decision makers.

If people are weak in their computational abilities and their understanding of economic concepts, this also can result in errors in decision making. But this problem can be addressed by improving people's level of understanding and by assuring that the choice environment works for people's level of understanding and education.

Chapter 8

How Norms, Peers, History, and Culture Influence Choice

In This Chapter

▶ Looking at the decision-making bubble that conventional economics built

▶ Recognizing the importance of social norms in making decisions

▶ Feeling the pressure of peers

▶ Seeing how history and culture affect the choices people make

*B*ehavioral economics argues that decision making is often influenced by social context — social norms, peers, history, and culture. All these factors influence how choices are framed and which defaults are set in place. They also are what makes each person unique — and that uniqueness impacts on his preferences and the choices he makes.

It may seem obvious that social context affects choice, but conventional economics assumes that people are all the same and that social context isn't important to the decisions they make. The sameness of all individuals flows from conventional economics' focus on what is called the *representative agent* (an artificial individual — the average person — whose preferences and choices are assumed to be representative of all individuals).

In this chapter, I explain how conventional economics approaches (or doesn't approach) social context. Then I describe how social norms, peer groups, history, and culture impact who we are and our preferences and choices.

Making Decisions in a Bubble, the Conventional Economics Way

In conventional economics, the simplifying assumption is that people make decisions as if social context doesn't matter. In other words, the choices people make in a social setting are no different from the choices they would make if they were in a bubble, isolated from everyone and everything around them.

By assuming that people make decisions as if they were in a bubble, and that those decisions are materially maximizing (because decisions are *always* materially maximizing in conventional economics), conventional economics assumes away the potential importance of social context. It also forces economists' analytical focus away from understanding how preferences are formed, why they are what they are, and why preferences differ from one person to the next.

Conventional economists end up paying little attention to things like the following:

- ✔ Why some people smoke and other people have never touched a cigarette
- ✔ Why some people like apples, some people prefer oranges, and some people don't like fruit at all
- ✔ Why some people are illiterate and others are extremely well read
- ✔ Why some people are drug addicts and others won't touch addictive substances
- ✔ Why some people from poor socioeconomic backgrounds engage in criminal activities while others from the same background don't
- ✔ Why some people are sensitive to price changes while others are not
- ✔ Why some people who are wealthy engage in significant charitable giving while others with the same socioeconomic standing don't

Sometimes, with this type of bubble economics, conventional economics simply assumes a representative agent — an average individual. In this way, conventional economics assumes that differences in preferences across individuals are of no consequence to economic analysis. And, of course, conventional economics doesn't see the origins of preferences as important either.

The representative agent is a long-standing and dominant concept in economic theory. All individuals are either assumed to be identical or homogeneous in terms of their preferences. These homogeneous preferences are typically assumed to be of a materially maximizing sort. People's economic behavior is then modeled on the assumed behavior of the representative agent — the average person.

With a representative agent, conventional economics is assuming not only that one set of preferences exists for the entire population, but also that only one type of preference is rational — this is to maximize income and wealth. Conventional economics then tries to explain people's choices as being consistent with this assumption.

Conventional economics fails to examine how social context helps produce different preferences from one person to the next, and how these preferences can be rational even if they aren't income or wealth maximizing.

In the following sections, I delve a little deeper into the kind of decision making that conventional economics assumes.

Making decisions as if other people don't matter

A typical assumption in contemporary economics is that the behavior and opinions of other people don't affect your decisions. This is true even if these are the opinions and behaviors of people you know, people you respect, people you fear, people you want to cozy up to for promotion, people you want to date, or a spouse or partner you want to please. Your demand curve is unaffected by the opinions and behaviors of others.

In other words, conventional economics assumes that what another person does or says won't affect someone's preferences or choices for goods and services. The position and slope of that person's *demand curve* (the person's sensitivity to price changes) — different brands and models of laptops, for example — are immune to the influence of other people.

Making decisions as if history doesn't matter

In conventional economics, history is of no analytical consequence to an understanding of current decision making. Past experience, for example, is assumed not to influence current decision making. Whether you ate certain foods, drank certain drinks, experienced certain types of music, or experienced and understood members of other cultural, religious, or racial groups shouldn't influence your current behavior, according to conventional economics.

The relationship between isolation economics and free will and free choice

An important hypothesis of conventional economics is that everyone is endowed with free will and, therefore, with free choice. People's choices are their own, and their choices reflect their preferences. These preferences are based on their freely chosen wants and desires and contingent upon the assumed universal principle of income or wealth maximization.

A working implicit assumption in conventional economics is that free will is strongly tied to people not being affected by social context and social relationships. Being in some ways socially embedded would result in people's choices being determined by others. In this case, their preferences and choices couldn't reflect their wants and desires. Freedom of choice and freedom to choose would become meaningless concepts. People's choices would be determined by others — not much different from communist or fascist societies.

But the fact is that people's choices are socially embedded. They're influenced by the society and community people are a part of. For many behavioral economists, this clearly suggests that people's choices are very significantly beyond their control. For other behavioral economists, the fact that preferences and choices are socially embedded simply means that they're influenced by others — influenced by friends, family, enemies, history, culture, religion, and the like.

This influence helps explain behavior that can't be explained by relative prices and income, or behavior that flies in the face of the maximizing assumption. Even people rooted in the same social environment and sets of circumstances facing the same relative prices and income still make decisions that differ. People's choices don't appear to be determined simply by society or by economic variables. These variables set the environments within which preferences are formed and choices are made.

But Nobel Laureate Amartya Sen has pointed out another influence and, indeed, constraint on the freedom of choice: the legal constraints on the capabilities of individuals to choose based on their preferences. These constraints can even inhibit an individual's capacity to develop his or her own preferred preferences.

Social norms, often enforced by social ostracism and legalized forms of violence, can set powerful constraints on choice behavior. But these constraints don't obliterate free will. They do set serious limitations on it, however, perhaps even more so than relative prices, income, and social context.

Nor should a person's past behavior, such as deciding not to do drugs, impact a person's current decisions. Conventional economics assumes that there is no path dependence in the formation of people's preferences and with regard to their current choices.

Path dependency means that history matters in determining the choices people make today. These choices determine economic outcomes — both today and tomorrow. From this perspective, choices made today can't always be explained by relative prices and income. When history matters, different people can make quite different choices, even when relative prices and income are identical. Some of these differences can be explained by people's different and varied past experiences. Economists Paul David and Brian Arthur have pioneered the general concept of path dependency, which was developed to explain the adoption of particular technologies and the location of industry.

Making decisions as if society doesn't matter

In conventional economics, where people live — the societies and communities where they make their lives — are assumed to make no difference to their preferences and choices. Society and community incorporate a rich medley of factors that include history, culture, religion, and social norms.

In other words, conventional economics assumes that whether you place a human being in the United States, Canada, Mexico, Brazil, China, India, Japan, France, Germany, Italy, Greece, Turkey, New Zealand, Australia, Israel, Iran, Afghanistan, Sudan, Somalia, South Africa, Samoa, or the Cook Islands, that person's preferences and choices would be the same. What drives choices are relative prices and income and the desire to maximize wealth.

Introducing Social Norms to Decision Making

Social norms represent informal rules of the game or behavior. Norms are often rooted in history, culture, religion, and social engagement. They're known by members of society and often followed even in the absence of explicit forms of punishment. If you break a social norm, you don't end up before a court of law charged with norm-breaking behavior. However, soft penalties often exist when norms are broken. Your friends and family may disapprove of you, reducing your level of satisfaction and your well-being. You may end up damaging your reputation, which can diminish the trust that both friends and strangers have in you and have economic consequences if you're engaged in business.

When norms that have economic implications are followed, they can impact economic development in a positive or negative way. Norms that encourage trust reduce the cost of doing business — trust promotes economic development. But norms that encourage discrimination against women, for example, negatively impact development, by reducing female participation in the labor market and discouraging women and society from investing in their productive capabilities.

Real-world norms can and often do result in many people violating the conventional economics norms of wealth maximization. Behavioral economists tend to be particularly interested in this type of "deviant" behavior. For some, this behavior is evidence of errors in decision making and even, possibly, of irrationality. For other behavioral economists, this is just how some people behave as a way of improving their well-being.

Looking at some norms

In this section, I offer examples of how certain behavioral norms — tipping and charitable giving — influence decision making. As a consequence of social norms favoring tipping and charitable giving in many societies, most people end up tipping and donating to charity way more than conventional economics would ever expect. Both of these activities involve some material sacrifice that makes little sense from the materially maximizing perspective of conventional economics.

How tipping violates conventional economic norms

Many economists brought up on conventional economics theory believe that tipping is irrational — perhaps even stupid — and it shouldn't take place. Individuals who tip seem to be making an unnecessary material self-sacrifice, giving up money that they don't have to give up. Smart people wouldn't and shouldn't be so generous.

But this perspective flies in the face of the fact that tipping is so ubiquitous. Tipping is very much part of economic life throughout the United States and Canada, as well a good part of the global community. People spend many billions of dollars annually on tips throughout the world. In U.S. restaurants alone, people are tipping to the tune of at least $20 billion annually. Not exactly small change!

Tipping and the conventional economic wisdom

Just as being nice can make economic sense in the business world, there are good conventional economic reasons for some types of tipping behavior. If you frequent a restaurant or a hotel and these establishments have a regular staff, tipping well is a way of buying quality service. If you tip well, you earn a solid reputation as someone who rewards good service — and good service is typically what you receive in return. In these circumstances, tipping doesn't involve making an *unnecessary* material sacrifice — you're paying for quality service.

But conventional economics has trouble explaining large variations in tipping percentages and why people tip individuals employed in establishments that they believe they'll never return to in the near future. If you don't expect to return to a restaurant, why tip? The waitress can't retaliate on your return visit by providing you with abysmal service. So, why unnecessarily give up some of your income?

Indeed, well-known Harvard economist, Greg Mankiw comments that:

> Economists do not have a good theory of tipping. Normally, we assume that consumers pay as little as they have to when buying the products they want. Yet, when buying meals, haircuts, the services of porters, and taxi services, most consumers voluntarily pay more than they are legally required. Why does this happen? Why is it more true for some services than for others? Why do tipping customs vary from country to country? I have no idea.

Tipping and behavioral economics

Much of actual tipping behavior can be explained only if we move beyond the assumption that people are obsessive material maximizers.

Behavioral economists point to tipping as a consequence of a variety of factors, which complement purely economic considerations. These factors are not pulled out of thin air — they have considerable empirical support.

Some people tip to feel good. They get a warm glow by tipping. They feel good when they behave in a manner that their peers consider to be appropriate. If they don't tip when tipping is the norm, they may earn the disdain of others. In other words, what other people think affects our behavior. Contrary to what conventional economics says, people don't decide whether to tip in a social vacuum.

The feel-good factor helps explain different levels of tipping by different people. But conventional economics often treats all people as identical. From a behavioral perspective, tipping behavior can differ with people's differing levels of the warm-glow effect — some people feel better when they tip than other people do, and the people who feel better will likely tip more.

Tipping behavior can be, for some people, a pathway to avoiding guilt, and avoiding guilt is a way of improving your well-being. But to feel guilty about not tipping, you have to be raised in an environment where the norm for proper behavior is to tip.

Behavioral economists are increasingly focusing on norms as a driving force behind tipping behavior. Specific social norms help explain why most people tip even when they don't have to for economic reasons.

Material sacrifice and survival of the fittest

Norms obviously influence the extent to which people engage in tipping, charitable giving, donating blood, and volunteering. But none of these sacrifices imposes a significant economic burden on the altruistic individual.

In other words, these "good deeds" come at a relatively small cost to the donor, often yielding quite significant nonmaterial benefits. Overall, the evidence on individual material sacrifice suggests that, on average, tipping, charitable giving, volunteer work, and the rest of it represent a relatively small portion of disposable income and time. The individual who gives away, on a regular basis, most of his or her income and spare time is the exception to the rule, especially when this person is part of a family unit.

The fact that such altruistic behavior represents a small portion of disposable income makes the behavior quite consistent with the economic survival of the altruistic individual. Charitable giving, as a form of material sacrifice, doesn't threaten to undermine the survival of the altruist or his or her kin.

This is, no doubt, one very important reason why charitable giving has remained a staple of human life over time. Market forces don't drive out altruists, especially when they're not overly generous and their "good deeds" increase, sometimes quite markedly, their level of well-being.

Why charitable giving is the norm

In many ways, charitable giving is similar to tipping insofar as most people donate money, goods, services, and time to charity, even if they get no financial reward for doing so. In many countries where blood donation is not materially compensated, this gift of life is certainly not motivated by commercial factors. Overall, one estimate suggests that charitable giving amounts to about $200 billion per year in the United States alone.

For conventional economics, charitable giving is a violation of good old-fashioned behavioral norms. For this reason, some economists regard such behavior, such choices, as irrational.

Charitable giving, like tipping, is significantly driven by social norms. And by adhering to social norms on charitable giving, people end up with a warm glow. They earn the approval of their peers. But they also may end up building good reputations that can help them in the economic sphere.

Even given income, the extent of charitable giving varies enormously. In many cases, the poor give more than the rich as a percentage of income, and some of the rich give much more than others just as some of the poor give much more than others. Differences in norms across individuals and groups of individuals play an important role in explaining these differences.

Linking trust and development

There is some empirical evidence linking trust levels with levels of economic development — output or gross domestic product (GDP) per person. Countries with a lot of trust are wealthier than countries with little trust. And it appears that more trust actually results in more economic development and less trust results in lower levels of economic development.

Also, according to some estimates, if countries such as India, China, as well as countries in Africa, were characterized by relatively high levels of trust, they may double their per capita income. Even wealthy countries such as France, Germany, and the United Kingdom, could improve their economic standing with higher levels of trust. This point has been made recently by French economists Yann Algan and Pierre Cahuc.

Even though trust seems to pay off from a society-wide perspective, most of the world seems to be bereft of the trust heuristic — trust is in short supply. Some people — movers and shakers — do quite well in a world without much trust. This, in turn, establishes path dependency for a world with little trust. But those countries where people employ the trust heuristic — not exactly following conventional economics norms — fare best economically.

Identifying how trust impacts economic development

The level of trust in society is a function of social norms. In a world of bounded rationality — that is, the real world — trust is actually a fast and frugal heuristic. It helps people avoid a whole array of search costs to locate honest brokers and draw up and sign expensive contracts. But trust usually isn't given much play in conventional economics.

According to conventional economics, market forces should eliminate or scare off cheats and scoundrels, but they don't. Given that trust is partly based on intuition and emotion, many people believe that trusting is naïve and even irrational. But this conventional argument doesn't assume a world of bounded rationality.

In a world where trust exists, the cost of doing business and the riskiness involved in doing business diminish. In the narrow "buyer beware" world, the consumer is at much greater risk and carries much more stress into transactions than in a world where the consumer can use the trust heuristic. Also, in a world with little trust, consumers must invest much more time and effort in locating and identifying honest brokers.

Trust has a long tradition of being used by decision makers throughout the world. In the absence of legal guarantees, trust provides a second-best substitute. In a world *with* legal guarantees but bounded rationality, using the trust heuristic saves on transaction costs, allowing for speedy, effective, and efficient decisions.

Trust is the expectation that the other party in a transaction will deliver on promises made. They may deliver on their promises because they incorporate the interests or welfare of others into their understanding of their own well-being (what Adam Smith referred to as *moral sentiments*), which represents a type of reciprocity: You scratch my back, and I'll scratch yours. Or they may deliver on their promises because they're afraid that their reputation will be tarnished or they'll face social or legal repercussions if they renege — and this would, no doubt, have economic consequences. But moral sentiments and reciprocity appear to be key ingredients to trust relationships, with reputational, social, and legal factors adding strength to the mortar.

Seeing how discriminating norms can lead to a slow economy

When social norms rationalize, justify, and sanction discrimination, many people's identity and level of satisfaction (influenced by warm glow) are impacted by whether they conform to those discriminatory social norms. These norms often are enforced by false and misleading information about minorities or women, for example. To increase their utility, many people in these communities follow social-discriminatory norms.

Discrimination can result in exclusion from particular jobs, from the official labor market completely, from quality education, from quality housing, and the like. It also can result in genocide, where many participants aren't even true believers but are socialized enough to turn a blind eye and even participate.

In conventional economics, labor market discrimination should be beaten up and driven away by market forces. But it hasn't been. And, of course, acts of genocide continue.

With discriminatory social norms in place against women, for example, women are kept out of the labor market, the best people don't always get the job, and labor market competition is greatly reduced. This practice reduces labor productivity, and labor compensation tends to be much lower than it might otherwise be. Many discriminators benefit from discrimination (or they believe that they do), providing economic enforcement of these discriminatory social norms.

As social norms change, even many people who once celebrated or at least conformed to discriminatory norms sing a different tune. Their utility is now enhanced by conforming to and even celebrating and acting upon the newly evolving nondiscriminatory social norms. The children of those engaged in visceral discrimination often are most transformed in a new normative environment. This was classically the case in the U.S. South, especially starting in the late 1960s, and in post–World War II Germany.

Studying the role of education in the formation of norms and the shaping of preferences

Norms are not genetically determined. They're learned through education, experience, and example. Many religions celebrate and promote different forms of altruistic behavior.

There is strong evidence that educating children to behave according to the norms of conventional economics makes them behave relatively more selfishly. In conventional economics, greed is good and moral sentiments are bad — and this point of view is often promoted as being how rational and smart people should behave on the road to personal and social prosperity.

Education plays an important role in affecting people's preferences and the choices they make. Social norms are influenced and enforced by education. The extent of this influence is determined, in part, by the costs and benefits of following or breaking with the prevailing norms in society.

The carrot and the stick: Exploring the enforcement of social norms

Often, educating people to behave in certain ways is complemented by enforcing punishment and offering rewards for conforming to or breaking with prevailing social norms. People are told that they'll be rewarded for their good deeds and punished for their bad behavior.

Often peer pressure or socialized feelings of guilt do the trick. Social norms work best when behavior becomes intuitive, such as charitable giving. And this occurs most efficiently when warm glow and guilt work at a subconscious level.

But social norms can break down when even a few people attempt to deviate from the norm. Therefore, societies often evolve explicit methods for punishing norm breakers — either through ostracism or by legal action. After seeing other people get away with violating social norms, many of those conforming with prevailing norms often feel that they, too, must break the norms of trust to get ahead in life.

Peer Pressure: Seeing How Peers Affect Decision Making

One important reason why people don't behave as if they make decisions in isolation is that peers influence their preferences and choices. People don't have to listen to or care about their peers, and they have some choice over their peer groups. But breaking with peers and choosing one peer group over another often comes at a significant economic and psychological cost.

At the end of the day, peers and peer groups exist. People don't make decisions in a bubble. As economists, we need to model our preferences and choices as if peers matter, because they actually are important to the choices people make.

Past peer group behavior as it interacts with a person's own behavior contributes to the accumulation of a person's *human capital,* or his or her stock of knowledge, according to University of Chicago economist Gary Becker. This type of human capital affects the choices people make, such as taking drugs, committing armed robbery, pursuing education, or enjoying a particular style of music.

Related to this concept, Nobel Laureate George Akerlof and economist Rachel Kranton argue that a key determinant of behavior is whom a person identifies with. Whom a person identifies with affects his behavior and choices by influencing his level of happiness or utility (see Chapter 4). By making choices that enhance your identity, you increase your utility. By making choices that denigrate your identity, you reduce your utility. It makes a big difference whether you identify with drug dealers, terrorists, athletes, computers geeks, police officers, or teachers. Whom you identify with influences who you become and the choices you make.

We can model or predict the types of choices that a person will make based on the peer group that he or she is born into or chooses. Given relative prices and income, a person will make different choices, in part, as a function of his or her current peer group, past peer group associations, and other related social interactions. A person's initial and current social interactions affect the satisfaction he or she gets from the different choices he or she makes. A person's choices become somewhat path dependent. This doesn't mean that if the person associated with thugs in her youth, she will become a thug in the future — but a person's social interactions help determine who she is.

Changing current behavior becomes more difficult over time, given the accumulation of specific social capital. And choices can't simply and simplistically be explained by relative price and incomes — we need to move beyond this simplistic perspective on choice behavior.

A really neat example of the impact of peer pressure is the persistence of illiteracy. In many inner-city schools, there is considerable peer pressure by the uneducated leaders of gangs or groups to keep all students in line. Doing well in school is frowned upon. Breaking with one's peers is emotionally and socially costly. Some people do — they're willing to bear the cost — but this is often because they have alternative peer groups and social interactions.

Connecting with the wrong peers can result in sustained criminal behavior. Given relative prices and income, we can better explain a tendency to engage in criminal behavior if we know whom a person hung out with in the past. Of course, if someone ends up in prison, given the way prisons typically are run, the social interactions there often encourage future criminal behavior.

How History and Culture Affect Choice

Modeling choice is even more complicated than simply integrating norms, peer pressure, and social interactions into our understanding of decision making. The importance of history and culture also must be integrated into economic analysis, making our simplifying assumptions more realistic and taking us beyond the simplistic conventional economics view that relative prices and income are the only things driving choice behavior.

Rooting choice in history

History speaks to a person's past experiences and past choices. These experiences and choices contribute to that person's ability and desire to make particular choices. A person's past social interactions and identities influence his current choices. They influence the utility or disutility he gets or expects from the choices he makes.

If a person's history is heavily embedded in racism and sexism, this will affect his preferences and choices with regards to women and those who are different from him. If a person's history is embedded in eating steak and potatoes or fish and chips, she's less likely to take the risk of trying foods that are outside her realm of experience and understanding, outside her comfort zone.

Culture club: How culture affects the formation of preferences and choices

Culture is not an easy concept to define, especially with respect to determinants of economic development. But one scholar writing extensively on culture and economic development, economist Lawrence Harrison, defines culture as:

> . . . the body of values, beliefs, and attitudes that members of a society share; values, beliefs, and attitudes shaped chiefly by environment, religion, and the vagaries of history that are passed on from generation to generation chiefly through child rearing practices, religious practice, the education system, the media, and peer relationships.

Just as people's preferences for food, art, and music are affected by their culture, so can their attitudes toward saving, entrepreneurship, government, globalization, and the environment be affected by their culture.

Culture can affect people's preferences and, therefore, their choices for goods and services. Culture provides explanations for differences in spending patterns across communities and countries that can't be explained by the conventional reliance on relative prices and income.

Some economists argue that culture can help explain sustained and persistent differences in economic development, after we control for basic economic factors. This argument continues the classic narrative articulated by Max Weber in *The Protestant Ethic and the Spirit of Capitalism,* published in the early 20th century. Weber argued that differences in religious cultures help explain differences in economic development across countries.

Chapter 9

Why Gender, Children, and Age Matter for Economic Analysis

....

In This Chapter

▶ Understanding how gender affects decision making

▶ Recognizing the role that children's preferences play in a household's decisions

▶ Exploring the importance of aging to the choices people make

....

*W*omen and men have different preferences on a variety of issues, and those preferences often result in different choices. But gender isn't the only thing that affects preferences and choice — so do children and aging. Kids tend to have different preferences than adults do. And parents have different preferences than adults without kids do. Finally, some preferences change as people get older. You aren't who you were in the past, nor are you today who you will become in the future. Preferences evolve over time, and economists need to incorporate this evolution into our simplifying assumptions of choice behavior.

In this chapter, I focus on how gender, children, and age affect preferences and choice.

How Gender Affects Choice

Conventional economics wisdom says that men and women have the same preferences. In other words, gender makes no difference to choice behavior. Conventional economics also assumes that men's choices are excellent representations of the preferred choices of women. After all, if men and women have the same preferences, a man can stand in for a woman without any problem.

As you probably guessed, behavioral economics sees things a bit differently. Behavioral economics recognizes that women and men have different preferences on a variety of important issues. Recognizing these differences when modeling various economic problems allows us to better explain how events unfold and better inform public policy.

A good example of these differences relates to family planning, where women tend to prefer fewer kids than men do, regardless of economic incentives. Women also tend to care more about the well-being of children than men do. In this case, the gender of the person making the choices has a big impact on social and economic outcomes.

Not tonight, honey: Conventional choice theory

Conventional economics models work, up to a point, when gender is of no consequence. Men and women do have certain similarities in preferences at a more general level. For example, both men and women are sensitive to relative changes in price and income. But men are much more sensitive to the price of shaving cream than to the price of tampons. Ignoring gender has its place when and where gender truly doesn't matter.

But when and where gender matters is an empirical question. We can't simply assume that preferences are the same for men and women. If we do make this assumption, we move from a simplifying assumption to a simplistic and unrealistic assumption — one that misleads.

Demand for commodities when tastes are gender neutral

In conventional economics, the changing structure of demand is often assumed to be a product of a representative (average) individual, who has no gender and responds to changes in relative prices and changes in income. This sexless individual may drive the demand in different ways and even for new goods and services. But this individual can't model the impact of income changes by gender and can't address the impact of differences in income allocation by gender.

In the oversimplified de-gendered models, economists end up focusing their attention on relative prices and incomes. However, some empirical studies in economics often go well beyond this simplistic approach, introducing gender factors into the analysis.

Understanding gendered tastes and preferences

Behavioral economics insists on introducing gender into the building of models, where gender may play an important role in determining economic outcomes. Considering gender is critically important if economists want to figure out why people end up buying what they buy.

Good models help economists focus their attention on what actually drives the decision-making process and the choices people make, whether independently as men and women or jointly, through bargaining and discussion.

Household bargaining power and women's rights

Because everyone has at least some experience being part of a family, dysfunctional or not, we understand that family decision making is not a simple process. And it can't easily be modeled by assuming that all family members have the same preferences. Doing so would be pretty much the same as assuming that family decision making takes place in the absence of conflict.

Even on the face of it, you know that household decisions are, at a minimum, a product of calm discussion among individuals with different wants and desires. Often the decision-making process involves serious argument and negotiation. In a more egalitarian and respectful environment, household choices are a product of learning through discussion, compromise, and trade-offs (you get this, if I get that).

But the decision-making process can be full of conflict and aggressive. No one's true preferences have to be realized. No one gets what he or she wants. No one's utility is being "maximized." Households are simply doing the best they can. And the household stays together as long as the adults in the household find it worthwhile emotionally and materially.

When women have weak bargaining power, men's preferences dominate — there is little explicit bargaining or negotiation. The household's preferences are those of the male partner. Overall, women's bargaining power is enhanced quite markedly when their legal rights are strengthened and when the social norms are to respect and consider women's contributions to the decision-making process.

How employment impacts bargaining power

Critical to household decision-making outcomes is the bargaining between men and women. A woman's bargaining power is dependent on whether she earns an income and what percentage of the total household income she contributes. Often, the more income a woman earns and the greater her income's share of the total, the greater her power. The extent to which a household's choices reflect female preferences is greatly affected by how much money she brings into the household.

In modern democratic countries, women's participation rate in the labor market is now huge, often greater than 70 percent and in many countries greater than 80 percent. In countries with higher participation from women, such as the United States, Canada, Great Britain, France, Germany, Sweden,

Norway, Finland, and Denmark, women have gained an increasingly equal share in the decision-making process. But in these countries, women's labor market participation is combined with legal protection of a wide array of gender rights, creating an environment where women can speak their minds without fear of punishment.

In many less-developed economies, female labor force participation is weak. And, often, so is the extent and protection of gender rights. In many of these economies, men's preferences dominate household decision making.

Policies in less-developed economies that promote institutions such as microfinancing have enhanced the bargaining power of women. *Microfinancing* provides loans to low-income individuals who have difficulty obtaining relatively low-income loans from traditional financial institutions. Microfinancing has played an important part in providing investment funds for women. Successful businesses that follow from microfinancing both increase household income and reorient household choices toward women's preferences. Because women tend to spend more money on their families, as opposed to on themselves, microfinancing helps to improve the well-being of the family as a whole.

Gender rights and household bargaining power

Women haven't always had the same legal rights as men. Equality before the law for women and men is a relatively recent phenomenon — not much older than a century in most parts of the world. And even today, these rights are nonexistent in many countries. In many countries, even when women have the same legal rights as men, if these rights aren't enforced and if they can be violated by men at a low cost, the rights exist only on paper.

With limited gender rights, women's influence in household decision making is at the behest of the husband. So, women tend to have a limited say on the choices made within the household. Or the decisions women have some input in are determined by social norms, and what the husband decides is in the household's and his own best interest.

In this type of environment, women have a much more limited ability to develop their preferences than they do in environments in which they're equal before the law and where the law is taken seriously.

Education and bargaining power

Education plays an important role in determining the bargaining power of women. As economists put it, all other things remaining the same, on average, the more educated women are, the more bargaining power they have. Their bargaining power is connected to the respect they earn and the quality of information they contribute to the decision-making process as a consequence of having more education.

But in societies where gender rights are limited, females don't have the same access to education as males do. Gender rights directly contribute to increasing the bargaining power of women by empowering them. But it also indirectly increases the bargaining power of women by providing them with more education.

Social norms and household decision making

Expectations of what roles people play in the household and in the larger community affect the capacity of women to influence the choices made in the household. Very often, people do what is expected of them. As economists George Akerlof and Rachel Kranton point out, people increase their level of satisfaction by affirming their sense of identity, a sense of identity often evoked by social norms.

Some women who have been brought up in a tradition where having as many children as possible increases the self-esteem and social esteem of the man will want to have as many children as possible. Older women in the community may acquire their own sense of identity by nudging younger women to behave in accordance with the social norms of how women are expected to behave.

Social norms may induce mothers to underfeed daughters as compared to sons. So, in many countries, girls are poorly nourished compared to boys. Social norms may induce mothers to provide more education to their sons than to their daughters. Sometimes this is also a product of the perceived economic benefits that sons are expected to bring to their families, which may be a product of rules, laws, regulations, and social norms that discriminate against women in the labor market.

On the other hand, social norms also can induce traditional women homemakers to maintain high levels of household cleanliness, regardless of their income level. Evolved and contemporary social norms can induce young women to aspire to jobs that were traditionally thought to be the domain of men.

Social norms impact women's preferences and, in turn, household decision making.

Understanding household choices when women have a voice

When women get their way, they shift household spending toward products that tend to benefit their children. Women also tend to have a stronger preference for saving. So, when women have more bargaining power, we would expect spending patterns to shift toward meeting the needs of kids and toward increasing savings.

Also, when women have more bargaining power and, therefore, a voice, spending decisions tend to differ between couples who have a more harmonious relationship and those where conflict and aggressive behavior dominate. Where there is more harmony and the expectation of divorce is lower, couples spend a larger share of their income on more expensive, indivisible products such as cars, housing, and collectibles such as art and designer furniture.

Exploring population growth when women's preferences count

The conventional economic analysis of population growth assumes the following:

- ✔ Men and women have identical preferences for the number of children they have.

- ✔ Men and women have equal access to information while forming their true preferences on family size.

- ✔ Women have the same capabilities as men to express their views on family size and to actually determine how many children they'll have.

An implicit assumption of the standard model is that if the husband wants ten kids and the wife wants only three, the final number of children will approach the woman's preferences for kids, not the husband's. In other words, the number of kids in a household is consistent with the wife's true preferences. Because the preferences of men and women are assumed to be identical, it's also assumed that the bargaining power within the family makes no difference when it comes to family size and population growth.

According to conventional analysis, population growth is largely a product of the relative cost of having kids and the quality of the child. It's assumed that people (both men and women alike) prefer fewer kids when kids are more expensive. This representative or average individual also has a clear preference for higher-quality children (children who are more educated, skilled, and sophisticated) — and higher-quality children are more expensive.

Children become more costly when women get jobs in the labor market — the household must sacrifice income to have children. In this case, the demand for kids should fall. However, when income increases, the expectation is that people would demand more kids. It's assumed that kids are normal goods. Like ice cream, the more money people have, the more they want. But people are supposed to be increasingly fond of higher-quality children. So, this means that we should demand fewer kids, because higher-quality children require more of an investment. Higher quality comes at a price. It increases the cost of having children.

The history of population growth

In the late 19th century, population growth exploded in the more economically advanced economies. With more money and more food, death rates collapsed and birth rates initially remained pretty steady.

Where once a family needed six to ten kids to end up with two of them surviving to adulthood, as economies began to advance a family needed only three or four kids to end up with two living to adulthood. Today in the wealthier economies, you need only two kids to end up with two adults. So, until birth rates dropped, population growth rates skyrocketed because people were used to having more kids.

Think about it: If only two of your kids will survive into adulthood, you'll have a population growth rate of zero, which isn't far removed from the world's population growth rate until the 19th century. From 1880 to 2000, the world's population increased from less than one billion to over six billion. Now that's a population explosion!

But population growth rates have fallen quite dramatically at least in the past few decades. One reason for this is that women have gained more control over the decision of how many children to have, driving population growth downward. Irrespective of the costs of having kids and income, population growth tends to fall when women become empowered and more educated.

A problem with this approach, pioneered by Gary Becker of the University of Chicago, is that its predictions on population growth are a wee bit ambiguous. This is for the simple reason that the price of kids increases at the same time as income. There is no reason why the negative influence of increasing price (the substitution effect) should overwhelm the positive impact of increasing income (the income effect).

And, it's not always clear why people would necessarily want higher-quality kids as income goes up. It also isn't clear why this effect should be large enough to overwhelm the income effect.

Looking beyond the conventional economics world of relative prices and income, the evidence suggests that women's bargaining power, as well as the education of women (which affects their preferences), plays an important role in determining how many children there are per household. In societies in which women have little bargaining power and aren't well educated, population growth rates tend to be very high. But the opposite occurs when women are empowered and are relatively well educated, especially on the availability and use of contraceptives.

A shift toward lower population growth rates can be expected when women prefer fewer children than men do and when women have the knowledge and power to realize these preferences.

Education provides women with the knowledge of how to control the number of children they have and why having fewer children than their spouses want is okay. Empowerment and education provide women with the capability to realize their preferences for fewer children.

This isn't to say that the relative costs of having kids don't matter — they do. So, too, does the demand for higher-quality children (however weird that term may sound). But female preferences matter big time in the determination of population growth. Assuming that men and women have the same preferences for the number of children assumes away the possibility that non-economic factors can play a major role in determining the rate of population growth.

In the wealthier countries of the world and in countries where women are pretty much equal to men before the law and in terms of social norms, preferences for the number of kids tend to be pretty much the same for men and women. Male preferences appear to have converged with female preferences for economic and non-economic reasons.

Understanding why women go on welfare even if they want to work

In the standard economic model, everyone has a preference for leisure. People would rather not work. Working reduces their level of satisfaction. What they really like is money. If people have more money, more income, they'll work less.

If government provides social assistance to families or to mothers who have young children, conventional economics predicts that women will tend to drop out of the labor market. They get the income they need from the state, and now they can consume leisure, which is their preferred good. Get rid of welfare payments, and you get people back on the labor market, where they belong — at least according to conventional economics.

Conventional economics theory suggests that women are on welfare because they prefer not to work. But there are some missing links in this theory, which assumes that leisure is a preferred good and that preferences for goods and services don't change over time.

Typically, women with children on welfare are on welfare so that they can take care of their children, given that they're priced out of the daycare market. Their preference for leisure isn't what drives them out of the labor market — it's their strong preference to take care of their children that does so. With adequate daycare provision or a high enough income, the typical mom on welfare may very well shift to working.

In Sweden, for example, female labor force participation is exceptionally high. Affordable and quality daycare is critical to women being so active in the Swedish labor market.

In addition, most moms on welfare don't find the amount of income they receive on welfare as an adequate target income. They'd prefer more money. Actually, most people prefer more income — as income increases, their desire for more goods and services increases. If this weren't the case, people wouldn't be working as much as they do in developed economies. In most of these countries, people would have to work less than one day per week to earn as much as middle-income people did in the early 20th century.

Moms go on welfare in spite of the fact that most of them end up earning very little. Welfare provides low-income moms with the opportunity to provide better care to their children in the absence of affordable alternatives.

Moms aren't attracted out of the labor market by welfare payments, as conventional economics maintains. But the conventional prediction that cuts to welfare payments will reduce the percentage of moms on welfare holds true, under certain conditions. If moms don't have any alternative source of income, they have no choice but to abandon their kids and search for work.

But this shift to the labor market takes place only when labor market conditions are vibrant enough to supply jobs of the type that these moms have the skills to do. When labor market conditions improve, many moms move out of welfare on their own — it makes economic sense to do so. There's no love for leisure here.

Identifying why women are more risk averse than men

Evidence suggests that women tend to be more risk averse than men are. Women tend to have a strong preference for certain outcomes. They prefer lower economic returns than higher ones that involve more risk. They prefer more stable, lower-paying jobs to riskier, higher-paying ones. Women should also be less entrepreneurial than men, given the risks involved in entrepreneurship.

This, of course, suggests that men and women don't have the same risk preferences. And this helps explain choices women make that are, on average, different from men's, including education and job choice.

There are exceptions to every rule. Some women have male-oriented risk preferences, and some men have female-oriented risk preferences.

Some behavioral economists argue that this type of gendered risk aversion — the female preference for less risky options — is chemically motivated. It's a product of the higher testosterone levels in men. Men are, on average, driven by testosterone to take on riskier jobs, such as in the financial market, whereas women tend to veer toward less aggressive and more caring jobs like teaching. From this point of view, it's not discrimination, social norms, and the like that keep women from entering into certain occupations. Instead, it's differences in testosterone levels.

Other studies provide strong evidence that women's apparent distaste for risk is very much socially constructed. It's more a product of social norms than of testosterone. For example, some behavioral economists have found that girls raised in more matriarchal societies are just as risk oriented and competitive as boys raised in patriarchal societies. How girls are raised and the environment they're a part of contribute to the risk preferences and competitive nature of girls and boys.

In addition, when females are confronted with the same risky prospects as males, they make similar choices as males do in an all-female environment. Women are also as competitive. Only when the choice environment is mixed are female risk preferences significantly different from their male counterparts. And in the mixed environment, women are also less competitive.

Social norms, sense of identity, and the overall culture appear to play very important roles in determining the immediate preferences and choices people make. Not only do preferences related to risk and competitiveness differ by gender, but these preferences also are subject to change based on the environment within which females and males are raised and the choice environment that they face.

Exploring women's altruistic preferences

Economists have become increasingly interested in how altruism affects people's choices. And it has become increasingly clear that when it comes to altruistic behavior, people's preferences often differ based on gender. Women appear to be more altruistic than men — but the evidence is not 100 percent clear and unequivocal.

Altruism typically refers to a type of self-sacrificing behavior. For example, if you accept a relatively low-wage job for moral reasons, give money to charity, or donate labor time to an organization, you're engaging in a form of altruistic behavior. This type of self-sacrificing behavior hasn't sat well with conventional economics. But the times, they are a changing (albeit slowly).

Experimental evidence suggests that women are more likely to donate money than men are, but men give more than women do when they actually decide to be altruistic. Women also appear to be more sensitive to the "price" of being altruistic. Women tend to engage more in charitable giving when costs are relatively low.

One reason for women being more charitable overall is that women tend to be more sympathetic and subject to guilt than men are. But men tend to give more when solicited by beautiful women. Beauty helps drive male altruistic behavior.

No matter how much more altruistic women may be, their preferences aren't always realized. A lot depends on how decisions are made within the household. Single women can do their own thing and follow their own desires or preferences. But when a woman has a partner, her choices may not dominate. Bargaining power is a critical determinant of the extent of household charitable giving, for example, regardless of what a woman's preferences may be. And a critical determinant of charitable giving, channeled through bargaining power, is the level of a woman's education and market income. The more educated a woman is and the more she earns, the stronger her voice.

Examining labor market discrimination

Woman are paid less than men are. This is a long-established and undisputed fact. Multitudes of studies document the gender pay gap worldwide.

The gender pay gap has declined dramatically over the past 100 years or so, in largely democratic societies. Today the gender pay gap is around 20 percent in most developed economies. In Japan and South Korea, the gender pay gaps are over 30 percent. Denmark, New Zealand, and Sweden have gender pay gaps well below 20 percent.

Not all this pay gap can be attributed to discrimination. Education levels, experience, age, and career choice also matter. But discrimination appears to play an important role in explaining perhaps 50 percent to 60 percent of the pay gap in developed economies, where women tend to be equal before the law and social norms are increasingly antidiscriminatory.

Preferences play a role in sustaining the gender pay gap. Gary Becker, of the University of Chicago, long ago broke with conventional economics, arguing that discriminatory preferences can result in different groups of people being paid differently.

Employers can have a taste for discrimination. They aren't simply interested in maximizing their profits. Instead, they try to maximize their level of satisfaction or utility. Given their disdain for employing women, for example, employers need to be compensated by paying women less than men. This lesser pay to women compensates the employer for the pain the employer suffers when employing people it doesn't like.

But in Becker's thinking, which is pretty dominant, market forces can be expected to take care of the discriminatory portion of the gender pay gap. Non-discriminating employers should come to the rescue, hiring the lower-paid women, which should drive the discriminators, who have all these high-paid men in their employ, into bankruptcy or into changing their discriminatory ways. But the evidence suggests that this hasn't been the case. Gender pay gaps, based on discrimination, are more than just a passing or short-run phenomenon.

In the following sections, I cover some of the non-economic causes of gender labor market discrimination. I also discuss how women respond to labor market discrimination.

Socialization and perception and the gender pay gap

Discrimination in the household and in society at large socializes girls into taking jobs that are relatively low paying, and this appears to play an important role in maintaining a gender pay gap. As long as girls' sense of identity is connected with targeting the lower-paying jobs, gender pay inequality will remain. And after women are socialized as kids and young adults, it's very costly for them to change their career choices. They're locked into these choices even if they may regret their past decisions. Off-the-labor-market discrimination and its effect on preferences influence the gender pay gap.

In addition, if girls expect that taking on certain jobs won't pay, due to discrimination, they won't prepare themselves for potentially high-paying jobs. In this case, past labor market discrimination or perceived labor market discrimination influences the preferences and choices that women make for the labor market. So, even pay gaps that don't appear to be discriminatory may very well be so.

Effort variability and the gender pay gap

A standard assumption of contemporary economics is that how hard and how well individuals work is not at all variable — it can be assumed to be fixed, often at some maximum level.

But this isn't necessarily the case. For example, women still do most of the housework, including childcare, even in the most economically advanced and democratic societies. Doing housework and taking care of kids is draining, so women may not be able to put as much effort into their paid work, which can result in lower productivity and lower pay. This is yet another example of off-the-labor-market discrimination affecting the gender pay gap.

Some women are discriminated against quite directly on the labor market and are being paid less than men for the same job. Based on recent research in behavioral economics, we would expect that the lower-paid women would retaliate by working less hard, which would reduce their productivity. This, in turn, would reduce the chances of non-discriminating employers driving the discriminators out of the market. Cheap female workers would no longer provide the non-discriminators with a competitive advantage over the discriminators.

If a woman's pay is lower than a man's pay by 10 percent (both working the same number of hours) and her productivity is less by 10 percent, she's retaliated by reducing how hard and how well she works — she's now as expensive as the higher-paid but more-productive man. In this case, Becker's market solution to eliminating discrimination wouldn't hold any traction.

Preferences can play an important role in influencing market outcomes on the labor market. And they can have a lasting impact on the wages women earn compared to men. Changing preferences and changing social norms have played important roles in narrowing the gender pay gap over time.

The Role of Children in Economic Decision Making

Children's preferences are often different from their parents. But typically the preferences of children aren't directly taken into consideration by conventional models of household decision making. From this point of view, you can model household decision making as if kids' preferences are the same as their parents' because parents typically do what they want. Also, kids typically don't have much bargaining power in the household, although they learn and develop various tactics to get their way.

Even so, children can have a dramatic impact on household choices by impacting the choices parents make on behalf of their kids. Parents don't have to pay much attention to what their kids have to say in order for children to influence parents' choices on things like spending, jobs, and savings.

People who have kids typically purchase a different set of goods and services than people without children. Also, children tend to affect saving patterns — this effect can be positive or negative, depending on the weight parents place on the future, their income, and the goods and services that parents consider essential to their children's present well-being.

News Flash! Preferences Change with Age

A topic of great discussion among behavioral economists is that preferences often change with age. In conventional economics, preferences aren't expected to change over time. Preferences are definitely not expected to flip or reverse. They're assumed to be unaffected by the aging process.

A novel look at preference formation over historical time

An important insight on the evolution of future selves is provided by Sebastian Faulks in his novel *Charlotte Gray:*

> . . . there was no such a thing as a coherent human personality. When you are forty you have no cell in your body that you had at eighteen. It was the same . . . with your character. Memory is the only thing that binds you to earlier selves; for the rest, you become an entirely different person every decade or so, sloughing off the old persona, renewing and moving on. You are not who you were . . . nor who you will be.

Some behavioral economists dub this *preference reversal* as irrational, because it deviates from the standard assumption of stable preferences. Other behavioral economists regard this type of preference change as rational and consistent with the evolutionary nature of preference formation.

A classic example of preference change associated with getting older is the attitude many people have on saving for retirement. Many people, in their youth, prefer not to invest much for retirement — or at least they won't invest all that much unless they have a strong incentive to do so. Yet, when these same people get older, they become strong believers in saving for retirement. Of course, by then it's too late.

But who you are today is not quite who you were in the past. And you don't know and can't know who you will be in the future. Your future self can't regulate or influence the choices made by your present self. That's just not possible.

Given that economists know what people's future selves want, on average, when it comes to retirement — they want decent savings — many behavioral economists argue for the introduction of mechanisms to encourage or nudge the younger generation to save more for the future. Otherwise, the level of well-being of the average individual won't be maximized, at least from the perspective of our older selves who would prefer to retire at a decent standard of living.

Part II
Growing the Economic Pie: The Economic Importance of Ethics, Well-Being, and Culture

The 5th Wave   By Rich Tennant

"Sometimes I get the feeling we're not as free-range as we think we are."

In this part . . .

*O*ne very important reason why behavioral economics matters is that it offers interesting and often compelling reasons for why people behave in unexpected ways and how this affects the size of the economic pie. In this part, I explain why the payment of taxes and criminal behavior have very important non-economic dimensions.

I also explain how the labor market may be affected by social welfare, unions, minimum wages, and the like. Although conventional theory predicts that these types of institutions can cause serious harm to the economy, this doesn't have to be the case, and I explain why.

In this part, I discuss some of the inner workings of the black box of the firm, which goes largely unnoticed in conventional economics. How individuals relate to each other inside the firm can have a huge impact on productivity and, thus, on material well-being and even on the spiritual well-being of all firm members.

In addition, in this part, I explain how ethical behavior impacts the wealth of nations. Contrary to what conventional economics tells us, ethics can have positive economic effects. Ethics also can affect what people produce and how they produce it.

Finally, in this part, I elaborate upon the significance of institutions in moderating and facilitating economic behavior.

Chapter 10

Why Smart People Pay Taxes, Recycle, and Even Break the Law

C riminals and good citizens come from the same social and economic groups: You can find examples of rich criminals and poor criminals, rich law abiders and poor law abiders. Basically, controlling for differences in income and costs, we see a tremendous variation of behavior.

In conventional economics, however, differences in relative prices and income should explain differences in behavior. In addition, changing the price of criminal behavior or the price of being a good citizen should change people's behavior in the expected way. People should commit more crime if it pays and less if it's too costly. They should be more ethical if it pays and less ethical if it doesn't.

In this chapter, I discuss different perspectives on what causes a wide range of behaviors and choices — from paying taxes to recycling to committing crime. I also examine the relationship between economic and non-economic factors affecting choice behavior.

Why Most People Pay Taxes: The Big Stick versus the Warm Glows

According to conventional economics, people pay taxes because they're forced to. The big stick is what gets people to contribute to the public purse. If people know that they'll be penalized if they don't pay taxes, this increases the chances that they'll pay. As the penalties for dodging taxes increases, conventional economics argues, more people will pay their taxes and each person will cheat less. If penalties for not paying taxes are decreased, the number of people paying their taxes will decrease, and each person will cheat on his or her taxes more. If there are no penalties for defaulting on taxes, people will set out to maximize their income and utility or well-being by not paying taxes at all. Any deviation from this type of behavior would be irrational according to conventional economics.

In the real world, however, the penalties are not nearly as severe as conventional theory would predict to induce so many people to pay their taxes. In other words, non-economic factors — including social norms and peer pressure — are lurking in the background, inducing people to pay their taxes.

On the flip side, even in countries where severe tax avoidance penalties are in place, a large percentage of people avoid paying their taxes. This is especially the case when many people believe that tax rates are too high or that tax revenue is not used fairly or efficiently. In this case, too, non-economic factors, people's sense of fairness and fair play, influence the extent of tax compliance — the extent to which people pay the taxes that they are legally obliged to pay.

Both economic and non-economic factors are critical to explaining tax compliance. Together, these two types of factors also help to explain the large variation in tax payment across individuals and countries. Good economic tax analysis requires the introduction of non-economic factors into the discussion.

In all countries there exists something called a *tax gap* (the difference between the tax revenue that government should collect based on the various taxes it imposes and the taxes it actually collects). The tax gap in the United States, for example, is about 20 percent. Obviously, the tax gap is a product of non-compliance. The big question is whether the tax gap is a product of people trying to cheat the system and break the law to increase income or other things, such as errors in completing complex and difficult tax forms, social norms, or objections over the fairness of the tax system.

How the big stick induces tax payments

In conventional economics, people are assumed to be wealth and income maximizers — they make decisions based on their desire to maximize their own wealth and income after taking risks into consideration. But taxes reduce personal wealth and income. People aren't expected to think about the social implications of their tax-related behavior. They aren't expected to consider whether tax revenues to government may benefit them in the future (through spending on things like roads, schools, and law enforcement, as well as on regulatory agencies that may uncover financial malfeasance). Instead, conventional economics expects people to pass the buck to the poor sucker who decides to pay his or her taxes.

In all countries, the tax-compliance system involves a system of penalties and monitoring that includes random audits. But for the most part, direct monitoring is minimal. The big stick largely involves the government imposing a cost on those who are caught cheating — but if you're an American, Uncle Sam isn't going to knock on your door to collect your tax payment on April 15.

According to conventional economics, people are supposed to calculate the expected costs and benefits of cheating and decide not to cheat only if the costs are too high. The experts are supposed to determine a set of penalties sufficient to deter cheating by the typical individual. Some cheating can be expected to occur because real people are different from the representative taxpayer. And for some people, the penalties are not high enough to deter them from skipping out on their taxes.

The niceness effect

People tend to increase their level of tax-compliance when government bureaucrats are more helpful and friendly. Most people respond favorably when treated with respect — they reciprocate. There is no niceness effect in the conventional economics model. But in the real world, there is.

The manner in which government treats the public — how it frames its interaction with the public, in this case with respect to tax advice — has an important impact on the level of tax compliance.

It's complicated: How the tax system trips people up

The big stick isn't enough to eliminate the tax gap. But this gap between what government should be earning from taxes and what it actually earns is not simply a product of people deliberately trying to cheat the system. A good deal of the tax gap is a product of how complicated the tax system is. Many people make errors when they do their taxes — some because of simple calculation mistakes and other because they're financially illiterate. Either way, they end up underpaying their taxes.

As tax forms become more complex, more difficult to understand, and more costly to process, the rate of tax compliance diminishes. If information were free and the brain weren't a scarce resource, this wouldn't occur. But the real world is another matter. In at least some countries, tax agencies are beginning to take this reality into consideration when designing tax forms.

Social norms and taxes

People are much more tax compliant than what conventional economics theory predicts. In other words, the penalty stick is far smaller than is required to produce the extent of tax compliance that we find in most countries. If people were motivated only by penalties and meaningful threats, the tax gap in most countries would be much greater than it actually is.

In the United States, where anti-tax and anti-government rhetoric looms large, close to 90 percent of Americans oppose tax cheating and a large percentage support reporting tax cheats to the government. The vast majority of Americans believe that paying taxes is the right thing to do. Paying your taxes is actually the social norm in the United States and in many other developed economies.

A good portion of tax compliance in the United States can be explained by the prevailing social norm favoring the payment of your allocated tax. Some people would say that the *tax morale* (the attitude toward paying taxes and being tax compliant) is very high in the United States. Actually, tax morale in the United States is higher than in most countries. When tax morale is high, the penalty stick can be relatively small to generate the desired level of tax revenue. There is even some evidence that when penalties are excessive, this results in many people retaliating by increasing the extent of their noncompliance or shifting from compliant to noncompliant behavior.

Social norms on tax compliance differ across individuals as well as across countries. There is good evidence to suggest that being trained in conventional economics is enough to reduce tax morale and, therefore, the level of tax-compliant behavior. Many people who've been trained in conventional economics live by the social norm that noncompliance is morally acceptable, as long as you can get away with it. People from different educational backgrounds are much more tax-compliant. Obviously, education has an impact on tax morale and tax compliance.

A sense of fairness and tax compliance

Tax compliance is affected by whether government spending can be identified and supported. If people know what government is spending their tax dollars on, this in and of itself increases tax compliance. If people actually support the direction of government spending, this further increases the extent of tax compliance.

The fairer people feel the tax process is, the more tax compliant they are. A sense of fairness also feeds into tax morale. However, everyone tends to have a different understanding of what's fair. What a middle-income person understands to be fair can be quite different from what a wealthy person perceives as fair. The two groups actually may have conflicting understandings of fairness in taxation. That said, there is a positive relationship between the perceived fairness of the tax system and government spending and tax compliance.

Different Perspectives on Reducing Pollution

In conventional economics, there is no clear consensus on how to deal with pollution, but there is general agreement that creating a greener economy is costly. Regulating pollution will make for a greener and even healthier environment but at the cost of reducing the rate of growth of per-person income and increasing the rate of employment. Economists can provide estimates (and sometimes guesstimates) of these costs, and people have to decide how much they're willing to pay to produce a greener economy.

Conventional economics also focuses on the economic dimension of pollution regulation. The focus is largely on imposing costs and regulations on polluters to induce or force them into reducing their pollution. In this way, they're forced to reduce some of the negative effects they impose on others when they emit pollutants into the environment. But the conventional model tends to exaggerate the costs of pollution reduction. It also tends to pay little heed to how evolving preferences and social norms affect private- and public-sector policy on pollution remission. This is an important gap in the economic analysis of pollution reduction that behavioral economics attempts to fill.

In the following sections, I discuss the conventional economics perspective on developing greener economies, which assumes that greener production inevitably generates higher production costs. I also discuss a behavioral approach to more environmentally friendly production, which recognizes the possibility of greener production inducing cost offsets. Green production doesn't have to be as costly as the conventional model predicts.

Exploring the economics of pollution control

Conventional economics assumes that individuals respond best to economic incentives. So, to reduce pollution, we need to use economic incentives to induce polluters to change their behavior. Conventional economics tends to ignore non-economic factors, as if corporate leaders can't be motivated by ethical considerations, social norms, and peer pressure.

Becoming green for ethical reasons: The importance and limits of ethics in motivating corporate behavior

Even corporate leaders who have a strong sense of moral sentiment and are heavily influenced by pro-green social norms must think about the bottom line. And the corporate leaders of publicly listed companies must pay heed to their companies' share prices when thinking about and planning for a more environmentally friendly corporation.

When government imposes taxes, rules, and regulations on all corporations to induce or force pollution abatement, all corporate leaders have to at least try to comply. And if they actually are sympathetic with a move toward a greener economy, a new incentive and regulatory environment allows them to act upon their preferences for a greener economy.

A classic economic device to reduce pollution is to tax polluting firms, forcing them to internalize the costs that they impose on others by polluting the environment. Other interventions are simply to impose limits on the extent of an emission and, in the extreme, to ban certain emissions. But none of these interventions is oriented toward non-economic incentives.

Thinking about the green corporation

Being green is assumed to be a problem in conventional economics because of the particular assumptions made about what happens inside the firm in response to efforts to make the firm environmentally friendly. In conventional economics, becoming more environmentally friendly invariably increases the firm's average production costs, which will either reduce profits or increase prices. It can even make firms uncompetitive. If you buy into the conventional wisdom, even if you want your firm to be more environmentally friendly, you'll resist becoming greener for fear that doing so might drive you into bankruptcy. But behavioral economics introduces some very real possibilities that make the green corporation more than a costly pipe dream.

Becoming more productive

Firms can become productive as a function of become greener. Workers, managers, and owners can end up working smarter and harder. Plus, more productive technologies can be developed and adopted as a consequence of the firm becoming greener. If firms choose to be green or are forced into becoming greener as a result of government regulation or public pressure, they can increase productivity through increasing the quality and quantity of workers' effort. Also, by initially increasing costs, becoming greener induces technological change. Improvements in effort and induced technological change can offset the costs of becoming greener.

Such behavior is consistent with much of the evidence that becoming greener remains cost competitive and profitable. Moreover, many companies that have become greener show better-than-average returns on investment and stock performance.

However, because becoming greener is often cost- and profit-neutral — it doesn't increase or reduce cost or profits — market forces can't really force such firms into becoming greener. Unless you have a preference for being green because of your sense of moral responsibility or you're nudged by government or consumer pressure, you might stick to operating a dirty factory. This is the safer option. It's what you're most familiar with.

The theoretical narrative underpinning this discussion is explored in more detail in Chapter 12, where I discuss x-efficiency theory and induced technological change.

Understanding the links between green consumption and green production

Consumer preferences for greener production can push firms into becoming greener. But to do this, consumers must be able to identify which firms are more environmentally friendly. If you can't identify greener firms, you can't shift your purchases toward them. For this reason, trustworthy product labeling is key to developing and growing markets for products produced by environmentally friendly firms.

Also, when greener products are more expensive, consumers must be willing to absorb higher product costs to purchase a car or a pair of jeans that's produced in an environmentally friendly way. This is often the case, especially for higher-income individuals. Wealthier people and wealthier societies can afford more expensive products.

When green and "dirty" products can be produced and sold at the same price, consumer preferences for green products drive what's produced, as long as consumers can identify green production. And firms will produce green products if it's profitable to do so.

Studying social norms and the greening of the world

As social norms evolve toward a preference for a greener economy, profit-maximizing firms have no choice but to think of ways of producing in a more environmentally friendly way. These norms can be enforced by the consumption standards of our peers and communities. When people's sense of identity is enhanced by conforming to greener consumption norms, their level of satisfaction is enhanced by consuming greener products.

All other things remaining equal, greener norms increase the demand for a greener economy, providing firms with a sustainable market for greener products. This is especially the case when green production comes at the same cost as traditional production.

Also, when communities demand higher environmental standards, profit-maximizing firms are incentivized to adopt greener production processes. This is particularly the case when governments are expected to impose economic sanctions and supply economic benefits to firms that are more environmentally friendly.

Understanding the mix of economic and non-economic variables in determining green production

Social norms work in concert with traditional economic variables in determining the extent to which an economy becomes greener. Greener social norms incentivize firms to search for competitive technologies and methods of organizing production and sales to meet the revealed preferences of consumers. But people's income and the relative price of greener production still affect their desire for greener production — consumers can be priced out of the green product market.

Overall, the myth that greener production *necessarily* results in higher costs and lower profits helps sustain social norms that are skeptical of a low-cost, high-profit green economy.

However, it appears that firms tend to react to the pressure of greener social norms by innovating and becoming increasingly green so as to maintain or increase their market share. And many corporate decision makers are now strong advocates of a greener economy, given that such an economy can be shown to be profitable and economically sustainable, even in competitive markets.

Crime and Punishment

According to conventional economic wisdom, the big stick is the driving force to control criminal behavior. (This perspective was pioneered by Gary Becker of the University of Chicago.) Non-economic variables play a relatively small role in determining the extent of criminal behavior. Conventional economics says that people choose whether to commit a crime based on its expected costs and benefits.

Behavioral economics doesn't deny the importance of incentives in determining the extent of criminal behavior. But the conventional economics model fails to explain a good deal of criminal behavior or the lack of it. Non-economic variables like social norms, identity, addiction, emotion, and the weakness of will or lack of self-control all contribute to a more complete explanation of crime. In addition, the fact is that many people don't think through consequences of their immediate choices for the future influences whether they commit a criminal act.

The calculating criminal

The conventional economics model of criminal behavior assumes the following:

- ✔ People commit a criminal act if the expected benefit of doing the crime exceeds the cost.
- ✔ People consider the costs and benefits of committing a crime over a long stretch of time into the future.
- ✔ People behave as if they actually do these calculations prior to deciding whether to commit a criminal act.
- ✔ People have reasonably good information on the costs and benefits of engaging in criminal behavior.
- ✔ People are self-interested and don't take into account the cost they impose on others when committing a crime.

Crime is all about maximizing material well-being over time, according to conventional economics. And it's all about doing the appropriate calculations to get a good idea of the net benefits of committing a criminal act.

Conventional economics suggests that societies should increase the costs of committing crime. It also suggests that people should have to bear the costs that they impose on others — the social costs of engaging in criminal activity.

Behavioral economics agrees that potential criminals will respond to costly deterrents. Prospect theory and loss aversion both suggest that people place a greater weight on equivalent losses than they do on gains. This alone suggests that people should be more responsive to deterrents than conventional economics suggests. But in order for this to work, penalties for committing crimes must be well known and fairly certain. (See Chapter 6 for more on prospect theory and loss aversion.)

The emotional criminal: Murder without calculation

Crimes of passion are not easily subject to analysis using the conventional economics model. These crimes are related to the lack of self-control that characterizes some criminal behavior — pulling a trigger or striking out violently based on fear.

If a crime is a heat-of-the-moment decision, conventional cures likely won't do the trick. Certainly, crimes of passion can't be explained or regulated by changing the relative cost of committing a violent crime, when committing such a crime was not initially planned in a calculating, deliberative manner.

If a prospective criminal believes that it's pretty easy to avoid the maximum sentence or even get away with it, this increases the chances that he or she will commit that bad deed. This is one reason why members of organized crime groups are not always very sensitive to hefty potential penalties. If they expect that a top-notch lawyer will defend them and that no one will squeal, the anticipated costs of committing a crime are actually much lower than what the law would suggest.

One reason that white-collar crime is such a growth industry is that *white-collar criminals* (people who, without physical violence, rip off other people for millions or billions of dollars) expect to face light sentences. This is because our society often doesn't perceive these people as evil or bad, whereas someone who robs a local liquor store is often perceived as the epitome of evil.

Social norms of what is considered a "bad" crime influence the deterrents the society develops when it comes to different crimes. This, in turn, has an important effect on criminal behavior.

From the perspective of behavioral economics, public policy that reduces the net benefits of criminal behavior should have a big effect on decision making, but only if the penalties are clear and unequivocal. This is particularly important in a world of bounded rationality (in other words, the real world of decision making).

Interestingly enough, at least in the United States, the legal system has not only increased the relative costs of crime but also has made prospective penalties clearer and more certain. Both property crimes and violent crimes have fallen 30 percent to 40 percent during the past 20 years or so. Clearly, economic incentives matter in the world of crime, just as they do in the market for fruits and vegetables, fuel, cars, and trucks.

How overconfidence affects criminal behavior

There is significant evidence that many people are overconfident about the expected outcomes that flow from the decisions they make. Some behavioral economists argue that such overconfidence, referred to as an *overconfidence bias,* contributes to more criminal behavior than the conventional model would predict. Overconfident criminals overestimate the objective net benefits of committing a felony. This suggests that deterrents need to be greater than initially thought if society is to effectively reduce criminal behavior.

Addiction and criminal behavior

Once a person becomes addicted, he or she has much less control over his or her choices. The choices of addicts are heavily contingent on their past choices — choices that resulted in their addiction. Addiction is path dependant — it depends on past behavior, which paves a path for future behavior. Doing drugs, gambling, drinking too much alcohol, even smoking cigarettes are not purely a matter of free choice for an addict.

When consuming certain products is made illegal, regulating the consumption of the illegal substance becomes very difficult (if not impossible) even when this raises the net cost of consuming or selling the illegal product. The addict's demand for drugs, for example, is not very sensitive to price (including the probability of going to prison) — it's highly price inelastic.

To reduce crimes related to drug addiction requires helping addicts who prefer to go clean get clean. But this has little to do with changing the relative costs of doing illegal drugs.

Even explaining the origins of addiction to illegal products has little to do with economic calculation. It has more to do with social norms, peer pressure, and sense of identity. Whom you choose (or are nudged) to hang out with, social norms, and family values all play key roles in determining whether you become an addict.

The role of identity and social networks in determining criminal behavior

As economists George Akerlof and Rachel Kranton suggest, criminal and, more generally, deviant behavior can be products of the identity people choose to make their own and the choices they make to increase the utility or satisfaction they get from those chosen identities. This increase in utility may very well exceed the possible costs of engaging in criminal behavior.

Cognitive dissonance

People tend to feel bad (suffer a lower level of satisfaction or utility) when they make choices that initially conflict with their preferences or ideals. This conflict is referred to as *cognitive dissonance*. People may initially choose an identity that conflicts with their sense of what's right and wrong. To reduce this cognitive dissonance, they often justify their choices so that the choices become their desired choices. In other words, they rationalize everything from murder and robbery to having bought something they now regret buying. That bad choice becomes a smart choice, and the extent of cognitive dissonance is reduced, which increases their level of satisfaction or utility.

The choice of identity can be a product of socioeconomic circumstances. If you have no job and this diminishes your sense of self, becoming a member of a gang may restore your sense of self and increase your utility.

But the choice of identity also is affected by the alternative identities available to you. If people have more options of identities to choose from, and if this basket of identities includes being part of groups that direct them *away* from criminal behavior, there is a much better chance that the crime rate will be reduced, regardless of the net benefits of committing a crime.

Building a sense of community, offering things for kids to do (sports, music, reading, after-school care), providing training programs for the unemployed, and offering drug rehabilitation for addicts all provide alternative identities that people can choose from. These alternative identities can increase people's utility without cognitive dissonance (see the nearby sidebar) or criminal behavior.

Why most people don't commit crimes even when crime pays

Just as most people pay their taxes even if it makes economic sense not to, most people don't commit crimes even when committing a crime is economically profitable.

Social norms, education, family, sense of identity, available identities, different weights attached to gains and losses, level of confidence, and a person's sense of how his behavior affects his friends and neighbors — all these things play a role in determining why most people don't commit crimes.

Terrorism and behavioral economics

Most terrorists come from relatively well-off and well-educated families and are relatively well off and well educated themselves. Some of these well-off and well-educated terrorists are suicide bombers, where the self-selected ultimate penalty is death. For many others, the penalty for committing or abetting terrorism is a hefty one. And for those involved in terrorism, there is the anticipated cost of losing their relatively high incomes if caught and the cost that this imposes on the terrorists' families over time. In spite of these severe penalties, terrorism persists.

If people actually believe in life after death and that the new life is better than the current one, then the supply of terrorists won't be very sensitive to traditional deterrents.

Alan Krueger of Princeton University finds that one of the key determinants in producing terrorists is the absence of civil liberties. Just providing civil liberties has the dramatic effect of reducing the supply of terrorists and acts of terrorism. This is independent of any change in the cost of committing an act of terror. Simply increasing this cost has no discernable impact on terrorism. And we can't explain variations in terrorism across the world by looking at differences in economic variables such as levels of income and differences in economic deterrents.

Although members of particular socioeconomic or demographic groups commit the majority of certain crimes, most members of these groups never commit crimes. Non-economic variables play a critical role in explaining why this is the case.

Chapter 11

Labor Supply in the Real World

. . . .

In This Chapter

▶ Understanding the meaning of labor supply

▶ Investigating the conventional model of labor supply

▶ Introducing behavioral and social determinants of labor supply

. . . .

The conventional thinking is that people will supply more labor to the labor market as wages increase from relatively low levels. But conventional economics assumes that people prefer leisure to work and will drop out of the labor force when wages rise sufficiently or when they get income from government when they aren't working. So, for example, unemployment insurance or social benefits like welfare are thought to reduce the workforce because they provide potential workers with the capacity to enjoy a life of leisure.

In this chapter, I discuss an alternative view — one that finds that participation in the labor market is driven by a much more complex set of factors than economic incentives.

An Introduction to Labor Supply

Before capturing the essence of the conventional economics perspective on labor supply, I want to explain what exactly is meant by that term. I also want to give you a sense of what has happened to labor supply over time. Finally, I want to fill you in on what people do when they aren't working. (Here's a hint: They aren't sitting around eating bonbons.)

Decoding the reality of labor supply

Economists define *labor supply* as the supply of labor to the official labor market. Labor supply is made up of individuals who are employed in the official labor market plus those who are officially counted as unemployed.

A person is counted as employed if he's working at least a small amount of time per week. Even if he wants to work full-time, if he's working part-time, he's counted as employed. A person is counted as being unemployed only if he isn't working and he is actively searching for work. So, if you happen to be unemployed and you're no longer actively searching for work, even if you still want a job, you aren't counted as being unemployed and, for this reason, you aren't part of the official labor supply.

Labor supply doesn't include people who are in the military or in prison. It doesn't include people who work in the illegal sectors of the economy — someone whose paid job is dealing drugs, for example, is not part of the labor supply. And it doesn't include stay-at-home parents — someone whose main job is taking care of her own kids at home, without pay, is not part of the official labor supply.

Government estimates labor supply using a survey of a sample of the larger population.

Conventional economics is concerned about policy that pulls people out of the labor market. It's concerned about people withdrawing from the official labor market and entering into the world of leisure. The conventional prediction is that if you somehow get your hands on some extra income, you'll withdraw from the labor market, which will reduce the supply of labor available to employers. This, in turn, will increase wage rates and the cost of production. And that would be bad for the health of the economy.

Mapping out changes to labor supply

What's most interesting about the evolution of labor is that it hasn't fallen off all that much over the past 100 years. Changes to the supply of labor are made up of the following:

- ✔ Changes in hours worked per week
- ✔ Changes in the percentage of the population who are active participants in the labor market

Hours worked per week

In most developed economies, hours worked per week have decreased from about 60 hours to about 40 hours in most developed economies — a product of workers fighting for a shorter workweek — but much of this decrease took place prior to World War II. At that time, *real wages* (money or nominal wages corrected for prices changes) increased by more than enough to keep income from falling as the number of hours worked fell. So, people were able to work fewer hours per week without experiencing a drop in weekly income (wage rate multiplied by hours worked).

After World War II, there wasn't much of a change in hours worked per week even as real wages continued to increase. More recently, real wages have decreased in many developed economies with little if any movement upward in hours worked per week.

Overall, there is no clear relationship between changes in real wages and hours worked per week. Real income has increased quite dramatically over the past 100 years. For example, in the United States, most people would only have to work for a bit less than one day per week today to obtain the standard of living that a middle-income family achieved in the first decade of the 20th century in the United States — and by most measures, the United States was the wealthiest country in the world at that time.

For many economists, including those educated in the tradition of conventional economics, this very unclear relationship between changes in real wages and changes in hours worked per week doesn't bode well for the conventional understanding of what drives labor supply. Historically, in the Unites States, Canada, Europe, and elsewhere, when real wages go up, hours worked have gone up in certain periods and down in others. And when real wages have gone down, hours worked have increased in certain periods and diminished in others. Conventional economics can't predict these types of empirical relationships.

The percentage of the population who are active participants in the labor market

Changes to the supply of labor are determined by more than just hours worked per week (see the preceding section). They're also determined by the percentage of people who are active participants in the labor market, referred to as the *labor force participation rate*. The official labor force participation rate is found by adding the number of individuals who are officially employed and the number of individuals who are officially unemployed, and then dividing by the total working-age population (in most countries between 14 and 66 years of age). The labor force participation rate is about 70 percent in most developed economies.

A broader measure of labor force participation is found by adding the number of individuals who are officially employed and the number of individuals who are officially unemployed, and then dividing by the total population. In the United States, in 1950, about 40 percent of the entire population was either employed or unemployed. This means that about 40 percent of the population was participating in the official labor market. This number had increased to 51 percent by 2010. (Most developed economies around the world saw a similar increase in the labor force participation rate.) So, as real wages increased, so did labor force participation (see Figure 11-1).

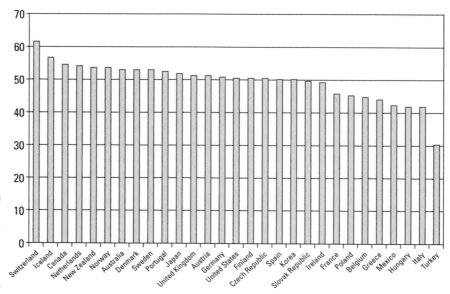

Figure 11-1:
Labor force
participation
rates
in 2010.

Source: Data from the Organization for Economic Cooperation and Development (2009)

The labor force participation rate is fairly independent of per-capita income. Among the countries with the highest labor force participation rates are countries with the highest per-capita income, such as Canada, Norway, and Switzerland. Many conventional economists would argue that, when per-capita income is quite high, people work less, enjoying more of their true object of desire: leisure. Among the countries with the lowest labor force participation rates are countries with the lowest per-capita income, such as Greece, Mexico, and Turkey. In this case, conventional economics would expect people to be more active in the labor market, earning income to cover their material wants and desires.

The active population does not include those who are in their late 60s and those who are younger than 15 years old. Definitions differ somewhat across countries.

Over the past 100 years, the female labor force participation rate has increased dramatically, climbing from about 20 percent or less in 1900 to 60 percent to 70 percent today. The female labor force participation rate has converged on the male labor force participation rate, and the male labor force participation rate has dropped somewhat over the years. All this has occurred as real wages have increased dramatically for both men and women over the past century.

These changes in labor force participation are quite difficult for the conventional theory to explain. Conventional economics anticipates that all people, irrespective of gender, should react in a similar fashion to changes in the wage rate, but that isn't what has happened. Also, conventional economics can't pinpoint when people will react to increasing wages by reducing their labor supply. The traditional narrative is that labor supply will initially increase and eventually diminish. But at which wage rate this labor supply switch takes place is never made clear in conventional economics (see "Labor Supply When People Prefer Leisure: The Conventional Economics Perspective," later in this chapter).

Uncovering what people do when they aren't working

The critical simplifying assumption of conventional economics is that when people don't work on the market, they indulge in leisure activities. But this assumption is highly simplistic and misleading.

Through time-use studies, more and more information is available on what people actually do with their time. What's really interesting — and probably not all that surprising — is that when people aren't working for pay, they're working for free in the household, with some volunteer time thrown into the mix.

Taking the U.S. population between 15 and 65 years old as an example, we know the following:

- ✔ People sleep about 8½ hours per day.

- ✔ People spend about 1½ hours per day on personal care, such as washing and eating at home. They spend another 15 minutes per day on exercise.

- ✔ People spend about 2½ hours per day during the week and about 3½ hours per day on the weekends on unpaid work related to the household, but not including childcare. Women devote close to twice what men do to this type of unpaid work.

- ✔ People spend about 1 hour per day on childcare. Women devote more than two times what men do to childcare.

- ✔ People spend about 1½ hours per day during the week and about 2½ hours per day on the weekends on socializing and leisure activities outside the home.

- ✔ People spend almost 3 hours per day during the week and about 3½ hours per day on the weekends on leisure activities in the household, which includes watching TV.

Working less in the labor market does not *necessarily* mean increasing leisure time. It can translate into doing more work at home, including childcare and household repairs. Moreover, shifting to the paid labor market doesn't mean that people end up watching less TV or spending less time with their friends. It can very well mean that they spend less time taking care of their kids and send them off to daycare, if they can afford to.

Of course, some people who aren't working for pay may be simply slacking off and taking it easy. But the evidence suggests that this simplistic portrayal of the *typical* individual is far off the mark.

There's actually no trade-off between income and leisure time. Instead, the trade-off is often between income and non-market activities, which includes some leisure time and a large number of other activities that involve unpaid work.

Labor Supply When People Prefer Leisure: The Conventional Economics Perspective

The conventional economics model is pretty simple: It assumes that the labor supply is determined by the price of labor and by income. It models a world where people have 24 hours available to them each day — a pretty good reality-based assumption. People decide what to do with these hours based on the price of labor (the *wage rate*), which presents the sacrifice they make if they decide not to work on the labor market. If people don't work, they forfeit labor income, which is determined by the wage rate.

Often, people are told that they have a choice between working on the labor market or using their available time for leisure. But leisure time is actually comprised of sleep (something few people can do without), household work, and leisure. Often, if you aren't working on the labor market, you're taking care of the kids, cleaning the house, doing home repairs, cooking the meals, and, when there's some time left over, taking it easy (maybe going out with friends, reading a book, or watching TV).

A huge assumption of the conventional model is that this so-called "leisure time" is a *normal good* (a good that you want more of as your income goes up). So, working on the labor market is not your most preferred choice. Working is often assumed to be the inferior choice. People don't really like working on the labor market — working isn't what gives them satisfaction, nor is it what increases their level of happiness.

When income increases, it's expected that people will demand more leisure, holding the wage rate constant. As a consequence, they'll want to work fewer hours on the labor market if they can afford to. As their income goes up, they'll demand more leisure time and less work. If the opportunity arises, people will move out of the labor market entirely. Why work, if you don't have to? Or so the conventional thinking goes.

In the following sections, I cover the basics of the conventional economics of labor supply, with a special focus on the so-called income-leisure trade-off. I discuss why conventional economics argues that increasing income tends to pull people out of the labor market. I also elaborate on the implications of this approach for public policy.

The income-leisure trade-off: Bribing people to work

In conventional economics, life is all about a trade-off between income and leisure.

The classic model of income-leisure choice is presented in Figure 11-2. Here we have indifference curves and budget or price lines (see Chapter 5). The vertical axis measures income, and the horizontal axis measures non-market time, which is assumed to represent "leisure time" in the simple conventional model of labor supply. In this figure, the indifference curve indicates a given level of well-being, satisfaction, or utility for alternative combinations of income and non-market time. The budget line tells how much people can purchase with their income; the slope of the budget line reveals the relative price of non-market time and is given by the wage rate. When the wage rate goes up, people have to sacrifice more income for every hour of non-market time that they "consume." Increasing the wage rate increases the cost of not working in the official labor market.

If you start off with budget line CA and indifference curve $U1$, you'll be happy at point h. Here, you'll be consuming $0L$ of leisure and LC of market time. The LC of market time is what generates your market income. If the wage goes up, this is illustrated by a pivot of the price or budget line to CE. Now you're happy at the higher indifference curve $U2$ at point n. And you're supplying more market time (KC) and less leisure time ($0K$). But there is no reason why you have to supply more labor to the labor market when the price of labor goes up and when the cost of "leisure time" increases.

Figure 11-2:
The stan-
dard model
of labor
supply
examines
how
changes in
the price
of non-
market time
influence
the deci-
sion about
how much
time, if any,
people sup-
ply to the
official labor
market.

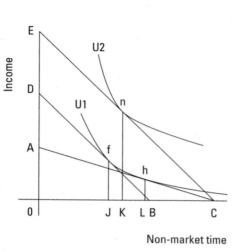

In conventional economics, everything depends on the interaction between the substitution and income effects (shown in Figure 11-3). When wages increase, it has the effect of increasing the cost of non-market activities and increasing your income. The substitution effect resulting from increasing wages is assumed to always decrease your demand for "leisure time" and, therefore, increase your supply of labor. This is illustrated in Figure 11-2 by a movement in the price line from *CD* to *BD* along your original indifference curve *U*1.

Simply because the price of "leisure time" has increased, your demand for "leisure time" falls from 0*L* to 0*J*. This is the substitution effect. But your demand for "leisure time" falls from 0*L* to only 0*K*. You end up at point *n* along indifference curve *U*2 because of the income effect. The increase in your income produces an increase in the demand for "leisure time" of *JK*. The income effect is given by *JK* — and the income effect is always positive for leisure time, which is assumed to be a normal good (you'll want more of it as your income increases).

A rise in total income always increases the demand for "leisure time" in the conventional model. In this example, the substitution effect outweighs the income effect, so you end up supplying more labor to the market. But this doesn't have to be the case: The income effect can outweigh the substitution effect. The problem is that conventional economics can't tell us when we can expect this to occur, if ever.

Figure 11-3:
The substitution and income effect illustrates how conventional economics understands how labor supply responds when wages increase.

1. The wage rate increases.
The Substitution Effect
2. This increases the cost of non-market time.
3. Non-market time becomes more expensive, causing you to demand more time of the labor market.
   The substitution effect always results in increasing labor supply.
The Income Effect
4. The increased wage rate results in more income.
5. More income causes you to demand more non-market time.
   The income effect always results in decreasing labor supply.
The Substitution Effect versus the Income Effect
   Changes to labor supply depend on the extent to which the income effect outweighs the substitution effect.

In Figure 11-2, if you start off with a price line of *BD* and there is simply an increase in income given by price line *CE*, according to the conventional model you end up with an unambiguous increase in the demand for "leisure time." Any policy or event that provides you with unconditional increases to real income can be expected to reduce your desire to work on the labor market.

If you were to just get some income by way of a government grant or inheritance or winnings from a lottery, you would be expected to increase your demand for "leisure time." More money buys you more of the good life in terms of "leisure time."

If society wants to get people to work, we must push and prod and bribe them. The biggest bribe is to increase wage or the cost of engaging in "leisure" activities. But this can and will be expected to backfire through the income effect, which is one of the unintended consequences of higher wages.

One of the classic predictions of conventional economics, which all students of economics learn at one time or another, is that higher wages are eventually accompanied by a reduction in the supply of labor. This point is illustrated by a backward-bending labor supply curve (see Figure 11-4). This labor supply curve assumes that individuals will eventually reduce the hours worked per week and per year as wages increase. It also assumes that more people will actually withdraw from the official labor market as wages rise. In both of these instances, the income effect eventually outweighs the substitution effect. And any income windfalls from any source shifts the labor supply curve inward to the left. People are expected to supply less labor for any given wage rate.

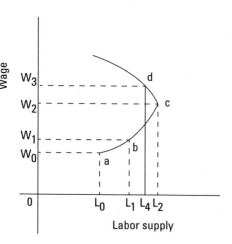

Why economics predicts that more income reduces labor supply: Work as an inferior good

Conventional economics assumes that people do leisure activities only when they aren't working in their paid jobs. So, it's an easy decision for people to spend less time in the labor market or to opt out if they can afford to. Conventional economics also assumes that most people don't get any satisfaction from working: Working yields a reduction in people's level of satisfaction or happiness. Not working — doing fun things off the labor market — is what makes people happy (or at least happier).

In conventional economics, work is treated as a type of inferior good. The more income people have, the less they want of it. Work is like having to eat sardines every day because you can't afford anything else on your budget. Increase your income and you'll cut down on the sardines and buy a steak or two.

Contrary to the assumptions of conventional economics, the evidence suggests that working makes many people happier and healthier. If you really like your job, all the better. But just being employed tends to raise people's level of happiness. Related to this, in a study conducted in Britain, being unemployed increases the difficulty of sleeping by 40 percent. Having a job makes you much more relaxed and comfortable than you would be if you were unemployed. From an American study, it's clear that employed men are much happier than unemployed men. But employed women aren't much happier than unemployed women. (The latter can be related to the happiness that many women get from raising their kids, which isn't something that characterizes men, at least on average.) Bottom line: In the real world, working in the official labor market does not appear to be a bad thing.

How to increase the labor supply when people dislike work: Using the big stick

Keeping people on the labor market has been a concern of politicians and academics for eons. There have always been economists who called for policy to keep wages low and economic assistance to the unemployed at a minimum to keep people on the labor market. Any efforts to increase minimum wages, introduce or increase unemployment insurance, or introduce or increase social assistance have been resisted by many economists because such policies are predicted to reduce the supply of labor. People are expected to buy more leisure if given the opportunity.

But this way of looking at the world assumes not only that non-market activities are equivalent to leisure, but also that most people have a relatively low and unchanging target income. If people aren't working, they're having fun. And the low incomes generated through government support policies are high enough to pull a large number of people out of the labor market.

In addition, conventional economics pays no attention to the possibility that non-market activities may includes things like childcare, which can be critically important to the future productivity and well-being of a society.

How Economic Necessity, Norms, and Love of Work Determine Labor Supply

A variety of factors, apart from the relative price of non-market time and income, affect the supply of labor. Economic factors, such as target income, are affected by social norms as well as economic imperatives. The supply of labor also is determined by the satisfaction that many people derive from working — work isn't all bad for all people.

In this section, I look at what behavioral economics has to say about the labor supply.

How target income affects labor supply

Behavioral economists have noticed that labor supply doesn't follow any clear pattern with respect to changes in wages or income. For example, I've modeled the supply of labor in terms of target income and the hierarchy of needs. The latter is a concept developed by the late American psychologist Abraham Maslow. According to Maslow, a good deal of decision making is driven by the expressed needs of individuals (as opposed to the economists' focus on relative price and income).

An empirical case, based on New York City cabbies, for a target income approach to labor supply has been make by behavioral economists Colin Camerer, Linda Babcock, George Lowenstein, and Richard Thaler. It appears that many New York cabbies stop working after reaching their target income.

Basically, one important driver of labor supply in behavioral economics is your target income. Given your wage rate and *non-labor-market sources of income* (income from relatives, friends, and government), you determine how much labor needs to be supplied to meet your target income. If your target income for the week is $2,000 and your wage rate is $20 per hour, you have to work 100 hours per week. This is way over what anyone could supply — there are only 96 hours in a standard five-day workweek and only 168 hours during the entire week. Assuming that most normal people won't work more than ten hours a day for six days a week, labor supply can't be expected to drop off until the wage rate reaches something like $50 per hour. With this wage rate, you'd have to work 40 hours to earn $2,000 per week. If you're earning a wage of $10 per hour and you receive a government wage subsidy of $10 per hour, this shouldn't affect your supply of labor if your target income is $2,000 per week.

The point is that if target income is relatively high compared to wages and non-labor-market sources of income, there is no reason to expect labor supply to fall as wages increase or non-labor-market sources of income grow. Only when the target income is hit can we expect a fall in labor supply.

Even more to the point: If your target income keeps increasing with your wages and with increases in non-labor-market sources of income, there is no reason to expect a fall in the supply of labor.

The decrease in labor supply that we've experienced over the past century is more consistent with the target income approach. What we've seen is a drop in hours worked per week from about 60 hours to less than 40 hours. In the meantime, there's been no dramatic fall in labor force participation over the past decades, although people are now retiring earlier than they did many decades ago. All this has occurred while wages and government support for people with low wages and poor skill sets have increased dramatically. It appears that people want more and more goods and services as they move along through time — target income is increasing.

Given that you're working at your target number of hours and you're earning less than your target income, your labor supply curve will be completely insensitive to changes in the wage rate. Instead of being backward-bending (as in Figure 11-4), it will be a straight vertical line. Plus, increases in non-labor-market income will not shift your labor supply curve to the left. Instead, it will stay where it is until your target income is reached.

Why increasing income doesn't reduce labor supply

Changes to target income are a product of a bunch of factors, but social norms and how people compare to others (known as *relative positioning*) are critically important. If people want more goods and services over time, they'll require more income. And this means that they won't want to reduce their supply of labor by much or at all, even with increasing real wages and non-labor-market sources of income.

Also, if people's preferences for goods and services are influenced by what they have relative to what other people have (and those other people are materially better off), this translates into the demand for more goods and services when those who are better off experience higher incomes and the consumption of more things they want. All this enforces either a disposition to increase labor supply or a reluctance to reduce it until that target income is reached.

With increasing target income, predicting the timing of decreases in labor time is difficult without knowing the targets and how they change over time. A lot depends on the extent to which target income grows as wages increase. A lot also depends on the labor supply that people think is reasonable given their various needs.

For example, few people believed that working 10 to 12 hours per day six days per week (which was the case over 100 years ago in today's developed economies) led to the land of milk and honey. And when they could afford it, workers bought a reduction in labor supply (in terms of hours worked) with higher wages.

It becomes difficult to argue that social assistance or unemployment insurance will reduce labor supply if these sources of income fall below the target income for most people. And it's important to keep in mind that these incomes are *relatively* quite low, even in most developed economies.

Labor supply when market employment is a superior good

When working increases your level of happiness, you're less likely to reduce your labor supply as wages and income increase. The more you like to work or to be employed, the less sensitive your labor supply is to changes in wages and income.

As long as most people want to work because working improves their level of happiness, it becomes even more difficult to predict that higher wages and income will invariably reduce their supply of labor, even if they meet their target income at current wages and given their non-labor-market sources of income.

One bit of evidence on the importance of work for well-being is that unemployment, especially long-term unemployment, causes many people to be physically ill and mentally depressed. People often feel helpless, losing their motivation to search for jobs.

Many people even see a diminishing capacity to exert themselves when they can't find jobs. The behavioral assumption of conventional economics wouldn't predict these outcomes. These unemployed people should be jumping for joy, gorging themselves on their newfound "leisure" time.

American economists William Darity, Arthur Goldsmith, and Jonathan Veum have found that the negative psychological impact of long-term unemployment can translate into a less productive workforce. It also can result in more people being out of the labor force. As a consequence, for psychological reasons, persistent unemployment can both reduce the supply of labor and reduce the efficiency of a segment of the labor force.

In this case, the current labor supply and current labor productivity depends in part on past rates of unemployment. They may even be heavily contingent on past rates of unemployment. The present state of the labor market is not independent of what's taken place in the labor market in the recent past.

Social welfare programs and labor supply

A number of people live off government income support programs, like welfare. But most of these people have disabilities of one type or another or lack the skills required in the labor market. Some are drug addicts and child runaways.

Traditional jobs as an inferior good: The price of art

Some people prefer not to work in traditional jobs and prefer to devote their time to low-paid or unpaid jobs as actors, musicians, and artists. This isn't the majority of the population, but many of these people, especially if they're single and have no family responsibilities, would and do reduce their supply of labor to the official labor market when government provides social assistance to those who are without jobs and who aren't eligible to collect unemployment insurance.

People in this category have low target incomes and do their preferred jobs at a pay rate that isn't viable. Sometimes artists and musicians use their time to practice their craft without pay. However, even in this case, in most developed economies, people who use government income support must search for employment and accept job offers if and when they get them.

For those individuals who use government programs to support their preferred non-market jobs or jobs for which they're paid under the table, this behavior is not driven by a preference for leisure as the conventional model would have it. Instead, it's driven by a desire to do their preferred work in alternative job markets. Government income support ends up subsidizing these preferred jobs.

Even in the world of the arts, many people work where they can to earn enough money to get by, even given the availability of income support programs. Still, there are some whose labor supply would be affected by cuts in government support, in the manner predicted by the conventional model. But some is not most.

These folks aren't on government support because of some higher-order preference for leisure. Cut government support, and many of these people would be even poorer than they are today. Some may even join the low-end unskilled tail of the labor market, driving wages down for all poorly skilled workers. This point is made by Nobel Laureate Robert Solow of MIT.

Just as important, people often are on support because of the absence of job opportunities. If you don't have a job, you may go on government support. And when job opportunities diminish, more people are on government support. But it isn't this type of non-labor-market income that's driving people off the labor market. Instead, it's the lack of jobs.

And this is what we would expect, given the target income of most people and the utility or satisfaction generated from being employed. As long as government support is not greater than target income and greater than what a person can earn in the labor market, people won't queue up for welfare payments. Only if non-labor-market activities are preferred over work might this be the case.

Labor force participation can be reduced if welfare payments are greater than the income that people can earn on the labor market and when government taxes labor market income that is earned when a person is off welfare. The same effect occurs when welfare payments are greater than the income that can be earned on the labor market and government bans labor market participation of welfare recipients. The latter is equivalent to a 100 percent tax rate of labor market income of welfare recipients.

Think of it this way: Say you're a single mom on welfare because you can't find a full-time or part-time job. You find a job that pays less than your welfare payment, but you're happy to take the job if you can keep most of what you earn while remaining on welfare. If the tax on your labor-market income (your job) is 100 percent, you won't take the job. But if the tax rate is, say, 20 percent, it pays to take the job. Eventually, your labor-market income may exceed what you would get on welfare, and the government can withdraw its welfare payment without pushing you out of the labor market. In this scenario, labor supply is restricted by taxing labor-market income at too high a rate. Some effective reforms to welfare simply reduce the rate at which welfare payments are cut when welfare recipients find employment, which increases the supply of labor.

Why women on social assistance aren't lazy: Childcare as a superior good

Non-labor-market time is not leisure time as the simplifying assumptions of conventional economics would have you believe. Many women choose to stay at home to take care of their kids, especially if affordable and quality daycare and after-school care aren't available.

Taking care of their kids would be at the top of the list of these women's hierarchy of needs. Here, women are sacrificing income from the labor market to take care of their children. Often the cost of childcare or after-school care would otherwise eat up much or all of their labor-market income.

Needless to say, mothers can make this sacrifice of income only when government or another agency provides them with some form of income support. Cutting support to such women would increase labor supply, but often at the cost of children being provided with quality care.

Women aren't drawn out of the labor market because they have a strong and unbinding preference for leisure. Instead, they have a higher-order preference for the welfare and well-being of their kids. Often, if mothers work and no proper childcare or after-school care is available, kids are left on their own, causing significant labor-market problems in the future.

There is very strong evidence that providing low-cost childcare has a very strong effect on increasing the labor supply of women. Many women would prefer to work than stay at home if they knew that their kids were being taken care of.

People want to work when market employment pays. There is no love for leisure driving labor supply here. It's how labor market income or welfare payments of welfare recipients are taxed that drives the supply of labor.

Norms, anchors, default retirement age, and labor supply

From the perspective of conventional wisdom, defaults or framing shouldn't affect a person's retirement decisions. But just as defaults influence our retirement savings decisions, defaults influence the timing of retirement.

A big question in many countries where mandatory retirement is in place is what may be the implications of ending mandatory retirement. With mandatory retirement, people must retire at a certain age (for example, 65). When this legal requirement to retire is removed, people can choose at what age they want to retire. Some economists have argued for reintroducing mandatory retirement in countries such as the United States, the United Kingdom, and Canada, as a way of creating job opportunities for younger people.

Evidence suggests that where mandatory retirement has been eliminated, the age of retirement is increased, but not by much. The original age of retirement appears to act as a social norm or anchor, signaling people when it's the right time to retire. Many experts worried that people would stay on in their jobs until they dropped dead — for love of money. But obviously, norms and anchors matter. When the mandatory age of retirement is eliminated, people no longer have this age as an anchor. Many people then choose their retirement age based on other social and economic considerations. Of course, the structure of the retirement program matters, too — economic incentives can affect when people retire, even if there is no mandatory age of retirement.

As an interesting aside, policymakers are thinking about eliminating mandatory retirement as a means to increase labor supply, allowing people to increase their savings for retirement. Obviously, if the would-be retirees haven't met their target income by their expected age of retirement, they'll want to work longer. But the evidence doesn't support the hypothesis favored by conventional thinking that ending mandatory retirement will cause any significant increase in the supply of labor. Behavioral factors and social norms about when to retire play an important role in determining a person's age of retirement, independent of economic factors. Simply changing economic incentives won't necessarily result in the hoped-for increases in the labor supply.

Chapter 12

The Black Box of the Firm: Human Relationships and Productivity

*A*ccording to conventional economics, what happens inside the firm is of little consequence for economic analysis. Conventional economics assumes that people behave in a manner that generates the best possible economic results. Behavior is, among other things, assumed to be narrowly self-interested, and the market is assumed to beat up and eliminate firms that don't perform efficiently.

But in behavioral economics, economic outcomes can be affected — big time — by how the firm is managed and by the preferences of workers, managers, and owners. Another key finding in behavioral economics is that both inefficient firms and efficient firms survive and can even do quite well in real-world economies. This chapter discusses the economics underlying how inefficient firms can prosper and why efficient firms don't conquer the universe.

I also explain how, from the conventional perspective, changing the wage rate should have no impact on productivity. High wages increase costs for the firm, while low wages lower costs. High wages are bad for the firm, and low wages are good for the firm — according to conventional economics.

According to the findings of behavioral economics, however, this conventional worldview can be dead wrong. Wages impact productivity in the real world because workers can and do vary how hard and how smart they work as wage rates change. When workers believe their wages are unfair, they may retaliate by reducing the amount of effort they put into their work. In this case, lower wages don't translate into lower costs, as the conventional perspective would have it. Similarly, high wages, when compensated for by more effort, don't have to result in higher costs. I explain this concept in greater detail in this chapter.

Survival of the Fittest, the Firm, and Contemporary Economic Theory

A basic premise of conventional economics is that people are preconditioned to work and think in a way that makes firms economically efficient no matter what. A softer version of conventional economics assumes that market forces impose a discipline upon workers, managers, and owners, which results in firms being economically efficient. Absent economic efficiency, inefficient firms are forced into bankruptcy.

In effect, the conventional wisdom makes the simplifying assumption that, as far as their place of employment goes, people tend to do the best they can. If they don't, market forces will take care of things.

The economic analyses and predictions that flow from the conventional model are quite clear-cut. They strongly suggest that there is little that can be done to improve upon economic efficiency. The market and human nature take care of economic efficiency. A key task of government is to make sure that the market is as free as possible. Only then will the economy perform at its very best.

In this section, I discuss some of the basic assumptions conventional economics makes about how hard and how smart people work.

Doing the best we can: From slave to free labor to the big boss

A fundamental assumption of conventional economics is that all individuals who work within a firm are doing their best. They're all maximizing the quantity and quality of effort that they're supplying to the firm per unit of time. Individuals don't have much choice in the matter. So, effort isn't variable. Conventional economics assumes that everyone is working as hard and as well as he or she can.

More generally, conventional economics assumes that the quantity and quality of effort supplied by workers is fixed. Wages and working conditions don't affect effort in the conventional model.

Even the slave is assumed to be an effort maximizer. Slaves are assumed to be no different in terms of economic efficiency than workers who are free to quit and, in democratic countries, go on strike when they're unhappy with their working conditions. But even unhappy workers are assumed to be effort maximizers. Effort isn't variable because it's fixed at some maximum level.

Conventional economics acknowledges that there can be conflict among managers, bosses, CEOs, and shareholders — something called the *principal-agent problem*. But at the end of the day, conventional economics assumes that this conflict is resolved by developing proper incentives. In most conventional models, these incentives induce agents, such as CEOs, CFOs, and managers, to behave in the interest of principals, such as shareholders. Agents end up doing their best for their principals, and principals are assumed to want economic efficiency to prevail. That's what makes them happy. Economic efficiency rules the roost in conventional economics. Many economists spend sleepless nights thinking about and building models demonstrating how the principal-agent problem is resolved and why firms are economically efficient.

Economies may still be far from perfect. But this is more a result of their not conforming to some ideal version of competitive markets as opposed to agents and principals not doing the best they can from the perspective of the economically efficient, profit-maximizing, cost-minimizing firm.

Determining industrial relations through market forces

Industrial relations are all about how firms are organized to deal with incentive issues — how workers, managers, board members, and owners relate to one another and engage each other inside the firm. When a key component of your economic model is that workers, managers, and owners are maximizing effort, thinking about and analyzing the firm's system of industrial relations can be no more than a passing interest. It's an exercise in description. It may even be an exercise in discovery about how agents and principals got it right. That they get it right is assumed from the get-go.

Although many economists assume that agents and principals get it right — they're economically efficient — if they *do* get it wrong, the market takes center stage. The market beats up, disciplines, or destroys the weak, the weary, and the slackers. Only the fittest and most economically efficient survive.

So, what we see, when we look at firms in action, should be the survival of the fittest. How firms operate, their preferred system of industrial relations, should be the best-practice system. Conventional economists tend to assume that economic efficiency requires principals and agents to behave in the careful, calculating manner prescribed by conventional economics.

Many non-conventional economists, including behavioral economists, have written about what are referred to as *superior work cultures* (cultures that generate higher levels of productivity and in which workers tend to be higher paid and have a greater say in the day-to-day operation of the plant). Toyota and Volvo are examples of superior work cultures. Worker cooperatives, where workers own and control the firm they work in, are another example. But conventional economics has turned a blind eye to these alternative systems of industrial relations. The argument is that if these systems are so great, they should dominate economies — they should drive out the inferior systems of industrial relations. Because superior work cultures *aren't* dominant, they can't be superior, by definition. And conventional economics assumes that the systems that *do* prevail are economically efficient. Work cultures that aren't economically efficient — ones in which workers, managers, and owners aren't working as hard and as well as they can — just aren't sustainable.

Maximizing profits and minimizing costs in the calculating firm

Every student of economics learns that firms are profit maximizers and cost minimizers. Conventional economics further assumes that profit maximizers must be productivity maximizers. Students are told that this is not only how firms *do* behave but also how they *should* behave.

A core truth of conventional economics is that firms must equate marginal costs with marginal benefits if profits are to be maximized. Following this rule allows firms to produce the right amount of output and hire the right amount of labor for profits to be maximized and costs to be minimized. Any other type of behavior would be irrational from the perspective of conventional economics.

In the textbook model of the firm, the *marginal cost* is the additional cost involved in producing an additional unit of output. The *marginal benefit* is the additional or marginal revenue to the firm from selling an additional unit of output. When product markets are highly competitive, the *marginal revenue* is the price that the product is sold for; this price is assumed not to change, no matter how much the firm sells. So, the marginal revenue ends up being the product price.

This is the case when each firm contributes only a small amount to the total sold on the market — 1 million apples in a market of 2 billion, for example. In this situation, the firm has no effective control over the market price of its product. Producing more or less output makes no sense, given the setup of the model, if you're maximizing profits (see Figure 12-1). At price P_0 and marginal cost $MC1$, the profit-maximizing firm produces $Q2$ of output. This is given by equating marginal cost and marginal benefit or price at point *b*.

If your firm is not maximizing productivity, however, you can still be maximizing profits. Your marginal costs will simply be greater than they would otherwise be. In Figure 12-1, the marginal cost curve shifts upward to *MC2* when productivity falls. Profits still are maximized when marginal costs are equal to marginal benefits at point *a*. You're simply producing less output (*Q1*) when marginal cost is higher.

Figure 12-1:
The relationship between the marginal product of labor and the marginal cost of labor, which is approximated by the wage rate, and the amount of labor that a profit-maximizing firm is expected to employ.

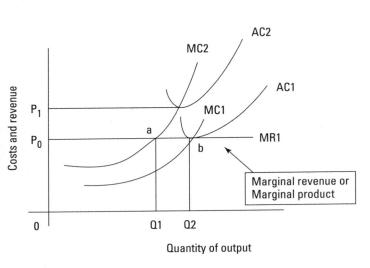

The relationship between marginal cost and productivity as well as the relationship between average cost and productivity are easily seen through the following two equations. In this very simple narrative, productivity refers to total output divided by total labor input.

$$MC = \frac{W}{\frac{\Delta Q}{\Delta L}} \text{ or } AC = \frac{W}{\left(\frac{Q}{L}\right)}$$

For simplicity, I assume that labor (*L*) is the only input in the production process. Wages (*w*) are assumed to be the only cost of production. Marginal cost (*MC*) is given by the wage rate divided by the change in labor productivity $\left(\frac{\Delta Q}{\Delta L}\right)$. The latter is also referred to as the *marginal product*.

All other things remaining the same, if you increase productivity, marginal cost falls. If you reduce productivity, marginal cost increases. The same relationship exists with regards to the determination of average cost (AC). Irrespective of the level of productivity, however, firms can maximize profit by producing a level of output consistent with equalizing marginal revenue and marginal cost.

In the conventional model, a profit-maximizing firm will hire additional workers or additional hours of labor time up to the point where the marginal cost of labor equals the marginal benefit of employing an additional worker or an additional hour of labor time. The marginal cost of labor is given by the wage rate and the marginal benefit is given by the marginal product of labor. This is the additional output generated by the additional amount of labor time employed. In Figure 12-2, the profit maximizing firm hires L2 of labor when the marginal product is given by MP0 and the wage rate by W0. If the wage rate increases to W1 and the marginal product is still given by MP0, the firm hires less labor, at L1. If labor productivity is actually not maximized and is at MP1 and the wage is at W0, a profit maximizing firm hires L1 of labor.

So, a firm can behave as a conventional profit-maximizing firm even if productivity is not maximized. And conventional profit maximization principles are consistent with firms not maximizing productivity.

Figure 12-2:
The relationship between the marginal product of labor and the marginal cost of labor, which is approximated by the wage rate, and the amount of labor that a profit-maximizing firm is expected to employ.

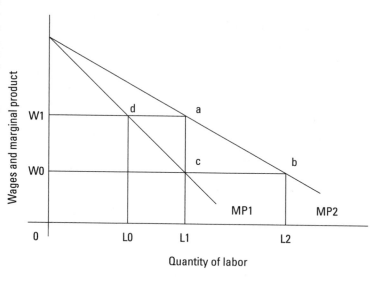

Understanding why the behavioral firm wins out

There is ample empirical evidence that firms engaged in a wide array of different types of firm management and organization survive and even do quite well over the long haul. Competition doesn't drive out certain forms or firm management or organization, forcing all firms to adopt a unique way of doing things.

More to the point, neither market forces nor our genetic makeup has forced us to converge to the behavior of the calculating firm of conventional economics. Even more interesting, some experimental economists, led by Nobel Laureate Vernon Smith, find that the conventional prototype of the efficient firm is least likely to survive. Smith, summarizing research findings in experimental economics, argues that failure is what investors should expect if they adhere to conventional economics behavioral fundamentalism. Firms that apply fast and frugal heuristics win out at the end of the day (see Chapter 6).

When People Don't Behave According to Conventional Economics: X-Inefficiency

Conventional economics assumes that everybody in a firm is always performing to the best of his or her abilities — that workers are always giving 100 percent. But if you've worked in the real world, you know that's not the case. *X-inefficiency* is the difference between what conventional economics assumes (the best possible effort all the time) and what happens in reality.

Types of x-inefficiency

X-inefficiency can be seen at every level of a firm, from the CEO and upper management all the way down to the line workers on the factory floor. There are two basic ways that x-inefficiency will come about:

- Managers are not working as well as they can. In this case, there is *managerial slack*.
- The incentive system is such that neither workers nor managers are working as well as they can.

The productivity difference between what the firm could produce *without* managerial slack and what it produces *with* managerial slack is one measure of *x-inefficiency*. More generally, x-efficiency in production exists when a firm's productivity is consistent with what it would produce if workers, managers, and owners were working as smart and as hard as possible. In a sense, this maximum is the implicit ideal of conventional economics.

Managerial slack: When managers aren't maximizing

Managerial slack occurs when the firm's movers and shakers are maximizing their utility or level of happiness by slacking off, which reduces productivity. All other things remaining the same, managerial slack, by reducing productivity, increases production costs.

In the managerial-slack version of x-inefficiency, it's important to emphasize that production costs increase. Both average and marginal costs increase.

The increase in costs is illustrated in Figure 12-1 by an upward shift in the marginal cost curve from *MC*1 to *MC*2. The profit-maximizing, x-inefficient firm produces less output than the profit-maximizing x-efficient firm does. But when the firm is relatively x-efficient, at marginal cost *MC*1, this firm is also covering its average cost or average total cost (*AC*1) and producing at the minimum of average total cost. With x-inefficiency, average cost increases to *AC*2. Given the market price, the firm is no longer covering its average costs. In the short term, the firm may choose to stay in business. But in the longer term, in order for the firm to remain viable, it either has to find ways to increase product price (to P_1) or increase its level of x-efficiency.

Work culture and x-inefficiency

X-inefficiency isn't just a product of managerial slack (see the preceding section). It's also a product of the firm's work culture or the incentive environment: the relationship between workers and mangers or owners, and even between workers and firm decision makers.

If a firm's work culture is one in which workers don't feel obliged to work as hard or as smart as they can, they won't. Given the complexity of even simple job functions and the cost of monitoring, detecting individual workers' shirking is difficult. And this makes the existence of this type of x-inefficiency all the more likely if the work culture and related incentives aren't strong enough.

When product markets aren't competitive enough

X-inefficient firms can survive only when they're protected from the pressures and discipline of competitive markets. If a firm is producing at higher unit costs (because of, say, managerial slack), it can't compete with more x-efficient firms. An x-inefficient firm should be wiped out or forced into becoming x-efficient by the ebb and flow of market forces.

Some scholars make the point that many product markets aren't very competitive (for example, in situations where firms have monopoly or near-monopoly power). Examples of this are providers of power, telecommunication services, and public transportation. Firms protected by tariffs from foreign competition, receiving subsidies from government, or protected by particular rules and regulations would also be protected from the wrath of the market.

Increasing inefficiency, managerial slack, and the art of lobbying

Firm decision makers who have a preference for x-inefficient behavior have a clear incentive to lobby government to provide their firms with some sort of protective belt so they can get away with being x-inefficient and, therefore, charge higher prices to cover their costs (including their preferred perks) and appropriate rate of return.

One argument flowing from this perspective on x-inefficiency is that less competitive pressure on the product market increases the extent of x-inefficiency. On the other hand, more competitive pressure results in more x-efficiency. One of the costs of reducing competitive product market pressure is increasing the extent of economic or x-inefficiency. This a cost assumed away in conventional economics. But it can be quite important in the real world.

Preferences, managerial slack, and x-inefficiency

One clear prediction from the x-efficiency model is that, given the possibility of managerial slack — which is a preference of managers and owners — less competitive pressure results in more x-inefficiency. This is consistent with firm decision makers maximizing their level of happiness. In addition, different preferences on the part of managers and owners can generate more x-efficiency, regardless of competitive pressures.

Finally, if firm decision makers have a strong preference for managerial slack, doing things x-inefficiently, severe competitive pressures would only be an unstable "equilibrium." The x-efficient solution to the productivity problem would revert to the x-inefficient solution when competitive pressures are relaxed, given the preferences of decision makers.

How low wages produce x-inefficiency and high wages contribute to x-efficiency

Conventional economics assumes that productivity is independent of wages and overall working conditions. This simply follows from the assumption that people work as hard and as well as they can. But this assumption isn't consistent with what occurs in the real world. In fact, one important source of x-inefficiency, with some overlap with managerial slack, is low wages and poor working conditions.

Everybody responds to incentives, both material and psychological. People also are influenced by the behavior of their peers and social norms. One important source of effort variability is changes to wages and working conditions. And there is a positive relationship between wages and working conditions and the quantity and quality of effort that we contribute to the process of production. The better people are treated, the more effort they contribute. The worse they're treated, the less effort they contribute.

But as effort inputs change, so does productivity. In this model, higher wages and better working conditions increase the level of x-efficiency. On the other hand, lower wages and poorer working conditions contribute to x-inefficiency in production.

In this x-efficiency model, changes in effort and, therefore, in productivity are directly related to changes in the cost of production. In the managerial slack model, firm decision makers aren't responding simply to changes in their compensation packages. They're behaving in accordance with their preferences and with what they can get away with in terms of performing x-inefficiently.

But if wages increase, for example, and this encourages increased effort and increasing productivity, the increased productivity can offset the increased cost of labor. And lower wages won't necessarily result in lower average cost if workers retaliate by reducing their effort inputs, causing productivity to fall. It's quite possible that a higher-wage x-efficient firm and economy will be as cost competitive as a lower-wage x-inefficient economy.

The following equation illustrates how average cost is a product of the relationship between wages (w) and labor productivity $\left(\dfrac{Q}{L}\right)$ or output divided by labor input:

$$AC = \frac{W}{\left(\dfrac{Q}{L}\right)}$$

If wages and productivity change by the same percentage, average costs don't change. If wages increase by 10 percent and productivity increases by 10 percent, there is no change in average cost. And when wages fall by 10 percent and productivity drops by 10 percent, there is no change in average cost.

Very rarely does labor make up the entire cost of production. Other factors include the cost of plant and equipment, land, management, and the like. To offset the cost of increased wages, productivity (output produced divided by labor input) must increase, but this increase doesn't have to be in proportion to the increase in wages. The increase in productivity can be less when, as in the real world, labor represents only a portion of total costs. So, if labor represents only 50 percent of the total and wages rise by 10 percent, productivity must increase by 50 percent of 10 percent, or by 5 percent. And, if labor represents only 20 percent of total costs, in this case productivity would have to increase only by 20 percent of 10 percent, or by 2 percent.

Overall, changes in wages don't have to affect the position of the average and marginal cost curves in Figure 12-1. As long as effort gains at least offset increases in wages, *MC* will not shift. And this is contrary to what is predicted in conventional economics.

In this type of scenario, inefficient firms very possibly could and would survive the wrath and discipline of the market. Of course, this is a reality that behavioral economists (and scholars from a range of disciplines) have long identified as important. There is no reason to expect that low-wage x-inefficient firms will be driven out by high-wage x-efficient firms. Therefore, there is no reason to expect that higher wages will cause economic harm and that low wages will benefit firms in the competitive process.

Another implication of this type of modeling of x-efficiency theory is that well-structured minimum-wage laws, union-inspired increases in wages, or increased wages produced by tight labor markets don't have to cause the economic harm predicted by conventional economics. They may even contribute to increasing the level of x-efficiency in the economy. This is not far off from what we find empirically.

In Figure 12-2, if increasing the wage from $W0$ to $W1$ raises effort, then marginal product curve pivots from $MP1$ to $MP2$. As a consequence, there doesn't have to be the predicted fall in employment from $L1$ to $L0$. Much depends on the extent to which productivity increases as wages increase. Also, if wages fall from $W1$ to $W0$, and the marginal product curve pivots from $MP2$ to $MP1$, employment will not increase as predicted from $L1$ to $L2$.

Introducing Adam Smith and x-inefficiency

Adam Smith underlined the important psychological relationship between wages and productivity. In *The Wealth of Nations,* he writes:

> The liberal reward of labor, as it encourages the propagation, so it increases the industry of the common people. The wages of labor are the encouragement of industry, which, like every other human quality, improves in proportion to the encouragement it

receives. A plentiful subsistence increases the bodily strength of the laborer, and the comfortable hope of bettering his condition, and of ending his days perhaps in ease and plenty, animates him to exert that strength to the utmost. Where wages are high, accordingly, we shall always find the workmen more active, diligent, and expeditious, than where they are low....

Efficiency wages: Connecting wages, effort, and productivity

One important piece in the x-inefficiency puzzle is referred to as *efficiency wage theory*. Efficiency wage theory was pioneered by Harvey Leibenstein and later further developed and enriched by many behavioral economists, led by Nobel Laureate George Akerlof.

The point made by Leibenstein is that when wages are very low and workers are very poor, they don't have the income to provide themselves with enough nutrition to work as hard or as well as they might otherwise work. Higher pay results in a more nutritious diet, which, in turn, results in workers working harder and smarter. And this causes productivity to increase.

The idea is a simple one: Malnourished workers tend to be relatively unproductive. And when a person is in the zone of severe malnutrition, even the nastiest of employers don't have the incentive to cut wages. Such cuts would simply result in an even greater than proportionate cut in productivity. Cutting wages may very well result in higher marginal and average production costs.

This point is made explicit by this now familiar equation:

$$AC = \frac{W}{\left(\dfrac{Q}{L}\right)}$$

The key idea here is that if wages (w) are cut by 5 percent and productivity $\left(\dfrac{Q}{L}\right)$ falls by 6 percent as a result, average cost increases. In the efficiency wage model, simply cutting wages does not generate a more competitive or profitable position to the firm.

Another possibility raised in efficiency wage theory is that there is some unique wage that minimizes average cost when effort is variable and when effort is affected by nutritional factors. This unique wage is referred to as the *efficiency wage*. Any other wage would result in higher average costs. In conventional economics, there can be no such thing as an efficiency wage. Moreover, all wage hikes should increase average costs.

Exploring fairness and gift exchange inside the firm

Efficiency wage theory has been modernized by George Akerlof and scholars influenced by his research. Akerlof makes the point, as does Leibenstein, that even very well-nourished workers vary the amount of effort that they'll contribute to the production process. Much depends on how fair they perceive their compensation and overall work environment to be.

When people are treated unfairly, they tend to retaliate by reducing their effort. Fairness tends to reap rewards, taking the form of more effort and, therefore, higher levels of productivity. This version of efficiency wage theory overlaps with one of the x-efficiency scenarios that I discuss earlier.

However, efficiency wage theory, based on arguments drawn from variations in nutrition levels or from changes in levels of fairness, focuses on the existence of an efficiency wage. Once again, this suggests that there is only one unique wage that minimizes average production costs. In x-efficiency theory, there doesn't have to be such a unique wage — there may be an array of wage rates consistent with a particular average or marginal cost. However, only a relatively higher wage is consistent with x-efficiency in production.

Understanding the relationship between conventional, x-efficiency, and efficiency wage theories

One way of comparing and contrasting conventional, efficiency wage, and x-efficiency theory is illustrated in Figure 12-3. Cost curve *CE*1–*CE*2 illustrates the conventional view of the relationship between wages and average or marginal cost, and it is unambiguously a positive one. Increase wages, and costs go up. Cut wages, and costs go down. In efficiency wage theory, there is a unique efficiency wage at W^*. Any movement away from this efficiency wage, up or down, increases costs. The efficiency wage should be sticky for profit-maximizing reasons — changing wages, up or down, away from the efficiency wage reduces profits.

One perspective on x-efficiency theory, which I developed, is represented by cost curve *CE*1–*XE*. At least up to wage *W*1, there is no change to costs because effort and, therefore, productivity change to compensate for changes in wages. After *W*1, effort can no longer increase sufficiently to compensate for increases in wages, and average and marginal costs can be expected to increase. Effort increases hit the brick wall of diminishing productivity. But there is no unique equilibrium wage here. Instead, there is an array of sustainable wages up to wage *W*1. At least in this diagram, the wage that produces x-efficiency or economic efficiency is *W*1. To the extent that increasing wages motivate firm decision makers into adopting and developing more productive technology, the x-efficiency cost curve shifts to *CE*0–*XETC*. In this case, wages can increase a bit more without increasing marginal or average production costs.

Figure 12-3:
The different relationships between wages and average and marginal costs and different ways of modeling the firms. Conventional modeling predicts a very different relationship than does either efficiency wage or x-efficiency theories.

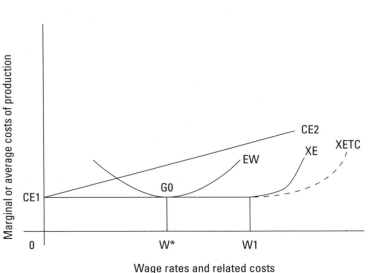

Chapter 13

The Good Economy: How Ethical Behavior Can Grow the Economy

A basic premise of the conventional economic wisdom is that rational people should be and are exclusively motivated by material self-interest. The conventional model pays no attention to nonmonetary factors. Market forces squash any other types of behavior. Also, ethical behavior is not considered to be consistent with rationality.

An important finding of behavioral economics is that consumers, workers, managers, and CEOs persistently engage in ethical behavior without being obligated to do so by the laws of supply and demand. In other words, ethical behavior exists and can be quite important — contrary to what most conventional economists argue.

In this chapter, I explain how rational individuals can and do engage in ethical behavior. In some cases, ethical behavior involves people making material sacrifices. But in other instances, ethical behavior can increase material welfare, increasing the size of the economic pie. Ethical behavior doesn't have be the pariah conventional economics thinks it is. Ethical behavior can induce higher levels of productivity or higher levels of x-efficiency (see Chapter 12 for more on x-efficiency).

Ethical Behavior: An Introduction

Ethical behavior is roughly defined as behavior that is acceptable and highly regarded in a particular community. Different communities have different definitions and related norms for ethical behavior. What counts as ethical behavior among neo-Nazis would be quite different from what counts as ethical behavior among Buddhists.

Milton Friedman and the conventional view of ethical behavior

Nobel Laureate Milton Friedman pops up all over the place, influencing the tenor of contemporary economics. In 1970, he penned a now-classic article in *The New York Times Magazine* entitled "The Social Responsibility of Business Is to Increase Its Profits." The piece is a manifesto for the conventional economics understanding of ethical behavior. In it, Friedman writes:

> When I hear businessmen speak eloquently about the "social responsibilities of business in a free-enterprise system," I am reminded of the wonderful line about the Frenchman who discovered at the age of 70 that he had been speaking prose all his life. The businessmen believe that they are defending free enterprise when they declaim that business is not concerned "merely" with profit but also with promoting desirable "social" ends; that business has a "social conscience" and takes seriously its responsibilities for providing employment, eliminating discrimination, avoiding pollution, and whatever else may be the catchwords of the contemporary crop of reformers. In fact they are — or would be if they or anyone else took them seriously — preaching pure and unadulterated socialism. Businessmen who talk this way are unwitting puppets of the intellectual forces that have been undermining the basis of a free society these past decades.

Businessmen who behave in a manner that is not consistent with profit maximization are behaving unethically, according to Friedman. And investing in community, greening the environment, and treating employees well are all warm and fuzzy behaviors that are inconsistent with profit maximization and the competitiveness of the firm. Friedman adds:

> . . . there is one and only one social responsibility of business — to use its resources and engage in activities designed to increase its profits so long as it stays within the rules of the game, which is to say, engages in open and free competition without deception or fraud.

Friedman has no objection to individuals behaving in a broadly defined, socially responsible manner — as long as it's only at their own expense. An owner of a company who isn't responsible to shareholders can do what he or she wants. But even here, Friedman contends, socially responsible behavior may very well result in job losses and even bankruptcy. Only socially responsible behavior that somehow fits into the norms of profit maximization is appropriate. If cleaning up a river is legislated or necessary to gain community buy-in for a corporation, then this socially responsible behavior is legitimate. Otherwise, such cost-enhancing behavior is illegitimate. Greed is great, and it's the appropriate norm for corporate behavior, unless businesses are mandated to behave differently.

Ethical behavior in business is often defined as doing good things for employees, suppliers, consumers, and your community. Such behavior is also referred to as *socially responsible behavior*. For example, coffee shops that purchase their coffee beans from fair-trade suppliers would be considered to be behaving ethically. The suppliers of the coffee are earning an income that, many experts would argue, is fair; at the very least, the farmers get a price for their coffee beans that is higher than they would otherwise receive. Paying workers higher wages and benefits than the "market" would provide is another example of ethical or socially responsible behavior. Producing in a more environmentally friendly manner is yet another example.

Conventional economics dubs such behavior as irrational and even unethical because it assumes that this type of behavior will threaten the economic viability of the firm. I also should note that conventional economics considers illegal behavior — for example, providing false or misleading information to customers, employees, or shareholders — to be unethical, too.

The Conventional Perspective on Ethical Behavior and the Economy

From the conventional economic perspective, increasing wages, improving working conditions, self-regulating safety conditions (for example, introducing safety devices in saw mills to minimize the loss of body parts), voluntarily reducing pollution emission, voluntarily implementing an antidiscrimination employment policy, and the like are largely regarded as cost enhancing.

Unless legally mandated to do so, policies like these, initiated by a particular firm, would increase average costs of production, reduce profits, and make the firm less competitive. Because of this, conventional economics says that such policies aren't smart. Not only are they not smart, but they also have negative effects on employment and on the overall economic well-being of society. The poor would be hardest hit by such socially responsible behavior.

This understanding of the economy follows from the assumption that ethical behavior will not and cannot stimulate and promote increases in productivity that will offset any of the costs involved in making production more ethical. Conventional economics assumes that, all other things remaining the same, increasing input costs — such as increasing wages, improving working conditions, or reducing pollution — will increase average costs (see Chapter 12 for a detailed discussion of this assumption).

Only if productivity increases as a consequence of ethical or socially responsible behavior inside the firm will average costs not increase in the manner predicted and feared by conventional economics. But such productivity increases cannot take place if firms are already x-efficient — when productivity is at a maximum, where employers and employees are working as smart and as hard as they can. And if costs increase in x-efficient firms, then ethical and socially responsible behavior will cause economic harm — possibly *significant* economic harm, unless the firm is protected from competitive pressures (see Chapter 12 for a detailed discussion of x-efficiency).

In this type of scenario, one that is so dominant in conventional economics, the preferences of decision makers for ethical or socially responsible behavior can be very damaging to the economy. The ethical bosses may be happy, but the workers forced into unemployment won't be happy, nor will the shareholders who experience relatively low rates of return.

Of course, if these ethical costs could be absorbed by the firm decision makers, ethical behavior wouldn't be the economic threat that conventional economics thinks it is. These ethical costs could be taken out of the pay package of ethical managers and CEOs. But typically, decision makers absorbing such costs isn't even within the realm of possibility for larger corporations — the costs of being ethical would be too large for even a CEO to absorb.

Figure 13-1 illustrates the conventional economics take on the implications of behaving ethically inside the firm. The number of ethical acts or the level of socially responsible behavior is measured along the horizontal axis. The average cost of production is measured along the vertical axis. Line segments C–$CM1$ and C–$CM2$ represent the conventional worldview. Basically, in both cases, as the firm becomes more ethical or socially responsible, average and marginal costs rise. There is always a positive relationship between the firm being more ethical and the average cost of production. With C–$CM2$, costs increase by even more than with C–$CM1$. The former scenario reflects the conventional assumptions of diminishing returns — the more you do of something, costs end up increasing at an increasing rate. Also, in conventional economics, as the firm becomes less ethical, its average cost falls along line segment C–CM. And, of course, this makes the firm more competitive.

As the conventional wisdom would have it, no "rational" businessperson would willfully increase the firm's average cost of production or reduce the firm's profit. The rational firm should be located at point 0 in Figure 13-1. There should be no elements of ethical or socially responsible production, according to conventional economics.

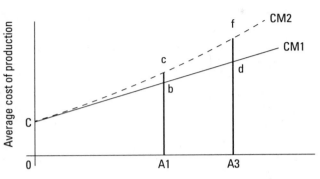

Figure 13-1: The conventional perspective on the cost implications of ethical or socially responsible behavior for the firm.

Number of ethical acts or level of socially responsible behavior

The Good Company

A *good company* is one that behaves in accordance with a particular set of ethical standards — standards that go beyond simply making a profit and remaining competitive. One perspective on the good company is that it engages in policy that improves the well-being of its employees and community.

Conventional economists denounce ethical or socially responsible behavior as being bad for business. But they're not alone: Advocates for ethical and socially responsible behavior within the firm often argue that such behavior is incompatible with capitalist production, the market economy, international trade, and globalization. From this perspective, being ethical and socially responsible involves somehow disconnecting from the market economy or recognizing and accepting the huge costs involved in being ethical and socially responsible in the economic realm.

But the fact is, ethical and socially responsible behavior *can* be compatible with capitalist production, competitive market economies, international trade, and globalization. The good company can be good for the economy.

In spite of what conventional economics argues, a growing number of firms are engaging in socially responsible behavior. As American economist John Tomer and other behavioral economists have argued, this behavior may be a product of firms' concern over how the wider community and customers will react if they don't move forward in this direction. Some firm decision makers are concerned about how government may deal with corporations that are perceived to be unethical and working against the interest of their communities.

The warm glow: Why people and companies are good or bad

Many firms actually behave like good companies, where ethical considerations play an important role in the design of corporate policy. Behavioral economists, as well as other scholars doing experimental economics and experiments in economic psychology, also have shown that many people engage in ethical behavior, even if doing so is costly. Being ethical, although not consistent with the norms of conventional economics, is more than eccentric, weird, oddball behavior. Being ethical is a means by which many people maximize their level of utility or happiness.

As American economist James Andreoni argues, people engage in ethical behavior even if it involves some material self-sacrifice, because of the warm glow it provides. People behave ethically because it makes them feel good. And when people don't behave ethically, they engage in such behavior because it makes them feel good — "unethical" behavior also can generate a warm glow.

But what's interesting is that this move toward ethical and socially responsible behavior by corporations hasn't damaged the bottom line. The change in the ethical orientation of for-profit corporations doesn't appear to have damaged their competitiveness. Most of these corporations' profits don't appear to have been sullied one bit — but their reputations are beginning to glow.

Detailed lists and rankings of corporations that are socially responsible are published and often updated annually. According to *Ethisphere* magazine (http://ethisphere.com/the-magazine/), the following are some examples of profitable corporations that are certified by some experts as operating consistent with socially responsible norms:

- ✔ **Aerospace:** Indra Sistemas, The Aerospace Corporation
- ✔ **Apparel:** Adidas, Gap, Patagonia, Timberland
- ✔ **Automotive:** Denso, Ford Motor Company
- ✔ **Computer hardware:** Hitachi Data Systems
- ✔ **Computer software:** Adobe Systems, Microsoft, Teradata Corporation
- ✔ **Consumer electronics:** Electrolux, Ricoh, Xerox
- ✔ **Consumer products:** Colgate-Palmolive Company, Henkel AG, Kao Corporation
- ✔ **Diversified industries:** General Electric
- ✔ **Energy and utilities:** Encana, Statoil, NextEra Energy

- ✔ **Financial services:** American Express, Housing Development Finance Corporation, NYSE Euronext, The Hartford Financial Services Group
- ✔ **Food and beverage:** General Mills, PepsiCo, Stonyfield Farm
- ✔ **Food stores:** Kesko, The Co-Operative Group, Whole Foods Market
- ✔ **Hotels, travel, and hospitality:** Kimpton Hotels, Marriott International, Wyndham Worldwide
- ✔ **Media, publishing, and entertainment:** Thomson Reuters
- ✔ **Restaurants:** Starbucks
- ✔ **Specialty retail:** Best Buy, Hennes & Mauritz, Sonae, Target, Ten Thousand Villages
- ✔ **Telecom hardware:** Avaya, Cisco Systems, Juniper Networks
- ✔ **Telecom services:** Singapore Telecom, Swisscom, T-Mobile USA
- ✔ **Transportation and logistics:** Autoridad del Canal de Panama, East Japan Railway Company, Nippon Yusen Kabushi Kaisha, UPS

Corporations often are considered to be socially responsible in one dimension but unethical in others. For example, Walmart, which is infamous for not being socially responsible in terms of how it treats its employees, is now building a supplier base for fair-trade coffee.

The cooperative as a dynamic corporation

One example of what some people would argue is a good company is the cooperative. Many types of cooperatives exist, including consumer, supplier, and worker cooperatives, as well as credit unions. Basically, in a cooperative, members control the direction of the company and share both the benefits and the risks of owning the firm.

Conventional economics has often decried the cooperative, especially the worker cooperative, as an inferior economic organization. Cooperatives aren't focused on narrow profit maximization objectives. Socially responsible factors often play an important part in decision making. In the workers cooperative, for example, wages and benefits are kept relatively high.

But there is considerable evidence that cooperatives are highly competitive, even with increasing globalization. United Nations estimates suggest that the "cooperative movement" had over 800 million members at the beginning of the new millennium and provided about 100 million jobs in over 100 countries in both developed and less-developed economies. About half of the world's agricultural output is marketed by cooperatives. In the financial sector, credit unions encompass about 120 million members in 87 countries. Healthcare cooperatives service about 100 million people in over 50 countries. Electricity cooperatives have become important, too — for example, in the United States, such cooperatives service over 30 million people.

There is strong evidence that companies that are considered to be socially responsible are more profitable than companies that are not rated as socially responsible. These socially responsible firms have outperformed the Standard & Poor's 500 (S&P 500) by a significant margin. In other words, there is increasing evidence that investing in socially responsible firms involves no material self-sacrifice.

It's possible to be good without being altruistic. This fits with the movement of highly competitive corporations into the realm of socially responsible production. And it should provide considerable food for thought for those versed in conventional economics, where such superior economic performance by ethical or socially responsible firms isn't thought possible.

The Compatibility between Ethics and Profits

When we drop the assumption that effort is a fixed input into the production process and that the quality and quantity of effort are unaffected by how people are treated by the firm, this opens the door to a better understanding of why and how socially responsible firms can be competitive and profitable. In addition, introducing the ethical consumer further weakens the conventional economics assumption that being ethical in the realm of production is a disaster waiting to happen.

Examining x-efficiency and the socially responsible firm

There is considerable evidence that people tend to be more productive if they're treated better by their employers. Being treated better may involve being paid better, receiving more benefits, working in a safer environment, having a greater say in how the firm is being run, and being treated with dignity. If a worker is part of a firm that's a good company, an increase in the worker's effort will increase the firm's productivity.

But an ethical firm isn't constructed in a costless fashion — there is no free lunch. But this does not mean that the firm must experience higher average costs of production. By being more socially responsible, the firm induces higher levels of x-efficiency. This increase in productivity can offset the cost of being socially responsible. So, there are clear and unequivocal ethical costs, but these costs don't undermine the competitive position of the ethical or socially responsible firm.

The limits of price gouging during crisis

The conventional model of the narrowly selfish individual would predict that businesspeople in the midst of an economic crisis would take advantage of acute shortages to increase prices in an effort to maximize profits. In fact, *not* taking advantage of such opportunities for gain would be considered irrational.

Basically, in a crisis, the supply of essential goods and services — like drinking water, essential foodstuffs, and shelter — falls and the demand increases. These movements in demand and supply increase the equilibrium price that businesspeople could charge. The higher price is supposed to then generate an increase in the supply for the necessary goods and services.

But behavioral economists and other scholars have found that many businesspeople don't behave in this type of profit-maximizing manner in times of crisis. And if they do, consumers remember and retaliate down the road, because they consider price gouging to be unfair and unethical.

Just as important, many businesspeople won't engage in price gouging for ethical reasons, which causes some upward rigidity in prices. In other words, prices won't increase to the extent that they would if market forces were able to determine prices without being interfered with by ethical considerations. Needless to say, many businesspeople do engage in price gouging during crises, especially if they figure they won't be easily identified down the road. (For consumers to retaliate, they have to know whom to retaliate against.)

Price gouging has long been recognized by scholars outside the realm of economics as being irrational, apart from any ethical considerations. Limiting the extent to which prices are increased during a crisis garners favor among consumers and avoids creating a sense of anger, which can result in less demand for a firm's products in the future.

Long-run profit maximization may very well involve keeping the lid on significant price hikes during periods of crisis, when ethics plays a role in determining whom consumers purchase their products from. And this would be quite rational from the perspective of long-run profit maximization.

One possible scenario that may unfold when effort is variable is illustrated in Figure 13-2 by line segment *C–D–XE*. Increasing the level of social responsibility along *C–D* does not affect average cost if the productivity increases sufficiently to offset the cost of being ethical — average cost remains constant in the face of increasing the extent of ethical or socially responsible production. The conventional perspective is illustrated by line segment *C–CM*. When effort is assumed fixed, as it is in conventional economics, ethical behavioral results in increased average costs of production.

If ethical costs increase by 10 percent and, through increases in the quality and quantity of effort, productivity increases by 10 percent, average costs don't change. And this refers to a firm where labor constitutes all production costs. As I discuss in Chapter 12, if the labor represents less than 100 percent of total cost, the extent of productivity increases required to offset the cost of being ethical would be less than 10 percent — maybe much less than 10 percent. If being ethical also induces technological change, the cost curve shifts to *C–D–XET*, which provides the firm with more flexibility to become even more socially responsible without increasing average cost.

Figure 13-2:
The behavioral perspective on the cost implications of ethical or socially responsible behavior for the firm.

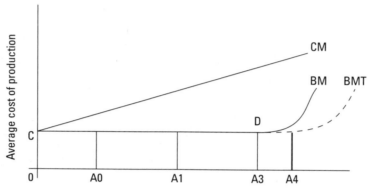

Number of ethical acts or level of socially responsible behavior

But this behavioral approach to the firm doesn't suggest that socially responsible firms can or should dominate the economic landscape. Even though being more ethical or socially responsible doesn't have to undermine the competitiveness of the firm, there is no clear incentive for firm decision makers to opt for the socially responsible firm. Being socially responsible doesn't necessarily put any more cash in their pockets. Also, if the socially responsible firm results in the relative power and income of the managers and bosses falling, there may be psychological costs involved in becoming more socially responsible. When relative positioning matters, firm decision makers will see their utility or level of satisfaction drop in the socially responsible firm.

Even if being socially responsible is cost neutral, becoming socially responsible requires either a change in the preferences of decision makers or changes in circumstances external to the firm, like changes in consumer and community preferences toward socially responsible firms. Otherwise, it's impossible to predict that firms will become more socially responsible on their own.

From the perspective of x-efficiency theory and an understanding of how human relations can influence the level of x-efficiency, it's much easier to understand how socially responsible firms can remain competitive. But remaining competitive by increasing the level of x-efficiency grows the size of the economic pie. Socially responsible production involves, in this case, increasing productivity to at least offset the cost of being ethical.

Nudging firms toward social responsibility

Typically firms need to be nudged into changing how they do business. Such nudging has already taken place in democratic societies through dramatic changes in consumer preferences, dramatic improvements in product labeling, and the enormous democratization of information on how, who, and where products are produced and delivered.

Nudging toward socially responsible production has largely taken place as a function of market forces, not through arbitrary government intervention. Consumers are voting with their pocketbooks and at the ballot box for what they consider to be more ethical production. Increasingly, firms are responding to these changes in consumer demand.

Plus, socially responsible behavior within the firm induces employees to work smarter and harder. When employees trust bosses and bosses trust employees in the context of socially responsible behavior, this encourages higher firm productivity. The cost of being ethical is not at the expense of firm profits or managerial income when the economic pie increases as a consequence of socially responsible behavior inside the firm.

Some economists would refer to this type of x-efficient solution to the productivity problem as the *golden rule outcome*. Given technology, the golden rule outcome is given at point $A3$ in Figure 13-2. Productivity increases with the level of socially responsible behavior. The size of the economic pie increases with the level of socially responsible behavior.

How ethical consumers sustain and grow ethical production

Consumers can have preferences for goods and services that are produced by ethical firms, particularly when the ethically produced product is pretty much the same price and quality as the product that the consumer considers to have been produced unethically or by a firm that isn't regarded as socially responsible.

For example, let's say that consumers prefer coffee that is fair trade. Moreover, fair-trade coffee is the same price and quality as regular coffee. Purchasing the fair-trade coffee provides the consumer with a higher level of satisfaction. Consumers with a preference for fair-trade coffee create a market for such coffee. As more consumers' preferences shift toward fair-trade coffee, firms are pressured to shift toward supplying what consumers want. This is even the case if firm decision makers don't care how or where the coffee is sourced. Changing consumer preferences force firms to change their ways.

The same scenario would arise if consumers prefer products produced by union labor, by firms that are greener, or by firms that appear to treat their workers better or more fairly. If consumers prefer such products, firms have to deliver. And if firms can produce these products at the same price as the less ethical firms, the market forces a shift to more ethical production.

If the relatively ethical firms are x-inefficient, and they initially produce their products at a relatively higher cost and price, competitive pressures can push these firms into becoming more x-efficient. And if this comes to pass, such ethical firms end up becoming cost competitive with the relatively unethical firms. These ethical firms could end up dominating the market if consumer preferences shift strongly enough in favor of products produced by ethical or socially responsible firms.

Even if the ethical firms can produce only at a higher cost and price, consumers often are willing to pay a premium for "ethical" products or the products of socially responsible firms. Being more expensive doesn't necessarily translate into economic demise, if consumers have a preference for ethical products and are willing to pay something extra for it. Higher-priced ethical firms can remain highly successful under these circumstances. Instead of being protected by tariffs or subsidies, they're protected by the preferences of consumers.

The limits of self-sacrificing consumer behavior

Although consumers are willing to pay more for ethical products, there are limits to what most consumers are willing to sacrifice. The poorer a person is, the less he or she can afford to sacrifice. So, income sets a serious or even binding constraint on how much consumers are willing to pay for ethical products. This doesn't imply that poor people are somehow unethical — it's just that the first priority of most people is meeting their own basic needs and those of their families and close friends.

There appears to be a negative relationship between the relative cost of ethical products and demand. The more expensive the ethical product, the less the demand.

Another constraint on how much consumers are willing to pay for ethical production is set by their preferences. Given income, some consumers would give up a large percentage of their income to pay for higher-priced ethical products, but these people are the exception to the rule. Most people are willing to make limited sacrifices. In contrast, the individual modeled in conventional economics wouldn't sacrifice one penny to pay for relatively higher-priced ethical goods.

The secret to the long-term success of ethical or socially responsible production is making such production cost competitive. And given the cost competitiveness of ethical production, consumer preferences force the hand of firms toward socially responsible production.

The importance of product labels for ethical production

Consumers can most effectively force ethical production in a world of bounded rationality and imperfect information when product labels are reliable and trustworthy. They need to know how goods and services are produced and delivered. Governments and government-sponsored agencies, as well as private certification agencies, are springing up, providing labels indicating whether a product is union made, made with child labor, or made with particular chemicals, whether animal products are free-range, where products originated, and much more. This information assists consumers in purchasing what they want. It also allows them to boycott products that aren't labeled — when a product isn't labeled, consumers don't know what they're buying.

Chapter 14

Why Institutions Matter

In This Chapter

▶ Looking at institutions from a behavioral economics perspective

▶ Introduction the New Institutional Economics

▶ Understanding why institutions matter for wealth creation

*I*n the world of economics, the term *institutions* is bandied about as if everybody knows what it means. But often economists use this word differently from the way non-economists do. In economic parlance, an *institution* consists of constraints that help structure behavior in the economic realm. Some examples of institutions include religion, culture, social norms, markets, and the rules and regulations that flow from government and their agencies.

A long-held assumption in economics is that institutions don't matter to economic performance because the right institutions will be in place to make for an efficient economy. There's no room for improvement.

There may be a few cents lying on the sidewalk (minor opportunities for gain), but certainly not billions of dollars. As the joke goes, if an economist sees a buck on the sidewalk, he'll step over it because he assumes that the money isn't there. The institutional environment is assumed to be just right to eliminate all waste and inefficiencies.

Contemporary behavioral economics doesn't pay much attention to the importance of institutions in determining economic outcomes. What matters to today's behavioral economists are psychological factors that have been long ignored or assumed away by conventional economics.

But following in the tradition of one of the pioneers of behavioral economics, Herbert Simon, this chapter discusses why billions of dollars actually *are* lying on the sidewalk because of institutional failure. I start by telling you what behavioral economics says about institutions. Then I introduce you to New Institutional Economics, which pays close attention to how institutions affect the costs and benefits to the individual of engaging in different types of businesses, only some of which are beneficial to society. I end the chapter by talking about how institutions matter to wealth creation, using two examples: government and culture.

Herbert Simon and the importance of institutions to behavioral economics

Nobel Laureate Herbert Simon, known mostly for his development of the concepts of bounded rationality and satisficing, paid close attention to the importance of getting our assumptions right about social norms, culture, and the law, if economists are to build rigorous models of the economy and economic behavior. In 1979, Simon argued:

> The principal forerunner of a behavioral theory of the firm is the tradition usually called Institutionalism. It is not clear that all of the writings, European and American, usually lumped under this rubric have much

in common, or that their authors would agree with each other's views. At best, they share a conviction that economic theory must be reformulated to take account of the social and legal structures amidst which market transactions are carried out. . . .

The social and legal environment provides the incentive structure within which decisions are made. In many key instances, without an understanding of this environment, we can't truly understand why, how, and what decisions are made, even if we get our psychological assumptions right.

What Behavioral Economics Has to Say about Institutions

Contemporary behavioral economics has downplayed the role of institutions in explaining economic behavior. Instead, the focus has been on constructed models that better reflect the reality of human behavior. However, getting our simplifying assumptions right about institutions when building models was important to early pioneers of behavioral economics. Institutions set the incentive environment within which choices are made.

In conventional economics, institutions are also of little importance. Instead, it's assumed that the institutions in place will induce or entice people into making optimal decisions at all times. If you assume that institutions will always be optimal, you can assume that institutions don't matter when building models to explain and predict economic decision making.

A key distinguishing feature of behavioral economics is that assumptions matter for building rigorous models. This is true not only for psychological assumptions, but also for the design of institutions that structure the decision-making environments people face in the real world. Starting with simplistic assumptions about institutions can lead economists to conclude that people are making biased or irrational decisions for embedded psychological reasons, when in fact their decisions are what they are because of the institutional parameters and related incentives that they face.

Getting all our relevant assumptions right — psychological, sociological, and institutional — is critical in order for our models to effectively explain important aspects of decision making and economic outcomes.

The decision-making context

Although the recent focus in behavioral economics has been on psychological variables, some people have tried to model institutional considerations. Psychologist Gerd Gigerenzer has paid careful attention to environmental factors (the decision-making environment) in addressing why people tend to behave in a way that often goes against the predictions of conventional economics. And these environmental factors often overlap with institutional factors. Gigerenzer argues that psychological and environmental factors must be brought together to best explain human decision making.

Experimental economists, led by Vernon Smith, also pay close attention to the environment in which experiments are conducted. They pay close attention to how markets are designed in experimental settings. The environmental parameters — a stand-in for real-world institutions — impact how the subjects of experiments will respond to different questions or options. They affect the incentives that influence decision making.

More specifically, discussing how people deal with imperfect and asymmetric information introduces institutional factors to the modeling toolbox. When government provides the means to deliver more accurate information on goods and services, people make different decisions than they do when the quality of information is highly uncertain and unreliable.

People also make different decisions on questions involving risk when they have better information on risks and when they're insured or protected from risk by government or other institutions. A farmer would treat his land differently if he's guaranteed a certain return on his investment. Not investing in the future productivity of land may be quite rational under certain institutional constraints. A renter can be expected to invest less than the owner of a small tract of land.

The theory of the firm

A theory of the firm would inform people about the firm's inner workings — how and why individuals interact in a particular fashion, and how and why particular decisions are arrived at. Conventional economics has little to say about a theory of the firm — the firm is assumed to be efficient because its incentive problems are assumed solved from the get-go. Early contributors to behavioral economics, who paid close attention to the inner workings of the firm — the essence of a theory of the firm — examined the firm as an institution. The institutional parameters within the firm and the decision-making environment within the firm were considered critical to the decision-making process.

These behavioral economists invested a lot of time and effort to better understand the inner workings of the firm (often referred to as the *black box* of the firm). X-efficiency theory, pioneered by Harvey Leibenstein, was critical to these early efforts. The behavioral model of the firm developed by Richard Cyert and James March, once of Carnegie-Mellon University, also was important.

The designation *black box* stems from the fact that most economists treat the details of the inner workings of the firm as unimportant — they're part of a black box that somehow generates efficient economic outcomes.

In these models of the firm, outcomes were not of the productivity-maximizing sort envisioned and predicted by conventional economics. Psychological variables play an important role in affecting outcomes, but institutions are allocated an important role, too. This is especially the case in x-efficiency theory, where the industrial relations system impacts whether and the extent to which output is maximized — whether x-efficiency is achieved. Institutions can help fix the incentive environment inside the firm. Institutions also can help resolve the coordination of decisions and behavior of individuals inside the firm, which is necessary for the firm to operate efficiently.

The New Institutional Economics

Institutional economics has a long history in the economics profession and was once the dominant approach to economics in many universities, especially in the United States before World War II. But it was displaced by a more mathematical approach, which didn't pay much attention to institutions and decision-making environments.

A resurgence of sorts took place through the work of economists Douglass North, Oliver Williamson, and the late Mancur Olson. North and Williamson were awarded the Nobel Prize in Economics for their efforts. These and other scholars contributed to the development of what is referred to as New Institutional Economics (NIE). Unlike much of the "old" institutionalists, the NIE has much more of a theoretical bent.

North and Olson, for example, show how institutions have been marginalized by conventional economics. For this reason, conventional economics can't explain fundamental economic problems such as persistent differences in economic development. For the New Institutional Economists, the fatal flaw of conventional economics is that it's simply a theory that explains the allocation of scarce resources by "rational" individuals in a frictionless world.

Douglass North and the New Institutional Economics

Douglass North, noted for his research in economic history, pioneered efforts to return institutions to the economic analysis. This has met with some success, as key international organizations such as the World Bank and the United Nations are increasingly integrating the importance of institutions into their analyses of economic development. A critical point made by North and other scholars involved in developing the New Institutional Economics is that conventional economic theory contains a fundamental defect when it comes to understanding the evolution of economic efficiency. North writes, for example:

> . . . not only that institutions are designed to achieve efficient outcomes, but that they can be ignored in economic analysis because they play no independent role in economic performance.

The conventional wisdom assumes that efficiency-facilitating and -promoting institutions will develop by force of circumstance. A key point made by North and others is that it's quite possible for inefficient institutions to persist over time, such as in many third-world countries today and during most of world history. This occurs when institutions make it more profitable for individuals to secure economic gain through redistributing income as opposed to increasing income. This is often referred to as *rent-seeking behavior*. In other cases, individuals may simply be exploiting resources in a manner that doesn't maximize returns to the wider community. Many of the oil-rich countries in the world remain poor, for example, although those controlling these resources are among the wealthiest in the world.

For the New Institutional Economics, these types of perverse incentives are related to the relative transaction costs of engaging in productivity-enhancing activity and the preferences of decision makers. The bottom line for the New Institutional Economics is that economic problems persist due to the lack of sufficient competitive market forces and to rules of the game that reward utility-maximizing inefficient behavior. For this reason, institutions make a huge difference to economic outcomes even when we assume the rational decision makers of conventional economics: narrowly self-interested, utility-maximizing individuals. The errors-and-biases approach that's so important to much of contemporary behavioral economics plays no role here in producing significant economic inefficiencies. Problematic institutions form the backbone of the problem.

No mention is made of x-inefficiencies in production. The implicit assumption in the New Institutional Economics is that effort is, in some sense, being maximized. But institutional deficiencies result in utility-maximizing, rational individuals investing in low-productivity or productivity-reducing venues.

Unlike much of contemporary behavioral economics, NIE has no problem with the notion of rational individuals. In the context of NIE, decision makers can be smart and maximizing — there are no errors and biases causing problematic and inefficient decisions. Problems arise largely as a result of an incentive system that impedes the process of development and of efficient production.

Rent-seeking behavior

The concept of rent seeking was given a theoretical frame by American economists Gordon Tullock and Anne Krueger. The basic idea is that individuals seek to obtain and increase their income and wealth by achieving and exploiting political power as opposed to developing and growing the real economy. Instead of investing in new and more productive technology, producing at higher levels of productivity, and producing more goods and services, rent seekers find ways to exploit their political connections to increase prices and obtain subsidies and protection. They shift income into their pockets from others in society.

Rent seeking is very much about redistributing income and wealth as opposed to growing the economy. Harvey Leibenstein pointed out that rent seeking was also important to the development and maintenance of x-inefficiency in production. Lobbying plays an important role in creating a protective environment that allows x-inefficient firms to flourish.

Institutions, including legal institutions, affect the incentives that individuals face when they make decisions relevant to development, efficiency, and growth. There are no guarantees that current institutions will result in growth and development. In fact, throughout the world, economies are plagued by institutions that impede growth and development.

Figure 14-1 illustrates some of the points made by those who argue for the importance of institutions in determining the level of income per person. In some ideal world, decisions would be made such that income per person is maximized. Conventional economics predicts that the various world economies should end up on the arc *XE*, which represents the production possibility curve. The appropriate institutions are assumed to be in place such that *XE* can be achieved. However, if the appropriate institutions are not in place, an economy may be at production possibility frontier *ab* or, worse still, at *cd*. Line segment *st* would be one measure of big bills lying on the sidewalk. According to the analytical framework of institutional economics, new and old, a major cause of this loss in economic welfare is a product of institutional failure constructed by rational individuals in control of the decision-making process.

American economist Mancur Olson identifies one important example of big bills lying on the sidewalk and exciting opportunities for big bill hunting: the huge income differences between what individuals earned just before moving to the United States and what they earned just after moving to the United States from relatively low-income economies. Such immigrants have earned about 55 percent of what native-born American citizens earned with the same level of schooling, gender, and age — this, in spite of the great adjustment costs new immigrants face in terms of a different language and culture. These immigrants earned, in their countries of origin, 10 percent to 20 percent of what native-born Americans earned. Just by moving to the United States, the immigrants' income soared.

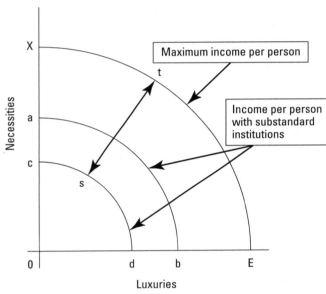

Figure 14-1: The production possibility frontier can be used to illustrate differences in output that are a consequence of differences in the quality of institutions and governance.

Transaction costs

A *transaction cost* is the cost of engaging in economic exchange. It often involves the cost of negotiating, drawing up, signing, and monitoring contracts. Conventional economics often assumes that transaction costs are so small that they can be effectively assumed away when constructing models of human decision making. In the New Institutional Economics, transaction costs are large enough to keep decisions that benefit society at large from taking place. As American economist Allan Schmid has discussed, relatively high transaction costs serve to maintain status quo arrangements, even if these arrangements are damaging from a broader social perspective. However, even with low transaction costs, difficulties arise when decision makers benefit significantly from the old institutional arrangements from an economic and power perspective. These benefits may be such that they help maintain status quo arrangements that maximize the utility or level of satisfaction of a small percentage of the population. At the same time, these arrangements cause society's level of material and social well-being to be much lower than it would be if current decision makers were characterized by a different set of preferences.

Resource-rich countries: Institutions make all the difference

Many resource-rich countries are quite poor, including many of the oil-rich countries such as Nigeria, Saudi Arabia, and Russia. Other resource-rich countries, such as the United States, Norway, Canada, Australia, and Botswana, have fared pretty well. Some economists have recently argued that being well endowed with resources such as oil, natural gas, and diamonds is a curse, incentivizing persistent economic underdevelopment.

However, many other scholars, based on analyses of a large set of resource-rich economies, have now come to the opinion that an abundance of natural wealth can facilitate and contribute to great prosperity across all members of an economy if the institutions are the appropriate ones.

Such institutions can't simply be assumed to be in place, however — such an assumption deflects attention from factors that can be critically important to building a better understanding of why some resource-rich economies develop while others linger in poverty. Economies can be cursed by bad institutions, which can be changed. Bad institutions prevent countries like Nigeria and Russia from taking advantage of their good fortune of being blessed with an abundance of natural resources.

This gap between what new immigrants earn in the United States and what they earn in their country of origin as compared to native-born Americans represents some very big bills lying on the sidewalk. Improvements to institutions in the countries of origin should reduce and eventually eliminate the big bills lying on the sidewalk. In Figure 14-1, the economy would move from production possibility frontier *cd* to *XE*.

In this approach to institutional failure, all individuals are rational and profit maximizing as well as utility maximizing. The problem lies with the inability of "rational" or smart people to shift to institutions that benefit the population at large.

Institutions and Wealth Creation

Unlike conventional economics, behavioral economics pays keen attention to the institutional factors that influence decision making when it comes to economic development that creates wealth. Not all institutions are conducive to economic development. In many cases, institutional constraints encourage behavior that results in economic underdevelopment, although such behavior produces tremendous wealth to individual decision makers. (What's good for the individual isn't necessarily good for society.) But certain types of institutional constraints encourage behavior that not only favors economic development, but also is consistent with creating a high standard of material well-being for individual decision makers.

In this section, I cover two examples of institutional constraints:

- ✔ **Governance:** The type of governance in place — which includes the rules of the economic game and how these rules are developed, monitored, and enforced — matters.

- ✔ **Culture:** The cultural factors that affect decision making are social norms. Not all cultural constraints are consistent with or conducive to economic development.

Governance

Adam Smith argued that good governance, which typically requires good government, is critical to sustained and relatively equitable economic development. Good governance has a lot to do with the rule of law — the provision of fair and equitable law and order and the protection of private property, as well as legal guarantees with respect to free labor. With good governance, slavery and other forms of servitude are forbidden and labor mobility is guaranteed.

This idea is very much what Douglass North, Mancur Olson, and other New Institutional Economists refer to as *good governance and efficient institutions.* But as Adam Smith recognized many years earlier, capitalism was no guarantee of good governance and the rule of law.

Markets have existed for thousands of years, but good governance has not dominated. The point Adam Smith made — one lost on many conventional economists — is that good governance has to be developed, if not constructed. And good governance incentivizes individuals to make choices that help grow the economic pie. It creates incentives that push and pull individuals away from rent-seeking behavior and toward productive activities.

But good governance has come to mean much more than the protection of private property rights. The protection of private property rights appears to be necessary for growth and development to take place. But the protection of private property rights is by no means sufficient to make growth and development happen. Transparency, the minimization of corruption, and accountability are now considered to be other necessary conditions for sustained growth and economic development.

Democracy, freedom of the press, and an independent judiciary are also thought to be critical if transparency, the minimization of corruption, and accountability are to take effect. (Nobel Laureate in Economics Amartya Sen emphasizes these points.) As an important aside, democracy and related democratic rights, as well as an individual's sense of empowerment, tend to have a powerful effect on increasing his or her level of happiness. So, democracy can positively affect development of both the level of material well-being and happiness.

In the following sections, I cover the importance to economic development of quality information, democracy, transparency, low levels of corruption, social capital, and cultural factors.

Good governance and bounded rationality

Democracy, freedom of the press, an independent judiciary, and so on all become critical in a world of bounded rationality where the brain is a scarce resource and information is both imperfect and *asymmetric* (some people are more informed than others). Institutions need to be in place to provide people easy access to good, honest information and to make sure that people aren't being lied to.

If these institutions aren't in place, people can't make fully informed decisions. Contrary to the conventional wisdom, we can't assume that such institutions fall like manna from heaven. With bad institutions, conventionally rational decision makers have all kinds of incentives to behave in a socially destructive way (for example, by displaying rent-seeking behavior).

Some of the pioneering studies on good governance, produced through the World Bank by Daniel Kaufmann and his colleagues, found that improving the rule of law and reducing corruption can have huge economic effects. For example, improving the rule of law in Russia so that it matches what exists in the Czech Republic (another of the economies that made the transition from communism to capitalism), or reducing the level of corruption in Indonesia so that it matches the much lower level of corruption in South Korea, would result in a twofold to fourfold increase in per-capita income. There would also be a similar drop in infant mortality and a 20 percent improvement in literacy. There is a clear cause-and-effect relationship between good governance and improved socioeconomic performance.

Democracy and economic development

The evidence strongly suggests that democratic governance affects economic growth if the governance is designed to constrain the behavior of corrupt officials. Keeping corrupt officials in check is partially achieved through a free press that monitors corruption. A free press also can expose corruption and corrupt individuals in both the private and public sectors so that decision makers are held accountable. Of course, politicians who are no longer approved of can be booted out of power.

In other words, democracy contributes to economic development and growth when it contributes to good governance. Democracy contains the tools to make this possible. And democracy has great potential to produce good governance.

Evidence also suggests that authoritarian societies that are characterized by significant growth are most likely to see their fortunes flounder if they can't produce institutions that contribute to good governance — which is often not possible or likely in authoritarian regimes.

The relationship between income creation, corruption, accountability, and transparency

Legal guarantees for private property carry with them no guarantees for minimizing corruption or maximizing accountability and transparency. These three variables — corruption, accountability, and transparency — are closely tied. Increasing accountability and transparency plays an important role in reducing corruption. The evidence strongly suggests that moving these variables in the right direction plays an important role in increasing per-capita income and per-capita income growth.

Drawn from a World Bank study by economist Daniel Kaufmann, Figure 14-2 illustrates the positive relationship between increasing control over corruption and increasing per-capita income. The more control there is, the higher the per-capita income. Improving governance has very large economic payoffs.

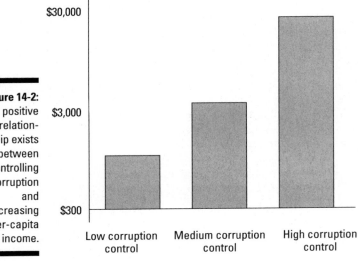

Figure 14-2: A positive relationship exists between controlling corruption and increasing per-capita income.

Strong private property rights alone won't make for a strong economy. With strong private property rights and corruption, for example, a small group of individuals with considerable power can end up being very well off and happy in this kind of society. Such self-interested individuals have little incentive to happily and merrily push for a less corrupt, more efficient, and wealthier society.

The importance of good governance and a vibrant financial sector

A sound financial sector is critical to sustained economic growth and development. But a sound financial sector also has to go beyond securing private property rights for individuals. Again, good governance — in the form of controlling corruption and maintaining high levels of accountability and transparency — is critical.

Figure 14-3, drawn from a World Bank study by economist Daniel Kaufmann, illustrates this point. Poor control over corruption, typically closely related to low levels of accountability and transparency, results in a banking sector that is fragile. In contrast, when corruption is under control, there tends to be a relatively sound banking sector. And a sound banking sector is necessary for sustained economic growth.

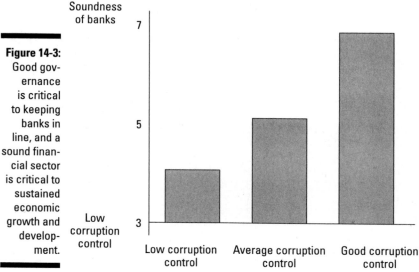

Figure 14-3:
Good governance is critical to keeping banks in line, and a sound financial sector is critical to sustained economic growth and development.

This back story is as relevant to countries like Russia, Ukraine, and South Africa as it is to the United States. When there are serious problems with accountability and transparency, all hell can break lose. The most recent financial crisis of 2008–09 (which many critics argue continues to this day) had at least something to do with the absence of good governance. And this had huge effects on the real economy not only in the United States, but also throughout the world.

Culture

In the economics realm, culture is about the social norms related to economic activity, such as work ethic, savings, investment, merit-based hiring and job promotion, and risk taking.

The brilliant German scholar Max Weber, writing over 100 years ago, pioneered the hypothesis that culture matters for economic development in *Protestant Ethic and the Spirit of Capitalism.* Weber argued that particular norms and values are critical for economic development. Without these norms and values, individuals and societies will be worse off (that is, poorer) than they might otherwise be. In other words, if societies deviate from these "ideal" norms and values, they'll be poorer.

There is some evidence to support the argument that culture can play an important role in either facilitating or retarding the process of economic development and growth. American economist Lawrence Harrison has been at the forefront of arguing for the importance of culture, which now increasingly overlaps with the notion that good governance and social capital are critically important for economic development.

Social capital and economic development

The contemporary concept of social capital was pioneered by American sociologist Robert Putnam, but it has become of increasing interest to scholars and policy experts interested in economic development. The World Bank has recently invested significantly in studies examining the importance of social capital for development.

Social capital has a lot to do with social relationships and the connectedness of individuals and communities. It relates to improvements in the ability of individuals to work and communicate with each other. One aspect of social capital is the level and quality of trust that individuals have in one another when engaging in economic transactions. Some experts argue that social capital also involves social cohesion across individuals and groups, which reduces conflict and increases trust.

There is evidence that social capital enhances economic development. For one, it reduces the cost of doing business by increasing trust and reducing conflict. Social capital also can contribute to increasing productivity by improving and facilitating networks in labor markets and between firms and by increasing trust within the firm. Social capital therefore contributes to increasing the level of x-efficiency.

The determinants of social capital formation have little to do with irrationality or errors and biases among decision makers. They have more to do with the decisions made by those in power. But social capital fills in important gaps that facilitate improvements in decision making in a world of bounded rationality.

Most economists reject the argument that culture matters. For example, Australian economist and economic historian Eric Jones argues that, eventually, market forces will result in eliminating the differences in cultural norms and values that matter for economic development. Basically, the whole developed and developing world should end up with quite similar cultural norms and values that are critical for economic development. This is largely because economies — more specifically, firms — with cultures that aren't compatible with economic development can't survive in a competitive global economy. In addition, as more individuals aspire to high levels of wealth and income, this convergence of cultural norms and values is forced in the economic realm.

This doesn't mean cultural convergence in the realm of food, clothing, movies, theater, literature, and the like. In fact, cultural convergence in the economic realm often has taken place without having much impact on the viability of local arts and culture.

McDonald's is a neat example of how economic success doesn't mean death to local culture. In different countries, McDonald's serves food and beverages that have a local bent (in terms of what's served, how its traditional dishes are prepared, and how the products are labeled). McDonald's in Manhattan is different from McDonald's in Warsaw is different from McDonald's in Helsinki is different from McDonald's in Glasgow. Think of having a beer with your Big Mac in Spain or having your Big Mac on rye bread in Finland. Maybe local flavor contributes to the economic success of McDonald's.

Even if productivity is relatively low, inefficient firms and economies can survive by keeping wages low. This keeps the average costs of inefficient firms from rising (see Chapter 12). Also, government can protect inefficient firms from market forces with, for example, subsidies and tariffs (taxes on imports). In addition, those in power in the inefficient economies may very well prefer the status quo, when these economies are the source of their wealth and power. This, despite the economic harm it causes to the majority of the population. In addition, those disadvantaged in these economies may not know what the actual causes of their economic deprivation are. They often blame the "outsider," such as ethnic minorities or the "West." Often, they're not even aware that they're economically disadvantaged.

Imperfect (basically bad) information also can play an important role in preventing economies from becoming more economically efficient. But the web is making a serious dent in this situation. It's becoming increasingly difficult for governments to prevent people from learning about economies and societies throughout the world. In part, as a consequence of the recent information revolution, the world has witnessed popular uprisings leading to economic and political change — the Arab Spring is one important recent example.

Part IV

When Bubbles and Busts and Inefficiencies Are Possible: Some Behavioral Insights into the Strange World of Economic Reality

The 5th Wave   By Rich Tennant

"We can't insure your happiness; however, we do offer an extended warranty on joie de vivre."

In this part . . .

Behavioral economics has a lot to say about the macro-economy, from unemployment, business cycles, and asset prices, to economic growth and the determinants of happiness. In this part, I discuss behavioral finance and, related to this, inefficient markets and asset bubbles and busts.

I also explain some of the insights provided by behavioral economics to understanding the business cycles.

Finally, I discuss some of the key sources of happiness. Of crucial importance is how happiness is affected by non-material variables in addition to income and wealth. Money can't buy happiness, at least not all the time.

Chapter 15

Deciphering Behavioral Finance

. . . .

In This Chapter

▶ Defining behavioral finance

▶ Exploring efficient markets

▶ Introducing irrational exuberance

▶ Examining bubbles and busts as a preface to inefficient markets

. . . .

*T*he conventional finance point of view assumes that financial markets are efficient — asset prices (the prices of bonds and stocks, for example) reflect the fundamental economic values (the nuts and bolts of the real-world economy) that they represent. It also assumes that individuals typically behave in a manner that's consistent with asset prices, reflecting their fundamental values. Only this type if behavior is considered to be rational.

Behavioral finance challenges this perspective, arguing that asset prices don't necessarily reflect the fundamentals in financial markets and, therefore, can be highly inefficient, with asset prices persistently deviating from their fundamental values. This can be reflected in booms and busts.

In this chapter, I discuss how financial markets can be inefficient and how such inefficiency can be a product of what some behavioral economists refer to as *cognitive biases and errors* in decision making and in the use and application of various types of *heuristics* (decision-making shortcuts). I also examine how institutional factors can cause booms and busts on financial markets that conventional wisdom can't predict or explain.

What Behavioral Finance Is

Two of the leading lights of behavioral finance, American economists Richard Thaler and Nicholas Barbersis, argue that behavioral finance is all about understanding why and how financial markets are inefficient. First and foremost, behavioral finance builds on a vast array of empirical studies that suggest that asset prices don't move in a fashion consistent with the predictions and modeling assumptions of conventional economics.

Just like behavioral economics, behavioral finance introduces psychological, sociological, neurological, and institutional factors to help explain the level and movements of asset prices, including levels and movements that appear to diverge from fundamental values.

Some behavioral finance scholars are also concerned about the possibility revealed through inefficient financial markets that big bills are lying on the sidewalk — there are pretty much always great opportunities for big-bill hunting in financial markets. These unexploited opportunities for gain in financial markets are vociferously denied by conventional finance theory. There is no way to beat the market, no matter how much is invested in expertise to do so. So, one other concern of behavioral finance is investigating the possible connection between inefficient financial markets and unexploited opportunities for gain.

Behavioral finance doesn't deny that eventually, in the long run, asset prices will converge with their fundamental values. But what triggers and sustains short-run deviations from fundamental values is critically important. In the short run, we see and experience asset bubbles and busts. These market inefficiencies can and often do wreak havoc in the real world, causing damage to the real economy.

Think of it this way: Wars are not a long-run phenomenon in most societies. Eventually, in the long run, societies converge to a relatively peaceful environment. But in the short run, wars can and do cause real damage. Recovery occurs — but short-run events can have long-run consequences, often masked by smoothed long-run trends.

The Efficient Asset Market Models and Their Limits

Behavioral finance tries to understand why asset prices usually deviate from their fundamental or intrinsic values. These deviations are considered to represent inefficient pricing of financial assets. The benchmark for efficient pricing is the fundamental or intrinsic value of what the financial asset represents in the real world.

If the intrinsic value of an asset, based on the real economy is 10¢, the total number of shares for this asset shouldn't be selling for $10 or even $1. Likewise, if the intrinsic value of an asset is $10, the total number of shares shouldn't be selling for 10¢.

If there is a difference between the market price of an asset and its fundamental or intrinsic value, then, according to conventional wisdom, no one — no matter how smart or well endowed with resources — can make money in financial markets by exploiting the difference. Exploiting this difference for profit would require being able to consistently predict movements in asset prices. It amounts to an individual knowing more than the market knows about what asset prices will be. For some people, this amounts to gazing into a crystal ball — a dream, but an impossible dream, even for the world's leading brokerage houses.

More often than not, efficient markets are assumed to consist of two key components:

- **Efficient market hypothesis:** This is the idea that asset prices and fundamental values are one and the same — or at least the two converge so quickly that differences aren't important for an understanding of real-world financial markets.

- **Random walk hypothesis:** This is the belief that no one has the ability to beat the market. On average, a person can't beat the average market rate of return. This is because nobody should be able to predict future share prices. But first a discussion of the first pillar of the efficient market hypothesis is in order: that financial asset prices mirror the fundamental values of what these assets represent.

The efficient market hypothesis

One part of the contemporary efficient market hypothesis, first formally developed by Eugene Fama of the University of Chicago, stipulates that in financial markets, asset prices always reflect available information. This information, in turn, mirrors the fundamentals of the real economy upon which these financial assets are based.

In an efficient market, asset prices are supposed to reflect only objective and best information related to the fundamentals that the financial assets represent. Asset prices move up and down because of the information about changes in the real economy conveyed to investors and speculators. Changes in the real economy and corresponding changes in information affect asset prices through the behavior of the good people buying and selling stocks and bonds.

It's important to emphasize that this information that people are expected to process efficiently is accurate and unbiased. If the information is flawed, people should be able to identify the errors and biases and stick with the good stuff. They should be updating the information at hand, so only the objective information affects people's decision making. This is referred to as *Bayesian updating*.

People shouldn't be subjectively influenced by the behavior of peers, by norms, or by psychological considerations. What counts is the objective information processing. So, unbounded rationality is assumed. People are expected to be aware of all relevant information related to financial assets. And they're assumed to have the capacity to quickly and effectively process this information so that they'll make smart and optimal investment decisions with respect to buying and selling stocks and bonds and the like.

Bayesian updating has become a shorthand for the notion that people's current set of beliefs and understandings is a function of their initial beliefs and understandings and *new* information relevant to a particular decision. In other words, people are willing and able to modify their beliefs based on new, objective information. But in a world of bounded rationality, people don't always know what good or objective information on the financial market actually looks like. Also, they don't easily modify their beliefs given the introduction of new information. They should, but they don't — at least not as quickly as they should. This point is often made, based on the evidence, by behavioral economists. If people don't engage in rapid Bayesian updating, for whatever reason (including the uncertain reliability of new information), asset prices won't be updated to reflect their fundamental values as predicted and expected by the conventional wisdom.

The random walk hypothesis

The idea that financial asset price movements follow a random walk was made famous by Princeton University finance scholar Burton Malkiel. He argued that past movements in asset prices don't provide you with the ammunition required to predict future prices. Price movements follow a random process, like flipping a coin over and over — you can't actually predict if the next flip will be heads or tails. If you can't use past data to predict future prices, devising investment strategies to beat the market is impossible.

You can't get rich by beating the market — but you can get rich selling advice to people who think that you can beat the market or getting hired by investment firms that sell advice and do financial investments and investment planning for people who think that these nifty firms can beat the market.

Behavioral economics meets the random walk

There is some good evidence that simply sticking with a diversified portfolio will serve you best. In one interesting example, psychologist Gerd Gigerenzer shows that using a $1/N$ approach to stock diversification does better than sophisticated approaches. In this scenario, you simply divide your money equally over N stocks. This, he argues, can outperform allegedly "optimal" rules for portfolio choice, in a world of bounded rationality (see Chapter 20 for more information).

Some behavioral economists actually support this perspective that financial asset prices largely follow a random walk. Therefore, using simple heuristics as an investment strategy is a smart, even income-maximizing, choice (after deducting all costs). These same behavioral economists don't accept the argument that a random walk implies efficient financial markets.

Other behavioral economists, led by Robert Shiller of Yale University, argue that there are big bills lying on the sidewalk waiting to be harvested by relatively smart investors. This is additional evidence, along with bubbles, that financial markets are inefficient.

From this perspective, you can exploit market inefficiencies to make money, above the market average, if you have the appropriate tools. Behavioral finance can provide insights into the realm of financial markets that would allow some investors to beat the market over the long run.

Key to this argument is evidence that asset prices do persist in one direction or another, contrary to the random walk theory. The past can predict the future, at least up to a point. And smart traders actually can do better than the average market returns, according to this argument. The fact that people can't predict day-to-day changes in asset prices, argues Shiller, doesn't mean that smart investors can predict nothing at all.

Trying to beat the market is like strategizing to win the lottery

Trying to make money on the stock market — that is, to do better than average — is like devising strategies to win the lottery. You may win, but it'll be pure luck. You'll just think you won because you're particularly smart. If you win a lottery applying a strategy you've cooked up, applying this same strategy to win the next lottery has almost no chance whatsoever of winning. If you do win, once again, it was pure luck.

You may be better off simply investing in a diversified stock portfolio and holding on to it than hiring a firm with a small army of Ivy League graduates to invest your money for you. This view is completely at odds with the self-proclaimed and often celebrated wizards of Wall Street, whose bread and butter (and sometimes gold) is based on your believing that they can beat the market average returns over the long term.

Of course, you may get rich if you have inside information — if you know how a company's strategy will impact share prices — but this would be illegal and has nothing to do with the random walk narrative.

However, in a world of bounded rationality, a key question is whether it's possible for someone to identify who these really smart traders are. If this task isn't feasible, then most people may do better applying something like the $1/N$ rule or seeking advice from someone who does. This would be the case especially if you're risk averse, loss averse, and have a preference for certain outcomes, even if there is some chance that betting on what appears to be a "smart" trader will cost some extra income down the road.

Distinguishing between inefficient markets and random walks

Proponents of the random walk and efficient market hypotheses, such as Burton Malkiel, recognize that asset prices can deviate quite significantly from their fundamental values. But efficient market theorists invariably argue that prices eventually converge to their market values.

Behavioral finance proponents wouldn't necessarily disagree with this long-run argument. They're concerned with what happens in the short run, which can actually last for quite a few years. In the short run, markets are inefficient in the sense that there can be marked differences between financial asset prices and their underlying intrinsic values. And within the short run, booms and busts, driven by psychological and other non-economic factors, can have quite significant effects on the real economy. This is clearly exemplified by the collapse of the stock market in the late 1920s and the implosion of the financial sector from 2007 to 2009.

Asset prices can follow a random walk even if they don't match their underlying fundamentals. For behavioral economics and behavioral finance scholars, the existence of a random walk is not proof of market efficiency. A random walk with inefficient markets simply suggests that beating the market average would be difficult and highly unlikely.

Irrational Exuberance: Smells Like Animal Spirit

The term *irrational exuberance* was coined in 1996 by Alan Greenspan, the former chairman of the Federal Reserve, at the beginning of one of the greatest surges in U.S. stock market share values. Greenspan thought the prices of stocks were probably rising too rapidly and getting out of hand. For example, the Dow Jones Industrial Average (DJIA) increased from 3,600 in early 1994 to almost 12,000 by January 2000. In 1982, the DJIA was less than 1,000. After the index peaked, it collapsed to about 7,000 in 2002 (see Figure 15-1). This period was also heavily influenced, if not dominated, by the boom and eventual bust in the share prices of high-tech companies.

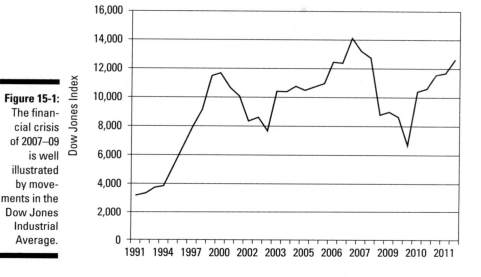

Figure 15-1:
The finan-
cial crisis
of 2007–09
is well
illustrated
by move-
ments in the
Dow Jones
Industrial
Average.

Robert Shiller made this term his own, introducing it as a key concept in behavioral finance. For Shiller, irrational exuberance is the psychological foundation for speculative bubbles. And he defines a *speculative bubble* (as opposed to a price increase based on increases in fundamental values) as an increase in price that is a product of news spreading about an increase in price. This news encourages investment confidence and enhances the animal spirits of investors, even if this news is not at all related to increases in fundamental values.

This confidence in price increases is based largely on psychological factors, which spreads like a virus across the investment community and draws more investors into the pool, further increasing prices. Decision making is based on investors being motivated by excitement and the behavior of others. This focus on psychological factors driving prices is similar to John Maynard Keynes's emphasis on animal spirits as a key driver of human decision making. American economist John Kenneth Galbraith in his analysis of the Great Crash of 1929 emphasized psychological and sociological drives, as well as the spread of misleading and overconfidence-breeding information, as key to the stock market boom and eventual crash.

Decisions are not made in isolation, as conventional economics would have it. And fundamental values are less of a concern as investors' confidence in prices continues to increase in the near future. Many behavioral economists refer to such behavior as irrational because it's tied to the behavior of others, not to the fundamentals of the economy. Other behavioral economists view much of this behavior as understandable and even rational, given imperfect knowledge and the knowledge at hand. But even rational behavior can cause market inefficiencies.

Bubbles and Busts: A Preface to Inefficient Markets

Bubbles in asset prices, such as for bonds and shares in the stock market, represent a deviation from their fundamental values. *Busts* represent an *eventual* market adjustment to fundamental values, usually after they fall below fundamental values.

Documenting bubbles and subsequent busts in asset prices has been critical to the development of behavioral finance. Cycles in assets prices represent movements around the fundamental values of financial assets. So, asset prices typically don't represent fundamental values.

Basically, movements in asset prices tend to differ or deviate from movements in the fundamental values of these assets. The facts challenge the conventional wisdom, opening the door to alternative understandings of the movement and level of asset prices.

The Dutch tulip bulb bubble

There have been many bubbles and busts over the past centuries, but one referred to often by economists is the "tulip mania" that took place in 17th-century Netherlands. In February 1637, the value of a single tulip bulb was worth many times the wage of a skilled worker. Some tulip bulbs were worth more than 2 tons of butter or 1,000 pounds of cheese. One bulb even sold for the price of a house in a really classy part of Amsterdam.

The Dutch brought the tulip to the Netherlands from the Ottoman Empire, reinventing it by creating a multicolored flower that become extremely popular. This rather rare and beautiful tulip was the type that eventually became subject to the buying and selling of speculators, increasing its price dramatically in the 1630s. Prices peaked in the winter of 1636–37.

A good amount of the buying and selling of the tulip bulbs took place using *future contracts,* in which buyers and sellers bet on the expected future price of tulip bulbs (a relatively new thing at the time). Buyers were betting that the price of their tulip bulb would increase at some specified future date. They paid some current price for the bulb written into a contract. The expectation was that prices would continue to increase. Many future contracts were purchased on borrowed money, or *leveraged.* Buyers needed to sell at expected prices to fulfill their loan requirements.

A *futures market* is based on futures contracts where buyers anticipate future prices to at least remain at the specified future price, known as the *strike price*. The sellers of the contract anticipate that prices will fall in the future and sell futures contracts to protect themselves from possible price reductions.

Leveraging in financial markets means borrowing to invest in financial assets in the anticipation that the returns will be large enough to cover the amount borrowed and the interest payments owed. People and companies can get in trouble if they're overly leveraged.

Figure 15-2 illustrates key characteristics of the tulip bubble and the consequent bust in the average price of tulip bulbs.

Figure 15-2:
The infamous tulip mania was characterized by a dramatic increase and then collapse in the price of tulip bulbs.

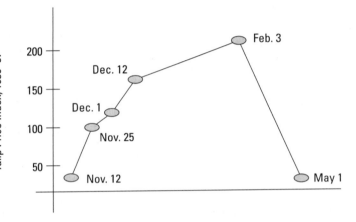

The increase in the price of tulip bulbs was remarkable and dramatic, and it had nothing to do with the cost of producing and marketing the bulbs or their fundamental values. Instead, it was the result of investors believing or hoping that prices would continue to increase, regardless of the fundamental values of tulip bulbs. Many people followed the lead of other people whom they believed to be really smart.

Eventually the bubble burst and prices collapsed toward the fundamental values of the tulip bulbs. There was a dramatic market correction following from the panic selling of contracts for the bulbs, with no parallel increase in the demand for the bulbs.

But unlike many of the more recent bubbles, the speculative tulip bubble remained on the fringes of the Dutch community. The well-established Amsterdam stock exchange didn't involve itself in this speculative venture. Although many people lost their pants when the tulip bubble burst, this speculative mania didn't drag down the Dutch economy. Nevertheless, it has come to exemplify speculative bubbles and inefficient financial markets, where asset prices are driven by psychological variables as opposed to the fundamentals of the assets in question. Of course, this was all because enough people thought they could get rich quick by buying and selling future contracts on tulip bulbs.

Contemporary bubbles: Evidence of inefficient markets

Among the better-known bubbles of contemporary times are the one that preceded the Great Depression in the 1920s, the dot-com bubble of the late 1990s, and the stock market crash of 2007–09. All these bubbles are evidence of asset prices veering severely from fundamental values. But the bubble of the 1920s and of 2007–09 also had dramatic effects on the real economy.

The stock market bubble of the 1920s

The U.S. stock market, as well as stock markets abroad, did spectacularly well for a short period from 1924 through January 1929. In Figure 15-3, this is illustrated by the movement in the DJIA, which increased from 96 to 381. On October 24, 1929 (known as Black Thursday), the New York Stock Exchange collapsed, with the Dow dropping to 299. By 1932, the Dow had dropped to 41. The Dow increased to about 150 by 1941, just prior to the Japanese attack on Pearl Harbor and the United States officially entering World War II.

Figure 15-3:
The collapse of the New York Stock Exchange played an important role in triggering and sustaining a depression in the real economy.

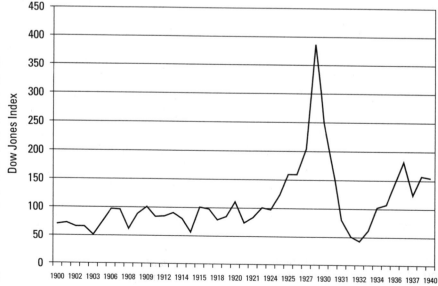

So, what led up to the Great Depression? In the 1920s, there was a severe speculative boom, in part based upon significant leveraging. Leading economists of the time, such as Irving Fisher of Yale University, were quite confident that the good times would continue. But the stock market collapsed, correcting for the unsustainably high share prices. This produced a severe liquidity crisis and a severe crisis of confidence among businesspeople and consumers alike. Given the lack of government response, the bubble soared and then collapsed. And this helped drag the economy into a massive depression, severely damaging the real economy.

The dot-com bubble of the 1990s

The NASDAQ, an index of high-tech stocks, tells the tale of booms and busts in the share prices of primarily U.S. high-tech companies. The movement in share prices is illustrated in Figure 15-4, which is drawn from Bloomberg Data Services. (Another perspective is provided by the DJIA in Figure 15-1.) From 1995 to 2000, the index of share prices for the listed high-tech companies skyrocketed from just less than 1,000 to almost 5,000.

Leading experts in the financial community predicted that prices should continue to climb. But by 2001, the index collapsed to 2,000, and it fell further to just above 1,000 by 2002. Not quite the tulip bubble, but significant nonetheless. Again, the smart money and those behind it were dead wrong. Eventually, the NASDAQ rose again to about 3,000 by 2007, and then fell below 1,500 by 2009. Unlike the tulip bubble, the dot-com bubble had some impact on the real economy. It also reflected movements in the fundamentals of important components of the high-tech industry that couldn't support the type of values generated by speculative bidding on the stock market.

The Dow didn't move with the severity of the NASDAQ, suggesting that industry share prices weren't as out of line with their fundamentals as were the share prices for the high-tech companies (refer to Figure 15-1). Speculators had congregated in the high-tech stocks where it seemed like a lot of easy money could be made quickly.

The big bubble of the first decade of the new millennium

Yet another bubble formed and burst with great effect on the real economy toward the end of the first decade of the 21st century. After increasing pretty much continuously from 8,000 in 2002, the DJIA fell from about 14,000 in October 2007 to about 6,500 in March 2009 — another market correction. By 2011, share prices had almost recovered to their pre-crash values. But the damage had already been done to the real economy.

The stock market bubble, filled with a lot of hot air supplied by access to significant leveraging, saw its value grow well above market fundamentals. Spurred on by easy access to funds and great confidence in increasing share prices, and egged on by experts everywhere from Wall Street to the inner sanctums of the universities, it appeared as if there was no end in sight to asset price growth.

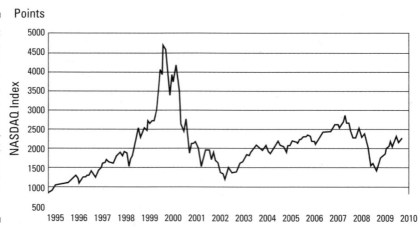

Figure 15-4:
The dot-com bubble and its eventually huge bust is illustrated in the NASDAQ price index of high-tech companies in the United States.

The bursting of this bubble almost took down the real economy. Government intervention saved the day, reducing the damage to the real economy from what it otherwise might have been. But it required significant bailouts of failing firms both inside and outside the financial sector. Throughout most of the developed world, real GDP or real income fell by at least 10 percent as a consequence of the financial crisis. Unemployment soared, almost doubling in the United States from its pre-crisis rate of 5 percent. Canada was one of the exceptions to the rule — and this was a consequence of its relatively sound financial sector, more effective financial sector regulation, and timely government intervention.

Bubbles in experimental economics

There's no denying bubbles in real-world economies. But bubbles also occur in the controlled environment of labs running experiments on human decision making.

One of the founding fathers of experimental economics, Nobel Laureate in Economics, Vernon Smith, and his colleagues have found price bubbles developing even in simulated competitive environments and even if experiments are repeated and subjects have opportunities

to learn. Price bubbles also occur even if subjects are well informed and highly intelligent. Eventually, prices converge to their fundamental values. But shock the experimental setting, and you'll get another bubble.

Bubbles are a product of the uncertainty people have about future opportunities to make more money and the uncertainty about when the bubble will burst — all of which are part and parcel of the human condition.

The causes of financial bubbles

Behavioral economists pay special attention to the causes of financial bubbles. Many explanations are offered, but key among them are herding behavior, relative positioning, and overconfidence. These psychological factors, sometimes referred to as *animal spirits* (following British economist John Maynard Keynes) and sometimes referred to *irrational exuberance* (following Alan Greenspan) not only can generate bubbles but also can produce greater volatility in the booms and busts. Both booms and the busts will be more severe than they might otherwise be because of psychological factors.

Following the herd: Decision making in a world of uncertainty

People tend to follow the herd, especially when information is uncertain, incomplete, and *asymmetric* (some people are more informed than others). Basically, in a world of bounded rationality, *herding* (following the herd) makes sense to most people. Herding is a fast and frugal heuristic that has been used by both human and non-human animals across the millennia.

Some behavioral economists see herding as irrational because people aren't basing their decisions on objective criteria. But with bounded rationality, herding may be a second-best solution where first-best solutions are nowhere to be found. Even if herding is rational, it can result in price cascades leading to excessive booms and busts in the prices of financial assets.

The role of relative positioning in investor behavior

Another cause of financial bubbles is *relative positioning*, which is a concern people have regarding their own economic and social status relative to other people. Any deterioration in a person's relative positioning should reduce a person's utility or well-being.

Herding behavior and trust

Trust, an aspect of herding behavior, is a heuristic that has been employed with relative success by humans for thousands of years. Trusting certain people and institutions allows people to save time, money, and aggravation in economic and social interactions. Some economists refer to trust as "saving on transaction costs."

Trust wouldn't contribute to the efficiency of decision making if this were a world of perfect information — people would know everything anyway. But the real world is another story. Many people follow people and institutions they trust because doing so is a proven fast and frugal heuristic. But if the people you trust mislead and deceive you, you can end up making very bad investment decisions. Just think of Bernard Madoff and his infamous Ponzi scheme, in which he defrauded many trusting people and institutions of billions of dollars.

The implications of institutional failure for financial markets

Herbert Simon emphasized the role of institutions in affecting decision making. Investment decisions that can be bad for society but good for the individual can be a product of the institutional environment. If decision makers face little or no downside risk when making very risky decisions, they'll take those risks. For example, some experts have argued that one cause for disastrous investment decisions is the fact that corporate decision makers and brokers often bear little or no cost for potentially bad financial decisions or for providing poor financial advice, and still take home rich compensation packages. Why not engage in these behaviors if you come out with a lot of cash in your pocket? Some people will refrain from behaving this way for moral reasons. But history has demonstrated that plenty of people will make decisions that harm society if those decisions benefit them personally.

This is a classic moral hazard problem where the individual or institution doesn't bear the costs of the decision. Nothing irrational is happening here, but such behavior can fuel bubbles and busts and can cause bankruptcies and liquidity crises.

Also, if regulations are not well designed, rational decision makers can provide misleading information to clients. Most recently, in the United States, financial assets were rating very highly even though high-quality assets were repackaged with high risk (referred to as *toxic assets*). And none of this was illegal. If proper regulation isn't in place or isn't enforced, unscrupulous investment behavior can occur. Bernard Madoff was able to get away with defrauding the public for well over four decades.

The quality of regulation and its enforcement play an important role in influencing investment behavior. In a world of bounded rationality and in a world where not all people are saints, regulators and regulations matter for the quality of financial decision making.

Many people will invest more as share prices increase for fear that otherwise their economic status will fall relative to those who are currently investing and making a lot on money, at least on paper. This fuels further increases in share values, but not on the basis of changes in the fundamental values of the assets.

Relative positioning is similar to herding, but with relative positioning, people aren't following the leader. Instead, they're trying to protect their relative economic and social status by keeping up with others in their reference group who are already investing.

Fueling the bubble: Overconfidence and underconfidence

Overconfidence is a belief, fed by emotions, that you can predict price movements better than you actually can. When you're overconfident, you're not as smart as you think you are. If you're overconfident, you'll invest more in financial assets than you would otherwise. Some economists argue that people invest in assets that they wouldn't invest in if they considered more objective criteria and weren't ruled by emotions — if they sat back and made more reasoned and cool-headed decisions.

Underconfidence is also emotionally driven. It's a belief that you have a less capacity to understand and predict asset prices than you actually have. When you're underconfident, you're actually smarter than you think you are. This can result in panic-driven selling of financial assets, causing many people to dump assets that they should keep, based on objective criteria.

Both overconfidence and underconfidence can fuel bubbles and busts.

People's level of confidence is often influenced by the behavior of others. Their confidence is often reinforced when people know that other people, including experts and the rich and famous, are doing the same. In a world of bounded rationality, such behavior may make sense — even though it can result in errors in decision making.

Financial education in a world of bounded rationality

In the real world, people aren't born with the ability to understand complex (or even not that complex) financial problems. People also aren't blessed with perfect information. Even if a person were endowed with the tools to make top-notch investment decisions, there is no guarantee that this would happen if he or she has to deal with tainted or incomplete information. In the real world, financial education matters because it can affect the quality of the decisions people make.

A leading behavioral economist, Robert Shiller, argues that one cause for bad investment decisions is poor and misleading information. He favors the provision of higher-quality information and the better dissemination of such information as one very important way of improving financial decision making. Shiller argues that improved information and good financial advice should be subsidized by governments "to help prevent bubbly thinking and financial overextension." Financial education is a public good that improves the efficiency of financial markets, as well as the efficiency of the real economy.

Shiller, among others, also argues for regulated labeling for financial products, similar to the required nutritional labeling for food products, as a means to improve financial decision making. Labels should be designed to provide consumers with basic information in a relatively easy-to-read and easy-to-understand format, one that doesn't send false signals to potential buyers of financial products. The fact is, human brains aren't designed to easily detect critical information somewhere in a dense document, often in small type.

The hope is that financial education can improve financial decision making by improving the decision-making environment and people's decision-making capabilities. Some people won't want to buy a house if they know that the mortgage interest rate will rise from 4 percent to 8 percent per year after a few months and if they understand the implication of this increase in interest rate for their budget.

Chapter 16

Looking into Recessions and Depressions

C onventional wisdom has paid little attention to the role that psychological and sociological factors — such as pessimism, optimism, fairness, envy, and reciprocity — may play in driving the real economy, affecting employment and output. The various schools of thought in macroeconomics all focus on institutions and aggregate variables such as central banks and money supply, tax policy, government spending, and wage flexibility as being responsible for booms and busts.

But behavioral economists have opened the door to non-economic factors as being vitally important as well. This perspective takes us back to John Maynard Keynes, the English economist who penned the influential book *The General Theory of Employment, Money, and Interest* in 1936. Keynes maintained that people's state of mind plays a large role in triggering booms and busts. Make the population feel bad about the future, and you'll keep the economy depressed for way longer than need be. Make people feel cheated and deceived, and they'll retaliate with real-world consequences.

How government impacts the psychological demeanor of the population can play just as important a role in impacting the state of the economy as real factors, such as changes in the interest rate. Of course, real factors also can affect people's state of mind. Bottom line: Both real and psychological factors play an important role in determining macroeconomic outcomes. That's the focus of this chapter.

Introducing Psychology in Business Cycle Narratives

Conventional economics — from left to right — have traditionally paid little attention to the importance of psychological factors causing booms and busts in output (gross domestic product) and employment. The basic underlying assumption is that psychological factors are all airy-fairy — not something that we should take seriously when trying to explain something as important as recessions, depressions, and unemployment.

This, in spite of the fact that one of the pioneers of modern macroeconomics, John Maynard Keynes, paid considerable attention to psychological factors. This side of his *General Theory of Employment, Interest, and Money* has been ignored by economists. Instead, focus shifted to much more easily mathematized factors, such as money supply, interest rates, and government spending.

But behavioral economics has introduced psychology back into the economic analysis of the macroeconomy, taking the lead from Keynes, whose psychological face was hidden in the closet for decades.

Grasping the meaning of macroeconomics, recessions, and depressions

Macroeconomics refers to the study of the larger economy such as employment, unemployment, gross domestic product (GDP), and *inflation* (average price increases). The *business cycle* is made up of the up and down movements in GDP. It involves booms and busts or upturns and downturns, which can be either mild or severe.

Market economies always have been characterized by business cycles. But since the 1950s, business cycles have been much less severe than during previous decades. And we haven't had a Great Depression like the one that severely scarred the world economy in the 1930s. But predicting with any precision the timing of the ups and downs is virtually impossible.

The typical business cycle is illustrated in Figure 16-1. The top of the business cycle is referred to as the *peak*. The bottom is referred to as the *trough*. Also, business cycles have been accompanied by an upward trend in total real GDP in most economics for many decades now. This is illustrated by the upward slope to the trend line *AB*.

Figure 16-1:
Business
cycles
involve
recurring
economic
downturns
and upturns,
with their
associated
troughs and
peaks.

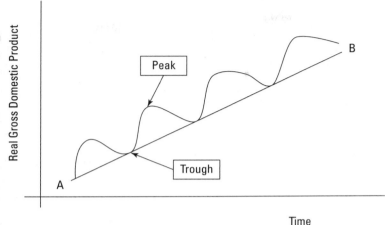

A *recession* typically refers to a short-term (usually three- to five-month) slowdown in the growth of GDP. This is invariably accompanied by an increase in the rate of unemployment.

A *depression* is far more severe than a recession, although there is no unequivocally agreed upon definition. One definition of a depression is a drop in GDP of more than 10 percent. Certainly, the decline in GDP is greater and lasts longer and the unemployment rate is higher and is more sustained than in a recession. However, you define it, recessions and depressions are bad news. And most people would like to see these events minimized in number and severity.

Figures 16-2 and 16-3, based on data from the Federal Reserve Bank of St. Louis, illustrate the evolution of business cycles in the United States from the 1920s through 2010. In both figures, periods of recession and, even worse, depression, are identified by columns. There were a whole bunch of recessions but hardly any depressions. In standard explanations of business cycles found in most macroeconomics textbooks, the virtual absence of depression since the 1950s is a consequence of government policy.

Figure 16-2 presents a picture of business cycles in the context of the level of real GDP over a long period of time. What's clear is that over the course of a number of ups and downs in the economy, total real GDP increased dramatically from the late 1920s through 2010.

Figure 16-3 illustrates business cycles in terms of the percentage change in total real GDP calculated on a yearly basis. For most years, total GDP has increased (it's positive in this graph), but the extent of this increase varies from year to year. So, most recessions consist of the rate of increase in total GDP falling from what it was in the preceding year. This fall in the rate of increase is often accompanied by an increase in the rate of unemployment. More serious is when the growth of real GDP is negative — when the level of real GDP in one year is less than what it was in the preceding year.

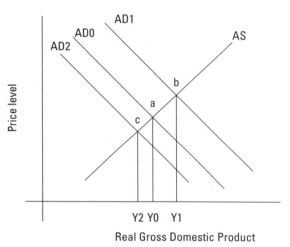

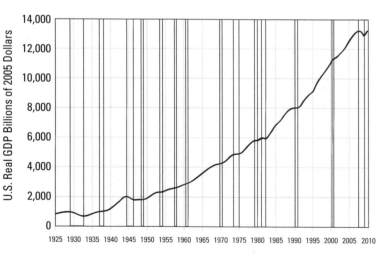

The size or volatility of these movements year-to-year in GDP has diminished by quite a lot since the 1950s. The type of severe drops in GDP of the late 1920s and early 1930s and following World War II haven't been repeated. We came close in 2007, as the level of GDP dropped, but this decline was by less than 5 percent. The severity of this drop was mitigated by timely government and central bank interventions in the leading world economies. By way of comparison, during the depth of the Great Depression, real GDP fell by almost 30 percent. Government did little to mitigate the severity of the depression, following the dictums of the then-conventional economic wisdom.

Understanding animal spirits

John Maynard Keynes refers to *animal spirits* as behavior that is motivated by emotional, as opposed to calculating or hard-core economic rationality, considerations. In *The General Theory,* Keynes writes:

> Most, probably, of our decisions to do something positive, the full consequences of which will be drawn out over many days to come, can only be taken as the result of animal spirits — a spontaneous urge to action rather than inaction, and not as the outcome of a weighted average of quantitative benefits multiplied by quantitative probabilities.

People just don't behave like calculating machines. We act based on our sensibilities that are rooted in our intuitive sense about what we expect will happen in the near future. These animal spirits typically have roots in the real world, related to what people see and understand is happening in the economy and how other people are responding to the economic signals around them.

For Keynes, psychology was one important additional tool in the economics toolbox that allows people to better understand the ups and downs of the economy. Non-psychological factors, such as wages, interest rates, exchange rates, and government spending, are also critically important.

Some behavioral economists have resurrected Keynes's animal spirits to help explain economic booms and busts or business cycles, reintroducing human sensibilities and emotions into modeling and understanding the macroeconomy. For much of conventional economics, assuming away animal spirits makes building mathematically oriented economy models much easier — but this ease comes at the cost of making the models poor tools for getting at the heart of critical economic issues.

Animal spirits have been introduced big time, for example, by American economists George Akerlof and Robert Shiller in their book, *Animal Spirits,* published in 2009. They argue that animal spirits, broadly embodying a wide variety of psychological factors, is key to understanding the macroeconomic landscape. With a good dose of psychology, we can better appreciate why economies get ill, sometimes seriously so, and how they might recover.

For Akerlof and Shiller, the notion of animal spirits goes beyond the idea of the degree of confidence that people have in the economy and the psychological factors that drive their level of confidence. It also includes their sense of fairness, trust and breaches of trust, and corruption, as well as *money illusion* (in which people may be under the illusion that their purchasing power *isn't* falling as prices increase in a world of bounded rationality).

Our emotions and computational limitations play an important role in determining how people react to changes in the economy, how other people behave, and how people are treated in the economy. Our emotions and computational limitations affect economic output as much as, if not more than, traditional, more easily measured, economic factors or variables. More to the point, there is an interesting tango between animal spirits and the straight-laced economic variables. Of considerable importance is how and the extent to which emotions and attitudes influence consumer and investor behavior. Emotional factors heavily influence the evolution of economic bubbles, and some of this relates to the role that over- and underconfidence play in driving consumer and investor decision making.

Driving consumer behavior with animal spirits

When, on average, consumers don't feel confident about the future, they tend to spend less money, because they choose to save more or borrow less. When consumers feel more confident, spending tends to go up — they save less or borrow more. For example, when consumers feel good about the future, they feel confident enough to borrow money to buy a house or to purchase big-ticket items like cars, washing machines, computers, and TVs.

Even if interest rates are relatively high, when animal spirits are high, consumer confidence can help push the economy out of a recession or help sustain an economic boom. On the other hand, if consumer attitudes are depressed, this can pull the economy into a recession, even if traditional economic indicators look quite promising.

When consumer confidence is on the rise, this shifts outward aggregate demand (*AD*) from *AD*0 to *AD*1 in Figure 16-4. This causes GDP to increase. When consumer confidence wanes, aggregate demand shifts inward from *AD*0 to *AD*2. And this reduces the level of GDP. Consumer confidence shifts the aggregate demand, just as changes in "real" economic factors (such as interest rates and income) would.

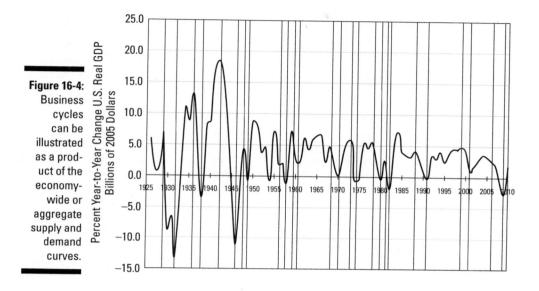

Figure 16-4: Business cycles can be illustrated as a product of the economy-wide or aggregate supply and demand curves.

Driving investments with animal spirits

Just as consumer sentiments help drive consumer expenditure, investor sentiments help drive investment behavior, such as the investment in new plants and equipment and in research and development. When business decision makers lose confidence in the economy, they won't invest or they'll reduce their investment expenditure. This reduces aggregate demand and can tip the economy into a recession, or make a recession worse than it might otherwise be. On the other hand, if investor confidence is high, this contributes to increasing aggregate demand and can help jumpstart an economy out of a recession or keep the economy in the upturn phase of the business cycle longer than it might be otherwise.

Changes in the level of investor confidence shift the aggregate demand curve (*AD*) in Figure 16-4, just as changes in the level of consumer confidence do. Increasing the level of investor confidence shifts aggregate demand from *AD*0 to *AD*1; decreasing the level of investor confidence shifts aggregate demand from *AD*0 to *AD*2. In other words, variations in investor confidence affect the level of GDP.

Generating business cycles through overconfidence and financial fragility

That business cycles can be driven by animal spirits and that this is an inevitable feature of market economies was seriously elaborated upon by American economist Hyman Minsky, who wrote in the tradition of John Maynard Keynes.

Minsky was held in considerable disrepute by most economists, who insisted that speculative bubbles and weird psychological factors motivating business cycles were wild-eyed and dangerous ideas. But Minsky's rendition of the Keynesian narrative has now gained considerable respect in the world of business, the media, and even among some academic economists.

Minsky's *financial-instability hypothesis* argued that, as the economy moves into an upturn, confidence builds among investors who want to purchase assets of all sorts. Financial institutions caught up in the spirit of the moment are willing to loan money on easier terms, betting on ever-increasing asset prices. More and more people borrow to play the market, and initially everything is fine as we scale the ever-rising walls of asset bubbles.

But eventually, many people have borrowed so much that they require ever-increasing asset prices just to pay the interest on borrowed funds. Sooner or later, someone panics, getting wise to the fundamentals. Lenders call in their loans, and borrowers have to sell off their assets (including non-speculative, fundamentally solid assets) to pay down their debts. We have a *Minsky moment* (a term coined by economist Paul McCulley). Asset prices fall, and more loans are called in. As asset prices spiral downward and defaults on loans occur, banks become increasingly reluctant to loan money even to good old-fashioned businesses that require short-term loans to run their operations.

A liquidity crisis emerges. Solid businesses have cash shortfalls. And the crises in the financial sector leaks its toxicity into the real economy, often sparking an overall economic crisis, as firms lack the financial capacity to operate.

George Katona and how consumer attitudes drive the business cycle

It may come as a big surprise to many conventional economists that consumer attitudes help drive the business cycle. But way back in the 1950s, George Katona, a psychologist with the University of Michigan, developed an important facet of economic psychology that's now being recognized as important to understanding and predicting business cycle behavior. Katona argued that the traditional reliance on business investment and government policy indicators are inadequate to forecast or predict business cycles. He pioneered consumer attitude surveys to better understand and measure consumer confidence.

Katona also argued that his consumer attitude surveys provide better predictions and understandings of business cycles. The more confidence consumers have in the future, the more they spend. The less confidence they have, the less they spend. Psychological factors help drive spending and, therefore, affect the business cycle. Even if specific economic indicators look good, such as low interest rates and low rates of inflation, the economy can remain in the economic doldrums if people feel bad about future economic prospects.

Minsky didn't believe that financial bubbles or business cycles could be eliminated. But he argued that, given that they're inevitable, careful government intervention and institutional change are required to moderate the extent of bubbles and minimize any damage that they may inflict on the economy.

Creating real estate bubbles

A *real estate bubble,* which incorporates *housing bubbles,* simply refers to an increase in the price of real estate from its fundamental or real value. (*Housing bubbles* are real estate bubbles in residential markets.) Because of the importance of housing and other property expenditure to the real economy, how the housing market performs can have large affects on the rest of the economy.

Real estate bubbles can be initiated by very traditional economic variables, such as lowering the rate of interest and reducing the percentage of down payment that prospective homeowners are required to put down (both of which make it cheaper to finance the purchase of a house) in order to obtain a mortgage.

With the economy strong and animal spirits vibrant, many people move into the housing market who can just barely afford their monthly mortgage payments. Any significant increase in the interest rate, a pay cut, or job loss results in defaults and economic disaster. In the early 2000s, many first-time homeowners in the United States, with a first taste of the American dream, had great confidence in the future, based on their understanding of the American economy and mortgage rate payments. This vision was enthusiastically promoted by experts and financial and political pundits.

Rising prices and great confidence in future price increases encouraged the purchase of real estate in expectation of future price increases. Many behavioral economists argue that this overconfidence in the future was critical to the housing and real estate bubble that preceded the American financial and overall economic crisis that began in 2007.

But no one knew for sure if and when the bubble would burst, especially given expert advice in a world of bounded rationality. People borrowed heavily based on their giddy expectations of the future. More hot air was being pumped into the housing and real estate bubble.

Real economic variables and animal spirits were both important to the housing and real estate bubble in the United States, which peaked in 2006. When the bubble burst, housing prices fell by over one-third from 2006 to 2009. This contributed to the economic crisis that hit the United States in 2007. In many ways, this bubble was quite similar to the one that developed in the United States, and elsewhere, in the 1920s, whose flames were fed by changes in both real economic variables and animal spirits.

John Kenneth Galbraith and speculative bubbles: Some things never change

John Kenneth Galbraith of Harvard University was one of the early pioneers investigating the origins of housing and real estate bubbles. A key point made by Galbraith is that

> . . . there is a basic and recurrent process. It comes with rising prices, whether of stocks, real estate, and works of arts, or anything else. This increase attracts attention and buyers, which produces the further effect of even higher prices. Expectations are thus justified by the very action that sends prices up. The process continues; optimism with its market effect is the order of the day. Prices go up even more. Then, for reasons that will endlessly be debated, comes the end. The descent is always more sudden than the increase; a balloon that has been punctured does not deflate in an orderly way.

But this is not all. Galbraith made the point that these type of bubbles often are initiated by changes in the real economy. However, they're also often sustained by leaders in the economic and political community whom the rest of us often follow, riding the wave of their advice and confidence. Given bounded rationality, this can make eminent sense, especially if we're out to make what, from all appearances, looks like easy money.

Robert Shiller of Yale University has taken Galbraith's research many steps forward, statistically examining the varied characteristics and causes of housing bubbles. As Galbraith pointed out, even the best critical economists can't predict exactly when housing bubbles will burst. But we can predict that disaster will eventually strike.

The most recent bubble burst quite dramatically, as confidence collapsed when a few investors grew wary about the viability of the bubble. It only takes a few pessimists to lead investors to unload now suspicious investments. In a world of uncertainly and imperfect information, people follow the leader up and down the bubble, creating cascades of boom and busts.

Deconstructing business cycles: The tango between psychology and "real" factors

"Real" economic factors — like wages, consumption, and investment — don't stand alone. An important insight from behavioral economics is that how people feel about the economy and its future also plays an important role in affecting their decisions. Only by examining real economic factors in the context of animal spirits — in the context of overall psychological variables —

can we explain decision making during the business cycle. Plus, any policy or event that affects our animal spirits and our confidence will invariably have an important impact on the economy.

Business cycles are affected by a mix of economic and psychological factors. No matter how good things appear, a good scare, no matter how unsubstantiated, can trigger a panic on financial markets, causing a liquidity crisis that impacts, big time, real income and employment.

Economic Psychology and Government Policy

Understanding the state of mind of the public is critically important if we are to understand how people tend to respond to government policy. People don't simply respond to changes in economic factors, such as interest rates or tax rates. They respond to these economic factors in the context of their state of mind, in the context of how they feel about the present and the future, and in the context of their level of confidence. If the public's confidence is undermined, it can more than neutralize government efforts to stimulate the economy by manipulating real economic factors. On the other hand, rejuvenated animal spirits can add serious punch to government policy.

The *liquidity trap* is a psychologically based concept made famous by Keynes and sometimes exploited by economists. But it lurked in the shadows of economic analysis for many decades until the 2008–09 global economic crisis. For Keynes, this concept was most applicable in times of economic distress, when animal spirits are weary and depressed. During such times, even when central banks reduce interest rates or the price of borrowing to very low levels, we expect little or no increase in the demand by consumers and investors for loans, including mortgages and credit cards. In other words, we expect a liquidity trap even at low interest rates.

In the standard economic argument, of course, when price goes down, demand should go up. The interest rate is essentially the rental price of a dollar for one year. Thus, lower interest rates should normally increase quantity demanded for loanable funds. But if you think that you might lose your job at any moment, or you don't expect your sales to pick up (or you think they might even drop), borrowing money doesn't make sense. Your low confidence keeps you from responding, in the expected way, to a drop in the price of borrowing money.

Government often uses tax policy to affect people's spending. And government officials and experts, including economists, often assume that people respond to changes in taxes as they would to changes in any other price. If taxes go up, people spend less; if taxes go down, people spend more. But this isn't necessarily the case — people's spending decisions also are based upon their expectations of future economic circumstances. If you expect the economy to remain weak or you see it heading for a recession, and if you expect that your job and purchasing power may be under attack, you probably won't spend more even if taxes fall — it's just too risky. Most people will simply save a bit more and even pay down some of their debt if they can.

The state of animal spirits can prevent monetary policy and tax policy from having much effect on the economy. Boosting confidence becomes critical to moving the economy forward.

How Fairness, Reciprocity, and Punishment Influence Wages, Effort, and the Business Cycle

One important model that dominates economics is that flexibility in wages and product prices is important to minimizing the length and depth of economic downturns. The assumption is that, ideally and rationally, prices should be flexible. During an economic downturn, prices — including money wages — should fall, making it more attractive for firms to hire workers.

The point is that in order for employment to be restored, money and even real wages need to be reduced. But price flexibility doesn't typically exist in either product or labor markets. That's simply a fact of life.

So, many economists actually blame the persistence of high rates of unemployment and also the depth and length of economic downturns on the irrational refusal of workers to accept the trade-off of lower wages for more employment and more job security. Workers are blamed for their own unemployment and considered to be voluntarily unemployed — people are unemployed because that's what they choose to be.

Behavioral economists have argued that there are good rational reasons for wage inflexibility. Many have also argued that wage inflexibility has little to do with causing and maintaining economic recessions. The behavioral arguments are closely tied to an understanding of how psychological factors affect workers' and employers' decisions. The perception of fairness and how workers can and do respond in the labor market when they feel that they're being unfairly treated are particularly important. Workers punish unfair treatment by retaliating against employers by reducing the quality and quantity of their effort, and they work harder and smarter and show loyalty to their employers when they're treated fairly.

In this section, I cover various reasons for wages being inflexible downwards. I discuss how money illusion in conjunction with mild inflationary policy can facilitate increasing employment. I also discuss how higher rates of sustainable employment can facilitate higher rates of x-efficiency and why higher wage rates don't necessarily impede achieving lower rates of unemployment. Finally, I discuss how higher rates of unemployment can undermine the confidence and productivity of workers, resulting in a less productive economy with higher rates of long-term unemployment.

How efficiency wages cause sticky wages and involuntary unemployment

Based on efficiency wage and x-efficiency theories (the idea that workers' effort isn't fixed), behavioral economists have argued that one important reason for downward wage inflexibility is closely tied to workers cutting their effort if their wages are cut. If workers retaliate because of unfair treatment, they can neutralize any economic benefits that their bosses may secure by cutting wages (see Chapter 12).

For this reason, cutting wages actually may be unprofitable. For rational reasons, wages are kept relatively high, even in the face of a drop in the demand for labor, which makes it more difficult for employment to be quickly restored to pre-recession levels. So, we end up with a large number of workers who remain involuntarily unemployed for longer than they would in a world of flexible prices. But this is only theory.

Why businesspeople don't like to cut wages over the business cycle

Truman Bewley of Yale University, a mathematical economist, wasn't satisfied with the conventional, standard, irrationality-based explanations of downward wage inflexibility. So, he did something quite unconventional for economists: He interviewed business and labor leaders to figure out why wages are inflexible downward. His findings were in line with the efficiency-wage-type explanations (see the preceding section).

Firm decision makers are reluctant to cut wages and salaries during an economic downturn for fear that employee morale will fall and employee loyalty to the firm will implode. Basically, cutting wages during an economic downturn is unprofitable. For reasons of fairness, reciprocity, and loyalty to the firm, wages are kept relatively high during the business cycle. This is a way for firms to maximize their long-term profitability.

Insights on money illusion: Tricking workers into cutting their wages

Most conventional economists argue that increasing the general price level will have no permanent effect on employment. This was not always the case. In the 1950s and 1960s, many conventional economists argued that inflation can increase employment by cutting real wages and making it more profitable for employers to hire more workers. As prices go up and money or nominal wages remain the same, workers' real wages fall. It's good news for the firm and the unemployed, or so the story goes. This argument was quite popular in the 1960s and was embodied in what has become know as the *Phillips curve,* named after New Zealand–born economist William Phillips, who formalized this idea.

But this Phillips curve argument has been rejected by most economists, because it would involve workers being tricked into accepting lower real wages. If prices go up and real wages fall, workers would soon realize what's happening and demand higher wages. The only real by-product of higher prices or a higher rate of inflation would be higher prices. Workers don't suffer from money illusion — they're smarter than that.

But this idea that inflation can increase employment by cutting real wages through money illusion has been resuscitated by Nobel Laureate George Akerlof. He argues that at low rates of inflation, workers suffer from money illusion. In a world of bounded rationality, worrying about the impact of small price increases on real wages is too costly. Plus, workers tend to make errors in calculating what their real wages would be following a small increase in prices. The consequence of this is lower real wages and more employment.

Going back a few decades, John Maynard Keynes argued that workers didn't suffer from money illusion. However, Keynes maintained that if real wages were required to generate more employment and job security, workers would knowingly accept lower real wages, as long as it was done in a fair and equitable manner. For this reason, Keynes believed that the level of real wages typically wasn't an obstacle to increasing employment, especially during a recession or depression. There was some trade-off between the rate of inflation and employment — more inflation leading to more employment — up to a point. But it was based on issues of fairness, not on money illusion. Fairness plus inflation can generate more employment, especially during a recession.

Why high wages don't necessarily cause higher unemployment

Higher wages don't necessarily prevent employment from growing either during the business cycle or in the longer run, as long as effort increases sufficiently with increasing wages and if increasing wages also induces technical change. In this case, increasing wages don't necessarily result in higher average costs.

According to the conventional wisdom, this is simply not possible. But when you look at labor productivity as a product of both traditional economic variables (such as plant and equipment per worker and education) and of fairness and reciprocity, higher wages aren't necessarily an obstacle to higher levels of employment. Then finding ways to cut real wages no longer paves the golden path toward economic salvation.

How higher wages may induce cost-offsetting increases in productivity becomes critically important. In this scenario, employment can grow both in the short run and in the long run, without money illusion or cuts to real wages, as long as there is enough aggregate demand to absorb the increased output being produced by the growing number of workers.

How unemployment undermines confidence and destroys productivity

There is some strong evidence to support the view that being unemployed can have serious psychological consequences on workers. It can undermine confidence, cause depression, result in a loss of will, and produce a sense of helplessness and a loss of self-esteem, which, in turn, can have a damning long-term effect on productivity. This argument is put forth by American economists William Darity and Arthur Goldsmith.

Simply put, unemployment reduces the productivity of many of the unemployed by causing them psychological damage. This makes many of the previously employed workers unemployable at current wages, after their productivity is undermined by a stretch of sustained unemployment. Also, the disillusionment of the unemployed may adversely effect the psychological well-being of the employed, negatively affecting their productivity as well. Finally, many of the unemployed find it increasingly difficult to engage in rigorous job searches because they're depressed and have low self-esteem.

If unemployment is allowed to persist, it can have long-term negative effects on the economy for psychological reasons. Poor mental health, produced by sustained high rates of unemployment, makes it increasingly difficult to reduce unemployment to the levels of the past. Many formerly vibrant and productive workers become unemployable or employable only at relatively low-wage dead-end jobs.

Chapter 17

The Art and Science of Happiness: Can You Be Happy without More Money?

onventional economics looks upon the level of wealth or income as a pretty good proxy for the level of happiness in a society. Increase income, and you can assume that you're increasing just about everyone's level of happiness. Behavioral economics, on the other hand, suggests that such a simplistic relationship between income and happiness doesn't hold, especially in relatively wealthier economies. In the short run, increasing income generates more happiness, but in the longer term the level of happiness reverts to prior levels. This is referred to as the *hedonic treadmill* — people adapt to higher level of income or material well-being.

In this chapter, I discuss the relationship between happiness and income and the multifaceted determinants of happiness, such as stable marriages, stable employment, and good health. Money isn't everything, but it remains one important determinant of happiness. What the individual and society *do* with increases in income matters, too.

Happiness and Conventional Economics

Conventional economics predicts that income buys happiness. This prediction follows from the assumption that a basic driving force of human decision making is income and wealth maximization.

If money makes people happy, then government should do its best to maximize the growth of per-capita income, at least according to the narrow view of human happiness assumed by many economists.

In this section, I discuss how conventional economics tends to measure happiness. I also cover the assumptions conventional economics makes about what people need to know to be happier and happier. I discuss the more nuanced conventional perspective on the relationship between increasing income and happiness, which assumes diminishing returns to money. I also explore some of the limits of the conventional analysis that assumes that the benefits of increasing average per-capita income applies equally to all members of society.

How happiness is measured

The conventional perspective on the determinants of happiness relates measures of individual happiness and life satisfaction to levels of gross domestic product (GDP) or changes to GDP. (Economists often use the terms *happiness* and *life satisfaction* interchangeably.) Happiness and life satisfaction are measured using indexes that are derived from answers to questionnaires.

In one type of survey, individuals rank their level of happiness in terms of very happy, pretty happy, not so happy, and not at all happy, and each category is assigned a number, with very happy being assigned the highest number. This approach is the one used by the very popular World Values Survey, which underpins much of the conventional wisdom on happiness.

Another survey, the Gallup World Poll, uses a ladder approach. Respondents to this survey are asked to position themselves on a particular step on a ladder, with the highest step representing the highest level of life satisfaction. Data from this survey is also important to the conventional wisdom on happiness. The Gallup World Poll is much more comprehensive than the World Values Survey.

All these data are obviously subjective in nature. They attempt to reveal what people think about their level of happiness or life satisfaction at the time that the survey is conducted.

The art of being happy

Two of the fundamental assumptions of conventional economics are that people know

✔ What makes them happy

✔ What they have to do to be happier and happier

Conventional economics also assumes that people are all income and wealth maximizers, when they take the riskiness of the economic outcomes into consideration. Many people are assumed to accept less income in exchange for less risk. This being said, income and wealth maximization is the most effective road to maximizing happiness. Conventional economics assumes that everybody knows how to best maximize his or her own income and wealth, and everyone's decisions are an expression of this deep-seated knowledge. Maximize income and wealth, and people will maximize their level of happiness.

So, utility maximization is assumed to be pretty much the same thing as income and wealth maximization. Deviate from this road, take a bit of a detour, and you won't be as happy as you might otherwise be. Of course, conventional economics assumes that people *don't* deviate from this prescribed road to ultimate happiness. If they did, they wouldn't be rational or smart, and conventional economics assumes that people are rational and smart.

Most conventional economists argue that the relationship between increasing income and happiness is pretty much a one-to-one or linear relationship. Increase income by 10 percent, and you'll increase the level of happiness by 10 percent. This perspective is illustrated in Figure 17-1 by line segment 0*F*. But, to be fair, many conventional economists argue that there are some diminishing returns to increasing income, so the relationship between increasing income and happiness is not quite one-to-one. This is illustrated by line segment 0*G*. This being said, increasing income is supposed to produce pretty large increases in happiness. And line segment 0*F* is a good representation of how conventional economics portrays the relationship between increasing income and happiness (for more details, see "Diminishing returns for income and wealth," later in this chapter).

Another key assumption of conventional economics is that each person's happiness or utility is determined completely independently from anyone else's income or wealth. Each person makes choices as if she were in a hermetically sealed box. A person's income or wealth relative to her friends' and neighbors', or complete strangers', has absolutely no effect on her utility or level of happiness. What makes people tick is the level of their income and wealth and changes to that level of income or wealth.

If your annual income increases by $10,000 (controlling for any increase in prices), you'll be happier. If this $10,000 raise increases your annual income by 15 percent, your level of happiness should increase by about 15 percent. Even if your friends and neighbors all get raises of 40 percent, your level of happiness will increase by 15 percent — you won't feel bad that you didn't get as big of a raise as your friends and neighbors did. What counts is your final level of income and wealth, not your *relative positioning* (how you compare to other people).

Figure 17-1:
There are
different
perspec-
tives on the
relationship
between
income and
happiness.
Line seg-
ments *F, G,*
and *E* illus-
trate these
different
worldviews.

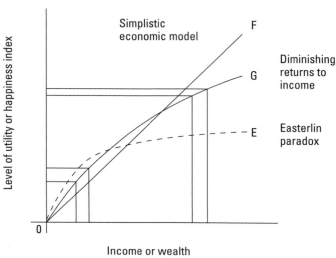

This type of model is thought to provide a great explanation not only for how people behave, but also for how people *will* behave and how people *should* behave.

Why conventional economics assumes that money makes you happy

Intuitively, the conventional approach seems to make a lot of sense. Most people would like more income and wealth. Sure, they also like to give to charity and help out people who are less fortunate, and some people would even accept job offers at a lower pay rate if it were a job they really liked for a firm they really liked.

But still, most people like pay raises because they allow them to buy more things, improve their lifestyle, give their kids more opportunities, and donate to charities. People around the world, in poor and rich countries alike, go on strike for higher pay and improved working conditions, a move that often involves significant short-term sacrifice.

All this suggests, as conventional wisdom would have it, that there is something to the idea that more money increases happiness. At least people's revealed preference is that they want more money and are willing to go to considerable length to get more money. (Read on for the behavioral economics take on happiness.)

Diminishing returns for income and wealth

Conventional economics has always been concerned with the idea of *diminishing returns:* The more people have, the more satisfaction they get, but at a diminished rate. You get more utility with each beer you drink — and the utility increase may even be proportionate to the increased consumption of beer. But after those first few beers, the level of satisfaction increases, but not in proportion to the amount of beer consumed. The last glass consumed increases your utility, but not by as much as the previous glass did. Eventually, drinking more beer can be painful, leading to vomiting and even blood poisoning. Now you have *declining returns* — your total utility is actually falling.

The same type of scenario can be envisioned when it comes to income and wealth. Increasing income or wealth increases your utility. But the more you have, your utility increases, but at a diminishing rate (refer to line segment 0G in Figure 17-1). At low levels of income or wealth, increasing income or wealth has a big effect on your utility. But when you're really rich, having more income or wealth increases your utility, but not as much as when you start off with low levels of income or wealth.

Overall, this suggests that the poorer people are, the more they benefit, in terms of happiness, from increases to their income or wealth. Wealthier people benefit less from any given increase in income or wealth than relatively poor people do. Introducing this diminishing-returns framework into an analysis of happiness also suggests that increasing the income to the poorer members of society increases society's total happiness by more than if the income of the wealthy increases by the same amount.

Still, according to this approach, the more income and wealth people have, the higher the society's happiness. Income and wealth remain key drivers to happiness. This more nuanced approach to the relationship between income and happiness often isn't at the forefront of conventional approaches to happiness.

What increasing per-capita income ignores

The ongoing discussions on happiness by economists have shifted focus away from the traditional focus on macroeconomic factors, such as per-capita income, as the key measure of well-being and happiness. Attention has shifted to what's happening at the level of the individual. Per-capita income is only an average — it says nothing about how this average impacts the individual. How individuals are affected by per-capita income depends on how this income is distributed and what types of public goods — such as medical care, education, and public safety — are provided by government. Two economies with the same per-capita income may have completely different income distributions and completely different supplies of these public goods. These differences in income distribution and in the supply of public goods have huge effects on the level of well-being of many of the individuals in those two societies.

The United States has one of the highest per-capita incomes in the world, but it has a very unequal distribution of income. Its supply of medical care, education, and public security also varies dramatically in quality and quantity depending on income, much more so than in most other wealthy economies. This means that even if per-capita income is the best measure of happiness, we really can't say very much about an individual's level of happiness in a particular economy just by examining national averages, such as GDP per person. We have to pay careful attention to the *distribution* of income and public goods as well.

Happiness and Behavioral Economics

Whereas conventional economics assumes that money makes people happy, behavioral economics says happiness is more complicated than that. Some behavioral economists argue that too many people don't know what makes them happy. Also, behavioral economics argues that if people know what makes them happy, poor and misleading information, as well as poor information-processing capabilities, can result in poor decisions. So, even if income increases, people can make mistakes that result in increases in income not producing higher levels of happiness.

There is some evidence that increasing per-capita income doesn't always increase the level of happiness to the extent expected by conventional economics. Some economists argue that increasing per-capita income produces only short-term increases in happiness and that after adjusting to the increased income, most people revert to their former level of happiness. This is especially true if you're already well off. It's not that more income kills happiness. It's just that happiness increases for other important reasons as well.

For example, happiness levels are very much contingent on the quality of institutions, especially how they affect mutual trust and levels of corruption. Low-quality institutions drag down the level of happiness of the poor and the rich alike. Happiness levels also are positively influenced by other factors, such as strong relationships, a good sex life, a good job, good health, a sense of community, and good governance.

What makes us happy: The individual versus the expert

Psychologist Daniel Kahneman and economist Richard Thaler make the case that conventional economics has it wrong when it comes to modeling and understanding the relationship between income, wealth, and happiness. Among its many sins and omissions, conventional economics errs in assuming that people actually can know what makes them happy.

Kahneman and Tversky argue that the conventional perspective on happiness or utility maximization

> . . . has focused on a necessary condition for utility-maximizing choices: an ability of economic agents to make accurate, or at least unbiased, forecasts of the hedonic outcomes of potential choices. The research we review shows that this condition is not satisfied: People do not always know what they will like; they often make systematic errors in predicting their future experience of outcomes and, as a result, fail to maximize their experienced utility.

If people can't figure out what will make them happy, then the implication is that some expert may be able to assist them in their pursuit of happiness, help them make the right decisions, nudge them in the right direction.

But there is considerable debate about whether an expert may know better than you what would make you happy. This is especially the case given that each person is different, and what makes one person happy may make another person sad (or at least not as happy as he or she might otherwise be).

But behavioral economists raise another important point: As a consequence of bounded rationality, people can make mistakes when they make decisions that they hope will result in more happiness. However, such mistakes can be corrected and don't have to be repeated if people have better information, a better understanding of the information, and better tools to process the information. Experts can help in this domain — but experts shouldn't make decisions for people, or even nudge them in one direction or another.

Even if we accept the proposition from conventional economics (shared by many behavioral economists) that people know what makes them happy and they make decisions that can further advance that goal, that doesn't mean they'll end up at a higher level of happiness if their happiness also depends on the choices of other people and the choices made by government. For example, say your happiness is contingent on the quality of education, healthcare, and your sense of public safety. If you have a government that makes poor decisions in these areas, your level of happiness may not increase with more money, or it may not increase by as much as it would with better government. Money helps buy these public goods, but only if government makes the right decisions.

Why money alone can't make you happy (at least if you're well off)

In the early 1970s, American economist Richard Easterlin first challenged what had become the conventional economics wisdom on the relationship between income and happiness. After Easterlin, the simplistic view that there is a one-to-one relationship between an increase of income and an increase of happiness appeared to be dead in the water. So, too, was the view that we can simply assume that GDP per person and changes to GDP per person could be used as a proxy measure of happiness for everyone. Averages can't capture nuanced individual portraits. Averages are too abstract and reality is much too complex for this type of simplistic perspective to hold much water.

Some scholars even argued that money buys you no additional happiness at all — even if we *think* it does, it doesn't. This view introduces important psychological factors into the discussion, as well as the fact that we're interested in how people fare relative to others. People's relative economic position can be even more important than the total amount of income or wealth they have or the increases to their income or wealth. By this logic, a rich person can be much less happy than a poor person, depending on the rich person's income compared to another person's income.

Understanding the Easterlin paradox: Money doesn't buy happiness

Named after Richard Easterlin and following upon his research, the Easterlin paradox suggests that, in many instances, within a country, the richer people appear to be happier than those who are less well off. But comparing countries, in terms of per-capita income or GDP, increasing income doesn't appear to have much of an effect on the level of happiness.

From about $15,000 per person, increasing income appears to do little for the level of happiness. Even within countries, according to Easterlin, after many of the basic physiological needs are met, increasing per-capita income does little to increase the happiness levels of the population.

But most people pursue increases to their income and wealth because they *think* it will make them happier. And it may very well do that in the short run, before they find out that their friends and neighbors have experienced the same type of increase or realize that they're commuting too long, working with people they don't like, or sacrificing time with their families. After all that effort, people end up at the very same spot that they began their race to increase their level of happiness.

The empirical challenge to the Easterlin paradox

Recent empirical research on the Easterlin paradox has challenged many of the findings of the traditional research on happiness. There is now considerable evidence to suggest that there is a positive relationship between happiness and per-capita income, regardless of income levels and across time and across countries and even within countries. Wealthier people tend to be happier. But there may be some diminishing returns to increasing per-capita income with regards to happiness. (People end up with a happiness curve that looks more like line segment 0G in Figure 17-1.)

But these revisionist empirical findings don't undermine a key finding of the research on happiness: that people's relative standing in society also affects how happy they are. In others words, both absolute levels of income and *relative position* (how people fare compared to others) contribute to their evaluation of how happy they are. Happiness also is affected by factors other than income or wealth. What people do with their money and what government does with people's money also play important roles in determining their level of happiness.

Introducing the hedonic treadmill: More money leads to more happiness (but not for too long)

Many economists have argued that a fundamental reason why more money doesn't buy more happiness after people meet their basic needs is that they're most concerned about their relative standing in society. What counts isn't how much they have, but how much they have relative to other people. Also, as per-capita income increases, people's expectations and norms of what they need also increases. People's level of happiness is linked to the norm for the necessary level of income.

People start off increasing their income, and the race begins. This increases their level of happiness. But as soon as they realize that their friends' and neighbors' incomes have also increased by the same percentage, and the social norms about the amount of money necessary to support their lifestyle has increased with income, their level of happiness falls back to what it was initially (see Figure 17-2).

No matter how much income people are able to obtain, it can give only a temporary lift to their happiness. Some scholars find that people tend to adapt to higher income levels within four years — they have maybe a four-year bump in happiness. But they end up running around in circles.

If this argument is correct, it appears that people are simply wasting time and energy running though this maze. Some experts argue that government should intervene, nudging people to get off this hedonic treadmill. According to this argument, the world would be a better a place (and no less happy) if people stopped seeking higher incomes to no effect, at least in terms of increasing their level of happiness.

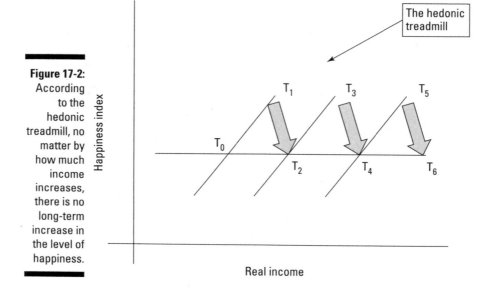

Figure 17-2:
According to the hedonic treadmill, no matter by how much income increases, there is no long-term increase in the level of happiness.

Going beyond the hedonic treadmill

Easterlin's basic argument has been substantially enriched, but his basic message remains: Increasing income and wealth per person won't increase levels of happiness after a certain threshold level of income has been met. Other things are much more important than increasing per-capita income.

For example, a leading proponent of the "money doesn't make people happy" argument, Canadian economist John Helliwell, argues that even when it appears that people in richer countries are happier than people in poorer countries, it's more smoke and mirrors than reality. Helliwell makes the point, based on his own empirical analysis, that people with the highest levels of happiness are those living in societies "where social and political institutions are effective, where mutual trust is high, and corruption is low."

It just so happens that these characteristics often are found in the wealthier economies of the world. But individuals in wealthier countries scoring low on these characteristics would be much less happy than individuals living in similarly wealthy countries scoring high in good governance and trust. To be happier requires much more than more money.

More money won't necessarily make you happy, but less money sure makes you sad

There is some suggestion that because increasing income doesn't make people any happier, maybe people would be just as happy if they were poor. They would simply adapt to these lower levels of income along the hedonic treadmill. So, lower levels of income should not lower people's level of happiness. Or, taking a less extreme perspective, maybe society should keep per-capita income at the same level, because increasing income doesn't make people any happier.

Of course, this viewpoint assumes that the revealed preferences of most people favoring increasing incomes shouldn't be respected. And this follows from the assumption made by some behavioral economists that most people make choices that aren't happiness enhancing. But it's quite possible that most people would resist such policy, at least in democratic societies.

Another point to keep in mind is that even if increasing income doesn't increase happiness, decreasing income or keeping income growth static may cause a permanent reduction in people's level of happiness, especially if this decreased income or no-growth policy weren't of people's own choosing. There is mounting evidence that for most people in most countries, reducing the level of income reduces the level of happiness (see the section "The new empirics of the happiness debate," in this chapter).

The new empirics of the happiness debate

Daniel Kahneman, one of the most significant contributors to the happiness debate, now accepts the argument that money plays an important role in determining people's level of life satisfaction. This type of happiness is based on how people feel about their successes (or failures) and their prospects for the future.

Kahneman writes, referring to the Gallup World Poll, that

> . . . the most dramatic result is that when the entire range of human living standards is considered, the effects of income on a measure of life satisfaction (the "ladder of life") are not small at all. . . . The GDP differences between countries are enormous, and highly predictive of differences in life satisfaction. . . . Humans everywhere, from Norway to Sierra Leone, apparently evaluate their life by a common standard of material prosperity, which changes as GDP increases. The implied conclusion, that citizens of different countries do not adapt to their level of prosperity, flies against everything we thought we knew ten years ago. We have been wrong and now we know it.

This idea is supported by a variety of statistical studies showing that, on average, the level of life satisfaction increases with per-capita income. Some researchers have found that there may be a one-to-one relationship between the two. There is even evidence that the relationship between income and happiness is, on average, no different in low-income countries and high-income countries.

People may adapt somewhat to their increasing level of income. There may be a particular type of hedonic treadmill. But they end up going a few steps forward in happiness, even with some pull back from the hedonic treadmill. The happiness gained from income increases is not neutralized by whatever adaptations to higher levels of income actually take place. Also, at lower levels of income, there tends to be lower levels of life satisfaction.

But as with just about all empirical findings in the social sciences, there are exceptions to every rule. In some poor countries, people are happier, on average, than people in rich countries are. And among the richer and poorer countries, there are differences in the level of happiness.

The United States stands out as one country where increasing per-capita income hasn't had a major impact on the average level of happiness. This is in part due to most of the increasing income in the United States being captured by a very small percentage of the population. Most Americans haven't seen much increase to their income. This is one good reason for there not being much of a relationship between income and happiness in the United States. Most Americans aren't experiencing the type of income increases that economists expect would make them happier.

So, although it does appear that being wealthier makes people happier most of the time, in terms of life satisfaction, other factors must be brought into the mix. The complexity of the determinants of happiness has always been a mainstay of the non-conventional contributions to the research on happiness. Money isn't everything.

Some of the recent empirical findings are illustrated in Figure 17-3, which is drawn from Gallup World Poll data on life satisfaction and World Bank data on per-capita income. The life satisfaction numbers have a maximum value of 100 for individuals who were at the very top of the life satisfaction ladder. Here you see a positive relationship between income and happiness. But it's also pretty evident that there is a lot of variation in the level of happiness for a given level of income. A given level of income is associated with a range of levels of life satisfaction. Having a high income is no guarantee of a relatively high level of life satisfaction or happiness. And there is a range of per-capita levels of income for a given level of life satisfaction as well. Explaining these variations requires the introduction of non-economic variables and differences in the provision of public goods that affect people's level of life satisfaction.

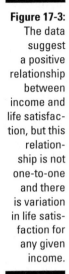

Figure 17-3:
The data
suggest
a positive
relationship
between
income and
life satisfac-
tion, but this
relation-
ship is not
one-to-one
and there
is variation
in life satis-
faction for
any given
income.

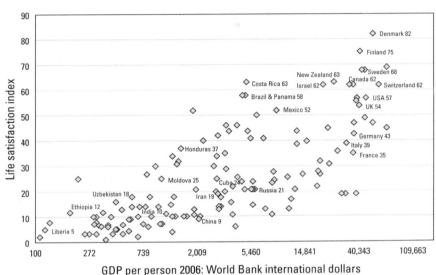

The results of the Gallup World Poll differ from those of the World Values Survey, which dominated the empirical research on happiness. The Gallup World Poll is more comprehensive, capturing a much wider array of poor countries, as well as the poor and illiterate in all countries. Therefore, the Gallop World Poll data provides a basis for more representative results.

What money can't buy (at least not easily)

Money can't buy everything. For this very reason, life satisfaction can't be determined simply by looking at the relationship between per-capita income and happiness. Nor can public policy simply be fixated on increasing per-capita GDP if one aspect of policy is to increase the level of happiness in society.

Another point to bear in mind is that increasing per-capita income doesn't necessarily mean that everyone is sharing in the dream. Only a small percentage of the population may actually see any significant increase in their income. In order for income to buy happiness in a society as a whole, increases to GDP have to benefit the many, not simply the few.

Some key factors best explain differences in happiness levels across individuals. Some of these factors also do a good job of explaining many of the differences in happiness levels across countries.

Explaining differences in happiness levels across countries

Many of the non-economic factors that help explain differences in happiness levels between individuals also help explain differences in happiness levels across countries. For example, a leading happiness economist from England, Richard Layard, finds that about 80 percent of the variation in happiness levels across 50 countries can be explained by differences in the divorce rate, unemployment rate, level of trust, membership in nonreligious organizations, percentage of the population who believe in God, and the quality of government.

A strong relationship

Being divorced or separated has large negative effects on happiness. But separation hurts more than being divorced. Being widowed also causes a large reduction in happiness, but not as much as being separated or divorced.

Not being married reduces happiness from what it might otherwise be by as much as being divorced, or about 5 percent. Despite the complaints we frequently hear about spouses, the data suggest that being married increases the level of happiness from what it would otherwise be.

A good sex life

Economists David Blanchflower and Andrew Oswald find that increasing the frequency of sexual activity with partners increases the level of happiness. This is true for both men and women. Moreover, this finding has nothing to do with a person's level of income. So far, we know that this relationship holds true for Americans, but the sex effect may very well apply to other countries as well.

A job you enjoy

Being unemployed has a large negative effect on happiness — it can cause a 6 percent drop. Job insecurity and increasing the rate of unemployment also negatively affect people's level of happiness. Good working conditions and pleasant working relationships have a positive effect on happiness.

Unemployment may reduce productivity by psyching out the unemployed, but it also makes people less happy, and less happy people are less productive. When people are happier, they become more productive. There is also a "happiness bug." If people are happy, their happiness positively affects the level of happiness of those they work with. So, colleagues can become more productive, being "infected" by one person's happiness. The increased productivity that comes from making workers happier may help increase the wealth of nations.

The great happiness debate: Money as the handmaiden of happiness

More money appears to make people happier. Wealthier people appear to be, on average, much happier than poor people. This is the case in both richer and poorer countries, as well as across countries and over time. But there are some diminishing returns in the relationship between income and happiness, just as economists writing generations ago maintained. In some countries, this is more the case than in others — for example, in the United States, diminishing returns aren't as great as they are in other countries.

Although money is not the only determinant of happiness, it is important. And more money causes no harm — most people wouldn't be upset with a pay increase, a bonus, or a winning lottery ticket.

But even if we grant that increasing income plays an important role in increasing the level of happiness, there are, without a doubt, significant variations in happiness between individuals with the same income and between countries with the same level of per-capita income. Nonmonetary factors also matter quite significantly to people's happiness. We can't explain differences in happiness levels or changes in happiness levels without bringing non-economic factors into our economic toolbox.

Trust and a sense of community

In a society where people feel that they can trust one another and where there is a sense of community, they tend to be happier. If people aren't worried about being ripped off, if they don't feel like they have to double-check every transaction to make sure they aren't being cheated, if they don't fear that their employers are always trying to get the better of them, if they don't need security guards to escort their kids to school, they tend to be happier. If people belong to social or religious organizations that provide a sense of belonging and community, this also increases their level of happiness.

Note: An improved work environment appears to have a much more powerful impact on people's level of happiness than increasing trust or an increased sense of community.

Good health

Being healthier improves people's level of happiness. Put another way, reducing health by 20 percent reduces people's level of happiness by almost as much as getting divorced. But a small drop in health drops people's level of happiness by only a small percentage.

Increasing life expectation appears to have little impact on happiness. The abstract notion that life expectancy is increasing has no important statistical effect in predicting happiness. But it isn't clear how people would respond if they were told that their own life expectancy would increase by ten years or decrease by ten years.

Good governance and democracy

People tend to be much happier living in a democracy and in a country where government is less corrupt and more transparent. Also, their level of happiness tends to increase by quite a lot if they have the opportunity to participate more actively in government, such as through referenda or votes on particular issues of importance. If we compare two countries with the same per-capita income, people in a country that is more democratic with a touch of good governance would be much happier. And people in a wealthier country with a dictatorship that is corrupt to boot would be much less happy than in a poorer country that is democratic and well governed.

How Government Policy Affects Happiness

Even many of the happiness researchers argue that government shouldn't try to devise policies to increase people's level of happiness. People are too diverse to be subject to specific happiness-augmenting policies. Besides, too much Big Brother may actually reduce their levels of happiness.

However, government intervention is highly recommended by those who maintain that people are all on a hedonic treadmill and that they make bad choices when it comes to increasing happiness. For example, a policy such as higher taxes is supposed to nudge people away from working too much and too hard, according to the ideal benchmarks established by the experts. People also should be discouraged from buying luxuries and too much stuff by imposing more taxes and regulations.

The pursuit of more and more goods and services is viewed as a mistake, an error in decision making, and even irrational because, it is argued, it ends up not making people any happier. So, why waste all this time and money running around in circles? Of course, many people get pleasure from the act of running around in circles — the joy is in the act of doing — but this isn't taken into consideration among proponents of government intervention.

Even if we accept that, on average, more income makes people happier, there is room for government and society to take action that, in a non-paternalist fashion, can contribute toward increasing people's level of happiness:

✔ **Distributing income more widely through tax policy; investment in and access to public goods; higher minimum wages; and higher-productivity, higher-wage, low-end jobs:** Increasing income may make people happier, but not if most of that income is concentrated in the hands of a few — if income is very unequally distributed or income distribution is becoming increasingly inequitable. More income equality, so long as it *doesn't* damage growth, should increase the level of happiness of more and more people, as more people share in the wealth of our nations.

✔ **Reducing unemployment and increasing job security by proactively limiting the severity of business cycles and promoting economic growth and development:** Unemployment and employment insecurity seriously damage happiness. Government can play a role in mitigating the damage caused in these domains. Even at a given level of income, people in a society would be much happier if there were less unemployment and more employment security.

✔ **Providing more opportunities for citizens to participate in governance:** When people have more of an opportunity to participate in the decision making of the firm and their governments, this increases the level of happiness by increasing their sense of empowerment.

✔ **Facilitating improvements to social capital by facilitating more active positive interaction between people at all levels of organizations:** The capacity to improve social connectedness tends to increase people's level of happiness regardless of their income. Social capital serves to increase the level of trust between individuals and reduces the risk and stress of engaging in social interactions — pretty important for most people involved in real-world economies. One aspect of social capital is increasing civic participation in government, mentioned above. American scholar Francis Fukuyama argues that the rule of law equitably applied to all is critical for social capital to be developed.

✔ **Providing public goods such as improved healthcare and education:** With improved public goods, people tend to be happier. Improved healthcare reduces the stress people feel when access to quality healthcare is uncertain or unlikely. Less stress results in more happiness. More and better education increases people's life opportunities and sense of empowerment, which also tends to increase their level of happiness.

✔ **Providing people with better information and decision-making tools:** This gives people the means to make better decisions, given their own goals. Information and decision-making tools are critically important in a world of bounded rationality. Better decisions — where there is less regret or no regret — make people happier.

Part V
The Part of Tens

The 5th Wave   By Rich Tennant

"This is classic voodoo economics, Grace, right down to the chicken blood it's written in."

In this part . . .

The Part of Tens is where to turn when you're short on time but not on curiosity. In Chapter 18, I discuss some implications of behavioral economics for public policy. In Chapter 19, I delve into what experiments in economics teach about human behavior. And, in Chapter 20, I cover some of the lessons behavioral economics has for consumers and investors.

Chapter 18

Ten (Or So) Key Public Policy Implications of Behavioral Economics

In This Chapter

▶ Considering how behavioral economics can impact public policy

▶ Paying attention to everything from consumer rights to gender rights to tax policy

*B*ehavioral economics has an important role to play when it comes to public policy — and that means everything from institutional design, transparency, consumer rights, and gender rights to government intervention in the realm of consumption, tax policy, and the overall design of public policy. In this chapter, I point out ten (or so) implications of behavioral economics in this arena.

I frame this narrative in the context of the two leading worldviews in the field: One school of thought in behavioral economics argues that people are essentially irrational, and it requires experts to nudge or even force people to behave smartly. The other school of thought maintains that people often make good choices except when they face poorly designed institutions, misleading information and decision-making defaults, inadequate education or experience, or an inability to make their preferred choices.

Conventional economics assumes that people make appropriate choices to maximize their well-being and their happiness with little or no government intervention, apart from protecting private property rights and the maintenance of law and order. Both faces of behavioral economics recommend a more nuanced and vigorous role for government and public policy than conventional economics does.

Consumer Rights and Protection and the Framing of Information

We wouldn't need to worry about protecting consumer rights to accurate information if consumers could easily collect and process all the necessary information required to make informed decisions without being misled. But people just aren't made this way — we're affected by how and where information is presented. If deceiving or misleading consumers is profitable, there are businesses that will take advantage of this opportunity, especially if the costs of doing so are negligible.

If a product such as a financial security is presented in a positive light, consumers tend to presume that the product is trustworthy, and they may very well invest in it, even if the financial security is actually a risky and low-yield investment. If you're about to take out a mortgage, and critical information is placed at the end of the document and/or in very fine print, you may not realize that the interest rate, payments, or penalties are not what you anticipated.

The devil is in the details, and behavioral economics suggests that people are not mentally constructed to see that all-important needle in the haystack. This needle is so much more difficult to find because firms do their best to hide the needle. This is why consumer rights are critical. All those proverbial needles must be clearly exposed so that consumers aren't stuck with products they would never have purchased with full and honest disclosure.

Conventional economics, on the other hand, assumes that sellers worry too much about their reputation to willingly mislead consumers. But such behavior has occurred in the past — you just have to look back to the 2008 financial crisis to find proof. Consumer rights and protection would minimize the risk of such a crisis happening again and protect the integrity of the market.

Product Labeling and Consumer Choice

Consumers can't make the best choice unless products are properly labeled. Labels must have a certain degree of integrity (meaning, they can be trusted), and the information must be easy to locate and read. Without proper labels, consumers' purchases are based on inadequate or imperfect information, and they can't make the best use of their resources.

Government can play an important role in improving consumers' welfare by fostering the development of independent agencies that certify the integrity of labels. Government also can force suppliers to properly label their products. Consumers are still free to choose, but they can make intelligent choices based on quality information.

The importance of proper labeling is illustrated by the fair-trade label, which has become a big deal. The fair-trade label is supposed to inform consumers that the original producers are being compensated and treated in a fair way. But many fair-trade labels exist. Without appropriate universal and independently certified standards, what you see may not be what you get. This makes it much more difficult for consumers to choose products that they can be sure are fair trade.

Financial Markets and Information Deceit

Financial markets always have been plagued with information problems. Investments that appear safe (low risk) may not be. Consumers can't figure it all out on their own. And if they can't figure it out, they may end up with financial assets that behave in a way that they don't expect — and they may lose lots of money in the process. Losing a bunch of money when you gamble in a casino is one thing; it's quite another thing when you thought you were making conservative investment decisions.

One possible solution to this problem is the introduction of proper labeling for financial products, similar to what's required for food. If suppliers of financial products are forced to clearly disclose the risk of investment and historical rates of return to their financial products, consumers can make more intelligent decisions, which could force suppliers to provide safer financial products (if consumers demand it). But just as with food labeling, this kind of labeling requires an independent and trusted agency to validate the integrity of financial product labels.

Saving for the Future

People's saving behavior is heavily influenced by how saving is framed. When saving is not the default (meaning, money isn't automatically pulled out of your paycheck and put into a savings or retirement account), a large percentage of people won't save enough to meet their future needs. Defaults matter big time!

This idea is contrary to conventional economics, which assumes that people will and can calculate how much money they'll require over their lifetime and save appropriately. Conventional economics also assumes that people have the willpower to save adequately and can resist buying something they want today in order to save for the future. In many parts of the world, including the United States, private savings are not sufficient, given anticipated future needs.

Some behavioral economists argue that part of the solution is to change the default in favor of saving. If the default is *not* saving, people have to make inquiries and fill out forms that allow them to save more. On the other hand, if the default is to save, people remain free to withdraw from the default saving plan — but people incur transaction costs (searching for information, filling out forms, and so on), which are a high enough hurdle that many people will just end up leaving their money in savings. The evidence is quite clear that changing the default in favor of saving increases saving. In conventional economics, saving behavior should be independent of defaults — but it isn't.

If government forces a change in default, it's nudging you to save more. If the default is not saving, government is, in a sense, nudging you *not* to save.

Of course, if the nudge is shifted toward saving, government must ensure that people understand the relative risks of the savings instruments into which their money is being funneled. They also must inform people that saving is the default and that some percentage of each paycheck is being directed out of the person's present pocket into his or her future pocket (assuming that his or her default investment doesn't crash in value some time in the future).

Organ Donations

In the United States, organ donation at death isn't as common as it is in parts of Europe. Is this because Americans are more selfish than their European counterparts? The simple answer is no. Organ donation rates tend to be high where the default is that, at death, a person's organs are donated to those in need. Defaults appear to be more important than altruism. In the conventional view, defaults shouldn't affect a person's decision making, but the evidence says otherwise.

If Europeans didn't donate their organs by default, it appears that even many of the altruistic among them would not be donating their organs. And it appears that many altruistic Americans aren't donating their organs at death because organ donation is not the default. Of course, Americans can donate their organs if they make the right inquiries and fill out the right forms, but this appears to represent too high of a hurdle for most people.

To increase organ donation anywhere in the world, changing the default from not donating to donating one's organs will have a large effect. But this raises important moral issues that need be addressed. If the default is not donating, those of us who prefer to donate won't. If the default is to donate, many of us who prefer not to donate will.

The important point is that defaults matter here, and important moral concerns surface no matter which default is chosen. But if organ donation is the preferred option for most, and this preference is not the default, many people will end up not making the choices that they prefer. If donation is the default, some people will end up donating their organs at death even though this isn't their preferred option. By making organ donation the default, but providing avenues to opt out of the default option, government could improve the organ donation rate. Those who strongly oppose organ donation would opt out; those who favor organ donation or don't feel strongly one way or the other would donate; and the end result would benefit people whose lives depend on organ donations.

Weakness of Will and Self-Control

Contrary to what conventional economics says, people are often plagued by a weakness of will and a lack of self-control. You may *want* to eat less, but can't. You may *want* to stop smoking, but can't. An alcoholic may *want* to stop drinking booze, but can't. You may *want* to change your job, but can't.

Some behavioral economists argue that there is some space for public policy facilitating individuals who want to overcome their weakness of will with what is referred to as a *Ulysses contract*. In a Ulysses contract, you bind yourself (sometimes legally) to certain future commitments in order to overcome your anticipated future weakness of will. This idea follows from an ancient Greek myth in which Ulysses had himself bound to the mast of his ship in anticipation of hearing the Siren's song, which he knew would drive him insane and to his death. Ulysses anticipated his weakness of will and overcame it by having himself bound to the mast.

Government can help gambling addicts restrict their gambling by providing them with a means to be voluntarily added to a list banning them from gambling facilities. The gambling addict may not *want* to gamble, but he knows that he won't be able to resist the temptation, so he binds himself to a list that forces a level of self-control that he chooses.

Banning certain activities can reign in the weakness of will. But it raises the important moral issue of what to ban and who decides what to ban. When one person prefers to do something and another person prefers not to (but has little self-control), a ban improves the welfare of the person with a weakness of will and reduces the welfare of the person who wants to engage in the behavior. For example, many people enjoy drinking alcohol and do so responsibly; other people are alcoholics and can't control their drinking, putting their own lives and the lives of others in danger because of it. If government were to ban alcohol because some people can't drink responsibly, it would be reducing the welfare of all those who *can* drink responsibly.

Labor Market Regulation and Economic Efficiency

In behavioral economics, from the perspective of x-efficiency theory (see Chapter 12), various forms of government regulation can motivate increased economic efficiency, particularly when firms are motivated to produce more or less efficiently by how much they pay, how well they treat their workers, and other costs, such as whether they're required to be environmentally friendly. Increasing efficiency by motivating members of the firm to work smarter and harder and by developing and introducing new technology compensates firms for increased labor costs and the costs of becoming greener.

Conventional economics assumes that increasing how hard and how smart firm members work is not an option because people are already working as hard and as smart as possible. Also, technological change has little to do with increasing wages and improving working conditions. So, increasing wages ends up increasing production costs and generates unemployment.

In behavioral economics, public policy designed to maintain and improve minimum wages, working conditions, union rights, and environmental protection all can contribute to increasing economic efficiency. Such policy changes the incentive environment in the firm and affects decision making. Of course, taken to extremes, this kind of public policy can undermine economic competitiveness. On the other hand, undermining labor rights and ignoring environmental concerns contributes to relatively low levels of efficiency and economic well-being.

Big Brother and Behavioral Economics: Does Government Know Best?

Behavioral economist Richard Thaler and legal scholar Cass Sustein introduced the term *choice architect* to identify a type of expert who knows what's in people's best interest as consumers. This expert, or group of experts, can be designated with the power to nudge people into making choices that the choice architect considers to be in people's best interest. These choices may be the ones that the majority would choose under ideal circumstances. But even so, the minority would be short-changed and end up with choices that reduce their well-being.

Thaler and Sustein assume that, in the real world, all too often, people don't know what's in their own best interest or lack the willpower to make decisions that are in their best interest. Thaler and Sustein's perspective is not accepted by all behavioral economists, but they raise the important issue of what government can do to help people make the best possible choices.

Conventional economics assumes that each person is best able to make choices that are in that person's own best interest. But this philosophy assumes, among other things, that people have appropriate information, that there is no weakness of will, and that people have time to think through the information before them.

One example of choice architecture is regulating how food is displayed in school cafeterias. If fatty and unhealthy foods are prominently displayed, kids will jump at the unhealthy foods. If you present salads first and desserts later in the line, kids will tend to go for the salads — or at least they'll buy some salad and not mainly dessert. And if kids are exposed to healthy foods more often, they may actually develop a taste for healthy food and have a greater preference for it. All cafeterias place food in some order, so why can't the choice architect decide the sequence of things, if doing so improves the health of consumers?

Following this line of thinking, a big public policy question is: Should the expert be *advising* on how things should be done or should the expert be *legislating* choice? If the expert legislates, many people argue that the expert will limit individual rights. Plus, the expert may end up being wrong.

Crime, Punishment, and Identity

The conventional economics argument is that crime is best deterred by increasing the costs of engaging in criminal behavior. If you know that the punishment for robbing a grocery store is a few years in prison, this should be a disincentive to commit the crime. If the penalty is increased, we would expect this type of crime to decrease. If white-collar crime (such as deceiving clients or engaging in Internet-based theft) carries light penalties, we would expect the criminally minded to move in this direction and even to increase this type of criminal behavior. There is strong evidence that changing the relative cost of criminal behavior has strong affects. Also, providing people with non-criminal sources of income reduces criminal behavior.

Most behavioral economists would not deny these assertions. Instead, they would add that other factors are of importance, too. Non-monetary factors such as identity, addiction, and emotion also play important roles. In addition, of some importance is the fact that many people in prison do not (and often cannot) calculate even the approximate cost and benefits of criminal behavior.

People gain satisfaction from being part of a group with whom they identify. They also gain satisfaction when the group does well and they do well for their group. If your identity is tied to a group that celebrates criminal behavior, you have significant non-economic incentives to engage in criminal behavior.

From this perspective, government can reduce crime by supporting community groups that provide individuals with alternative sources of identity and self-esteem — a football, hockey, or debating team instead of a gang, for example. This solution can dramatically reduce the non-economic incentive to engage in criminal behavior without the add-on cost of the conventional solution (which is to incarcerate a larger percentage of the population). In the United States, over 10 percent of African Americans are in prison. Over 3 percent of the U.S. adult population was behind bars by 2010. Prisons are well-known breeding grounds for future criminal behavior. A prisoner's source of identity stems from groups within the prison population, which typically don't shine a light on those who aspire to be kind and gentle and who want jobs.

Addiction that results in criminal behavior is also difficult to address with conventional economic tools. Drug addicts can't be easily deterred from engaging in criminal behavior by increasing its relative cost. A drug addict's demand for criminal behavior is not very sensitive to price, just as a diabetic's demand for insulin is not very price sensitive. Government can reduce addiction-related criminal behavior by decriminalizing certain categories of drugs (recommended by the influential British magazine *The Economist*). In addition, government can facilitate efforts to reduce drug addition. Fewer addicts results in fewer people engaged in addiction-related criminal behavior.

Population Growth and the Empowerment of Women

Conventional economics suggests that population falls as the cost of raising children increases, so market forces should take care of things. For those who argue that continued rapid population growth can pose problems for economic growth and development, as well as environmental changes, market forces don't appear to work at a fast enough pace. The world's population has increased from about 1.6 billion in 1900 to about 7 billion in 2010 — a pretty big jump in a little over a hundred years. Much of this is growth is due to dramatic drops in death rates without corresponding drops in birth rates.

A woman who doesn't know about effective birth control believes that she has no say in the number of children she'll have and fears physical and psychological abuse if she argues for fewer children than her spouse would want. Nobel Laureate in Economics Amartya Sen argues that by providing girls and women with more information, power, and rights, population growth rates will fall. Women who are equal to men will be able to realize their desire for fewer children. And men may very well change their preferences for more children, too.

Tax Compliance: The Carrot Is as Important as the Stick

The conventional approach to tax compliance assumes that people are largely motivated by narrow economic considerations and pay taxes (or try to evade taxes) based on the penalties and chances of getting caught. Increase the penalty and the chances of getting caught, and tax compliance increases.

Behavioral economics doesn't deny the importance of these economic considerations. But non-economic factors such as fairness, sense of belonging to the community imposing taxes, and a belief that taxes are used to do good for society also contribute to improved tax compliance. If government contributes to making the tax system fairer, improves taxpayers' sense of belonging (building their sense of identity with the larger community), and demonstrates that taxes are being used productively, tax compliance will increase without any change in economic incentives. This last point relates to government making the tax system and its use of tax revenue increasingly transparent.

If taxpayers believe that tax revenue goes toward lining the pockets of politicians, tax evasion will increase irrespective of existing penalties. If taxpayers have no affinity with their country of residence and a very weak sense of identity, tax compliance can be expected to diminish. By improving non-economic incentives, sometimes even reducing the size of the stick, tax compliance increases.

Trust and Economic Efficiency in an Imperfect World

People develop *heuristics* (decision-making shortcuts) to save time and energy. Searching for all relevant information and processing this information in great detail takes too long.

One heuristic that people have used for centuries is the trust heuristic. Contemporary evidence shows that most people start off trusting another party in a transaction unless they suspect that something is fishy. People want to trust that product labels are truthful, that financial advisors are honest, that car salespeople are trustworthy, that their business partners are upfront and honest, and that their children's teachers and coaches will take care of them. To the extent that you can make decisions quickly based on trust, you're making decisions in a relatively effective and efficient fashion.

If people can't employ the trust heuristic, the cost of decision making increases dramatically. Government can facilitate the use of the trust heuristic by providing instruments to validate the trustworthiness of information and by providing relatively low-cost methods of punishing those who violate the trust that others place in them. In addition, encouraging and developing norms of trust and *reciprocity* (treating others well, if that's how they treat you) helps weave the social fabric of society. This increases the non-monetary incentives not to breach behavioral rules and social norms that make for more effective and efficient decision making.

The evidence shows that per-capita income is fairly closely tied to the level of trust in society. Countries where trust is more abundant tend to be the more prosperous. For example, Scandinavian countries are characterized by higher levels of trust than the United Kingdom, and the United Kingdom is characterized by a higher level of trust than African and Arabic countries. Russia and the Ukraine, with very low levels of per-capita income, are characterized by very low levels of trust. The United States falls below Scandinavia's trust level but well above that of most other countries in the world.

Chapter 19

Ten (Or So) Experiments in Behavioral Economics

In This Chapter

▶ Looking at key behavioral economics experiments

▶ Seeing the proof behind what behavioral economists claim

Many of the claims of behavioral economists are drawn from economic experiments and economic psychology experiments. In this chapter, I highlight some of the most important experiments that have informed behavioral economists.

Most economic experiments are done in college or university classroom settings with students. So, the results of these experiments often reflect how students (relatively young and well-educated people) behave in particular environments designed to reflect certain real-world circumstances. College students aren't representative of the wider population, which raises concerns among many economists about the validity of many experimental results. Even so, the results of these experiments are thought to provide some insight on how the wider population may behave under similar circumstances. Some of these experiments are now being replicated and refined, with more representative subjects outside the college or university setting, even in non-Western and less-developed economies.

The Ultimatum Game: Fairness and Punishment

The ultimatum game, pioneered by German economist Werner Güth, is a type of experiment that has played an important role in behavioral economics. The results of this game have challenged a key premise of conventional economics: that people are materially maximizing and won't sacrifice a penny in their calculating efforts to maximize their level of *utility* (happiness or satisfaction). In other words, it challenged the conventional notion that our final state of wealth is everything.

The basic ultimatum game has a pretty simple setup: You have two players, both of whom are typically anonymous to each other but whose identities are known to the experimenter. One player is the proposer, and the other is the responder. Who becomes the proposer is random — the name is picked out of a hat or by a computer — and the participants and experimenter all know that the proposer is randomly selected. A certain amount of money is allocated to the proposer; usually, the amount of money isn't much, but often the money is real, and the responder is told how much money the proposer has been given. If the proposer wants to keep any of the money, he or she has to strike a deal with the responder — for example, offering the responder a certain percentage of the money. The responder can either accept or reject the offer from the proposer; if the responder rejects the offer, neither player ends up with any money.

Typically, the proposer can make only one offer; if the offer is rejected, that's the end of the line. But when proposers can make multiple offers, the results don't differ by much from those of the traditional ultimatum game.

Conventional economics predicts and insists that the responder will accept any offer — however small — because any offer above zero increases the responder's level of income. No rational income maximizer would make a choice that would deprive him or her of an unequivocal increase in income. So, if the proposer knows that the responder will behave in this way — if this is common knowledge — the proposer will offer the smallest amount of money possible to get the responder to accept the offer. In other words, if all players are the selfish maximizers of conventional economic theory, and all players know this, the proposer will offer next to nothing, and the income-maximizing responder will accept the offer.

However, the ultimatum game doesn't turn out the way conventional economics predicts. Not only are lowball offers rejected, but average offers are between 40 percent and 50 percent. Proposers typically don't make low offers because they know that low offers will be rejected. Also, many proposers, at least in the context of the ultimatum game, believe that they should make fair offers.

Responders punish proposers who make what they consider to be unfair offers (say, below the 40 percent to 50 percent mark). Some responders even reject offers that fall in the 40 percent to 50 percent range. What this means is that most people playing the role of responders are willing to punish proposers for making unfair offers — even though they incur a cost when punishing the proposers (they don't get any money). In this sense, responders don't behave as conventional economics predicts. In addition, people expect other people — people they don't know, people they've never met — to think about fairness when making decisions.

The results of the ultimatum game played throughout most of the world are fairly consistent. This is true in both Western and non-Western economies, as well as in developed and undeveloped economies. There are limited exceptions to the rule, however. One well-noted example, from the research led by Joseph Heinrich of the University of British Columbia, is from an ultimatum game played among the Machiguenga people of the Peruvian Amazon. The Machiguenga have a very primitive economy and live in a society with relatively little social hierarchy. Among the Machiguenga, the average offer of the proposer is 26 percent, and these relatively low offers are typically accepted.

This exception to the rule still violates conventional economics predictions that people will accept anything that increases their income, even if it's next to nothing. But it also illustrates that some people's definition of fairness differs from other people's definition of fairness, and these different definitions affect behavior. Still, in controlled experimental settings, people don't behave in the income-maximizing manner predicted by conventional economics. Other things contribute to people's utility or well-being, apart from increasing their level of income.

The Dictator Game: Being Fair Because It's the Right Thing to Do

The dictator game is related to the ultimatum game in the sense that you typically have a proposer and a responder. But in the dictator game, the proposer plays the role of a dictator. And the dictator can make whatever offer he or she wants without fear of being punished by the responder. The responder can reject the offer, but the dictator keeps the portion of the money not offered to the responder. The dictator can't be punished for being unfair.

What is of considerable interest and consistent throughout just about all the published studies is that the average offers of dictators in the dictator game is less than what the average proposer offers in the ultimatum game, but average offers are still well above the predicted offers of conventional economics. When dictators and responders are not anonymous, dictators offer, on average, between 10 percent and 40 percent of the pie. However, when dictators and responders are completely anonymous, as they are in the classic ultimatum game, the percentage of dictators offering absolutely nothing to respondents varies from 15 percent to 65 percent. On the other hand, some dictators offer around 50 percent of the pie, even when there is complete anonymity.

Whether you know the proposer makes a big difference, even in an experimental setting where you aren't likely to be great friends with the responder in the future (you may never even meet this person again). But the fact that you know the responder and the responder knows you causes many dictators to behave in a non-materially maximizing manner. This behavior may be socially embedded — they may subconsciously fear future retaliation — or the dictator may just worry about being seen as unfair.

In some dictator experiments, using charitable giving as the experimental setting, dictators gave more for charities, particularly charities they knew. People tend to be more generous when they can identify and sympathize with the responder. However, when dictators don't like the respondents, they offer less than they would otherwise.

Fair Wage Experiments: Adventures into Labor Market Dynamics

Related to the ultimatum game are fair wage experiments, some of which have been pioneered by economist Ernst Fehr of the University of Zurich. In these experiments, subjects take on the role of employer/proposer and employee/responder. The objective is to test the hypothesis that effort varies with wage rates and the hypothesis that employees will retaliate against employers for what employees deem to be unfair behavior.

There is an abundance of real-world empirical evidence that effort is variable and that employees respond negatively to low wages and poor working conditions. But fair wage experiments provide a controlled environment that lets us examine the dynamic relationship between effort and wages.

In fair wage experiments, when responders *can* vary their effort, this is exactly what they do when proposers vary wages. There is the expected positive relationship between wages and effort: Responders increase their effort levels to reward proposers for paying higher wages and reduce their effort levels to punish proposers for paying lower wages.

Although the employee/responder is contracted to supply a specific amount of effort for an agreed-upon wage, the employee/responder can easily get away with providing much less than the contracted level of effort. Knowing this, the employer/proposer should offer the lowest possible wage, according to conventional economics.

But, as with the dictator game, employees don't minimize their effort levels and employers don't minimize their wage offers. Both parties expect each other not to behave in the narrowly self-interested fashion predicted in conventional economics. And when employers have the ability to punish employees who don't fulfill employers' expectations of effort levels, the effort levels increase. However, there is also evidence that building an environment of trust can have an even more powerful effect on effort levels than the threat of punishment does. Still, not punishing shirkers can result in the breakdown of the entire system.

Public Goods Games: Sacrificing for the Public Good

The public goods game is designed to test the hypothesis of conventional economics that public goods can be expected to be undersupplied in a world of materially self-interested or "rational" people.

A *public good* is defined as a good that is non-excludable — after it's produced, no one can be excluded from using it, even someone who contributes little or nothing to its production or maintenance. Examples of public goods are public parks, roads, sidewalks, bridges, street lighting, public restrooms, and water fountains.

Selfish people have the incentive not to contribute and take a free ride, because they can get something for nothing — as long as someone else pays the piper. In public goods experiments, free riders are known as *defectors*.

In the public goods game, all participants in the experiment get an equal share of the public good, whether they contribute or not. The value of the public good will increase based on how much is invested in it, by a fixed percentage. A "rational" selfish person won't contribute anything at all, but the size of the public good is maximized if everyone contributes. So, the cooperative solution is best from a social point of view — we end up with the best roads, sidewalks, parks, libraries, and museums.

For example, let's say we have three players, each endowed with $10 (either real or fake money). The percentage at which investments will increase is 80 percent, and all players are told this information upfront. If two players each contribute $5 to the public good, and one player contributes nothing at all, the public pool of resources is $10, and we can assume that the $10 will grow to $18. After the growth is calculated, the public pool is divided by three, so each player gets $6. The *cooperators* (those who donated to the public good) will end up with $11 each (the original $5 that they each held onto, plus the $6 of growth). The *defector* (the one who didn't donate to the public good) ends up with $16 (the original $10 endowment plus the $6 of growth). The defector comes out ahead, leaching off the goodwill of the others. If all three players had held onto their original $10, however, there would be no public good.

Public goods games have been played in both classroom and real-world settings, so the results are pretty robust. When the game is played only once, the results are completely at odds with the predictions of conventional economics: Most participants contribute *something* to the public good. Some contribute a large percentage of their endowment, and others contribute a small percentage (and there are large differences in contributions from one person to the next). But most people give cooperation a chance. Shirking is not the preference of most people. So, voluntary contributions appear to work.

If the game is played more than once, subjects tend to behave increasingly as conventional economics would predict. This is especially the case when cooperators become aware that there are defectors in their group. As the number of plays is increased, voluntary contributions decrease — people don't like to be used and abused repeatedly. The desire for fairness is significant.

Even in this type of scenario, some people remain cooperators, no matter what. What's interesting is that, if and when cooperators can match up with other cooperators, the public good will be maximized and everyone in the group will be better off. A society of defectors will do least well.

When the game is played more than once, the amount of shirking decreases if defectors can be punished. Participants are willing to punish defectors even if it comes at a cost to themselves — which isn't in line with conventional economics. Cooperation is enhanced when cooperative behavior is enforced by punishment. But in order to punish, the participants must be able to identify defectors. In the real world, it's much more difficult to identify defectors and, therefore, to punish them. So, sustained cooperative behavior is difficult to predict unless certain very special conditions are met.

There is some evidence, however, that in some instances, introducing punishment reduces cooperation. Introducing punishment can reduce the sense of community and upset certain individuals, making them less cooperative.

Still, in the classic public goods game, punishment increases cooperation. The bottom line is that even good people will take a free ride if they believe that everyone else is doing so. Most cooperators will cooperate when others reciprocate, but they'll defect if the other participants defect. The ability to punish defectors makes the cooperative solution sustainable.

Finally, the extent of shirking diminishes if participants can identify each other and aren't playing anonymously. Shirking is also diminished when participants communicate with each other during the experiment prior to each round of the game. If participants can talk, cooperation increases — even if no punishment is involved or expected. But the communication must deal with the issues involved in free riding and the essence of the public good — talking about the weather doesn't do the trick.

The Dark Side of Humanity: It Isn't All about Lovingkindness

Experiments examining the dark side of human behavior are on the rise. A lot of just plain nasty behavior is on display around the world, and this has been a part of the story of human and animal behavior from the beginning.

One example of this approach is seen in the work of European economists Klaus Abbink and Benedikt Herrmann. In one experiment, individuals are given endowments, and each individual is given the opportunity to destroy the endowments of the other participants, but they have to pay something for this opportunity.

In one scenario, participants can destroy another person's endowment anonymously — the subject on the receiving end of their nastiness can't identify them. In this case, about 25 percent of participants destroyed the endowments of other people.

In another scenario, participants can destroy another person's endowment, but their identity is known. In this case, about 10 percent of participants destroyed other people's endowments.

What flies in the face of conventional economics wisdom is that people are willing to self-sacrifice — reduce their own wealth — just for the privilege of causing harm to others.

The relatively destructive people are those who expect that other people will behave in a nasty way to them — in other words, that there will be reciprocal nastiness. Those who don't take advantage of the opportunity to be mean tend not to expect others to be destructive either.

So, the experimental evidence suggests that some people can be expected to be nasty even at a cost to themselves, especially if they can hide their identity. But even in the nastiness experiments, the majority of people choose *not* to be destructive to others, even if they can easily get away with it.

The Endowment Effect: How Ownership Affects Behavior

The *endowment effect* is a term coined to reflect often-cited experimental results that most people value an object more *after* they own it than they do *before* they own it. The endowment effect is related to the notion of *loss aversion* (the fact that people really don't like to lose what they already have, largely for psychological reasons). Loss aversion keeps people from behaving in the narrow, wealth-maximizing fashion predicted by conventional economics. This adventure in behavioral economics was pioneered by economists Jack Knetch and Richard Thaler and Nobel Laureate in Economics Daniel Kahneman.

In a large number of experiments, participants are asked how much they're willing to pay for a particular object. (This is referred to as *willingness to pay.*) In some of the classic experiments, coffee mugs and chocolate bars are used as the objects of desire.

There are variations on how this type of experiment is conducted, but in one version, participants are asked how much they're willing to pay for a coffee mug. Each participant pays his or her minimum amount, and now each participant owns a mug. The participants are then asked how much they're willing to accept to *sell* their mugs. According to conventional economics, the willingness to pay should be the same as the willingness to sell. The cup hasn't changed in any material manner — it hasn't been magically transformed into something new and different. A mug is a mug is a mug.

But contrary to the conventional wisdom, subjects are willing to sell their mugs only at a substantially higher price than what they originally paid. The willingness-to-sell price is much greater than the original purchase price. People's valuation of a good seems to change after they make the transition to ownership. Ownership in and of itself appears to confer additional value on the object. So, a mug is *not* a mug is *not* a mug.

Some behavioral economists argue that this is evidence of *preference reversal,* and preference reversal is thought to be impossible, at least among rational creatures, because it implies that people's preferences may be unstable. Stable preferences imply that if you value a mug at $5 *before* you buy it, you should value it at $5 *after* you buy it. Otherwise, your preferences for the mug, expressed in monetary terms, are flipping, for no good material reason. Regardless of whether this behavior is rational, it does appear that endowment effects are real.

Nobel Laureate in Economics Gary Becker, one of the pillars of conventional economics (although often a serious deviant with his introduction of social factors into the economic toolkit), has argued that the endowment effect *is* rational. He argues that preferences in some ways change after you own an object. There is now an additional characteristic that this object has: It grows on you. And if someone wants that object, he or she will have to pay a higher price — a price greater than your original purchase price. Your preferences haven't flipped, according to Becker, because the mug you own is not the same as the mug you initially bought.

The existence of the endowment effect also has implications for issues relating to law and economics. A long-held view, based on the Coase theorem (named after Nobel Laureate in Economics Ronald Coase), says that the distribution of property rights has no effect on economic outcomes, especially those related to economic efficiency. But the endowment effect suggests that, after you own something, you're less willing to accept offers to buy that thing, which, in turn, affects the bargaining outcomes between two parties. Who initially owns rights to a river will affect negotiations on pollution emissions or beachfront access to residents. According to the experimental evidence, the initial distribution of property rights has to be part of the economics toolkit.

Market Games: Markets Work Even When They're "Irrational"

One of the key pioneers of experimental economics is Nobel Laureate in Economics Vernon Smith. His focus is very much on what makes market economies efficient despite real-world markets not conforming to the strictures of conventional economics. In some of Smith's early pioneering experiments in the 1960s, which have influenced experiments conducted since, he examined the conditions under which markets clear (supply equals demand). More generally, Smith pioneered experiments examining how people might behave under different market conditions and environments.

A starting proposition of many economists is that markets shouldn't clear efficiently given that markets aren't competitive, information is imperfect, and people aren't calculating. This proposition was initially tested by Smith in a two-person exchange experiment, in which subjects represent buyers and sellers on the market. Sellers have the incentive to obtain the highest price; buyers, the lowest price. Sellers get information on simulated costs of production; sellers, on simulated resale values of what they can purchase in the experimental market.

Smith's simulated institutional setting for trade is the double oral auction, which is similar to the trading rules of the New York Stock Exchange (NYSE). In the experiment, both sellers and buyers (hence, the term *double*) publicly call out their offers or bids (hence, the term *oral*). Offers can be accepted or rejected by either party. Also, all sellers' offers are publicly posted, and subsequent offers from sellers sequentially fall below the initial offer. We end up with a downward-sloped sellers-offer curve; this is referred to as the *bid-asked-price-reduction rule.* On the demand side, after the first offer or bid is made, all subsequent offers from buyers sequentially increase above the initial offer. We end up with an upward-sloped buyers-offer curve.

No matter how many times this type of experiment was repeated, an equilibrium price was generated (supply equals demand), despite significant imperfections in information and lack of market experience. Also, an equilibrium price was generated even when there were a small number of buyers and sellers — so, experimental markets weren't highly competitive.

The moral of this story is that, given the institutional parameters of a double oral auction, markets will produce an equilibrium price and clear even when the assumptions of conventional economics don't hold. But a big question is, to what extent does the double oral auction experimental setup reflect real-world sensibilities? Too often, consumers and firms don't behave in a double oral auction market setup. Nevertheless, these experiments raise serious questions about many classic conventional economic assumptions.

Bubble Experiments: How Smart People Produce Economic Bubbles

Asset market experiments, pioneered by Vernon Smith, clearly show that asset bubbles not only can be expected to occur under not very exceptional circumstances but also can be affected by monetary policy. Experiments also show that, eventually, asset bubbles deflate. But still, some asset prices significantly deviate from their fundamental values in the short term. What happens in the short term often ripples in the long term — usually with big effects on the economy.

An *asset bubble* exists when the price of shares increases well above the real worth (or fundamental value) of the corporations that issue them on the stock market. The same can be said for bubbles in real estate and housing, for example.

In the experimental environment, participants trade assets and are provided with reasonable information to calculate the assets' fundamental values. They're given information on dividends and the probability of getting these dividends. The probability of getting dividends is the basis for the fundamental asset calculations.

In the initial trading, large bubbles eventually emerge and then there is the inevitable crash. Even if the same participants return to the market, a lesser but still large bubble emerges, because participants figure they can get out before the crash. Only with additional market experience will these same participants make trades that won't generate a bubble. So, experience determines whether a bubble emerges.

Of course, in the real world, inexperienced traders are always entering the market, making some sort of bubble par for the course. Plus, the evidence supports the hypothesis that experienced traders often partake in blowing bubbles with the younger folks. This could be a consequence of peer effects or the desire not to be outdone by the younger generation.

Experienced traders invariably produce bubbles in a lab environment if more cash (typically fake money) or liquidity is introduced into the system. Holding the quantity of money constant and reducing the amount of stock distributed to the participants has the same effect. The extra liquidity is used by traders to bid up asset prices, creating an asset price bubble. This is suggestive of the effect that monetary policy can have on the extent to which asset prices deviate from their fundamental values.

Experiments on Bounded Rationality

Conventional economic wisdom says that calculating behavior produces the most efficient decisions. But experimental evidence suggests that this doesn't have to be the case. Some of this research, pioneered by psychologist Gerd Gigerenzer, suggests for example, that being a wealth maximizer lowers a person's level of happiness and self-esteem.

In one experiment, there are two groups of people: those who can't let go of the remote control and are always flipping the channel, searching for something better, and those who flip channels until they see something they like and then stop. The latter are akin to the satisficers of Herbert Simon's bounded rationality theory. The former are maximizers; because they're always processing information, they have little or no time to enjoy a TV program. The maximizers are more unhappy, more depressed.

In another setup, one group of inexperienced investors is asked to name the stocks listed on the NYSE and the DAX (the German stock index) that they recognize. An investment portfolio is then constructed based on what's recognized by survey participants. The returns on their picks are compared with the returns of the stock choices made by experienced investors. So, the experienced investors have much information and much more experience in picking stocks, whereas the inexperienced investors' portfolio is based solely on name recognition. Those who know a lot have a wider basket of stocks to choose from and much more information to process. The stocks selected by the relatively ignorant investors outperformed, by a considerable margin, those selected by the more expert investors. This suggests that, in a world of bounded rationality, more is not always better, contrary to what conventional wisdom would lead us to believe. The fast and frugal name recognition heuristic ends up outperforming the more complex and time-consuming decision-making procedures recommended by conventional economic wisdom.

Chapter 20

Ten Decision-Making Lessons from Behavioral Economics

onventional economics pays little attention to errors in decision making. Conventional economists tend to focus on a lack of willpower and misguided decisions fueled by emotions. On the other hand, much of contemporary behavioral economics pays special attention to errors and biases in decision making. They pay more heed to decision making gone awry because of lack of information, misguided advice, inadequate education, and bad incentives.

In this chapter, I cover ten lessons from behavioral economics on how decision making can be improved or, on the flip side of the coin, how disastrous decisions can be avoided.

Be Wary of Overconfidence

Many behavioral economists believe that overconfidence bias is a major source of significant errors in decision making. *Overconfidence* is typically defined as believing that you'll do better (or much better than average) without much in the way of empirical evidence to back up that belief. Most people believe that they're doing better than average — but, obviously, most people *can't* be doing better than average. That's mathematically impossible.

It appears that people are wired to be overconfident, to go forward even if the odds are against them. This belief is at the heart of entrepreneurship. Sure, many entrepreneurs fail, but without all those overconfident go-getters, we might be further behind as a society.

On the downside, overconfident investors take greater risks than would be wise, based on the fundamentals of what they're investing in. They see themselves as smarter than the market — and they may lose their shirts in the process. Sometimes overconfidence is a product of a recent success and ignores past poor or mediocre performances.

Behavioral finance scholar Hersh Shefrin suggests that people would be better off if they were able to distinguish luck from skill and realize that not all risks are worth taking — even if, when all goes well, they might succeed spectacularly. There is a downside to risk: spectacular losses. You only have to look to the current economic climate in the United States and around the world to find proof of that.

What matters is that people are aware of whom they're investing with and how overconfident the decision makers in those organizations may be. Even *recent* performances shouldn't be taken as a sign of future performance. There are no guarantees that past greatness will repeat itself or that rumors of greatness will be fulfilled.

A proven way of reducing the extent of overconfidence in decision making and of encouraging more effective decision making is to force the decision makers to take responsibility for their decisions. If people have to significantly share in the losses that they might incur, or if their opinions are recorded and can be made public, they'll likely think twice before they make decisions that ignore the downside of risk. Forcing discussion on possible choices also forces people to think through the logic of what they're advocating.

You Can't Believe Everything You Read

Behavioral economics recognizes that people often use trust to make fast and often effective decisions. For example, consumers tend to trust product labels, but labels can be misleading. How reliable and trustworthy product labels are depends on the state of consumer protection where you live. In some places, what you see actually is what you get. In other places, you may end up with a product that doesn't do what it's supposed to do.

Conventional economics makes the simplistic assumption that information is accurate and that incentives deter false or misleading labeling. But reality tells a different tale.

Being aware of consumer rights and product labeling regulations can save you considerable aggravation and maybe even harm. Strong and transparent consumer rights and product labeling regulations dramatically reduce the transaction costs of shopping — for everything from computers and food to financial products. If you trust misleading labels, you'll end up making bad, even disastrous, decisions — no matter how smart you are.

Avoid Situations That Require More Self-Control Than You Can Muster

Most people lack self-control to some extent. For many behavioral economists, this lack of self-control suggests that people too often make decisions that they soon regret. For conventional economics, when you have another chocolate bar, another piece of apple pie, an extra scoop of ice cream, another muffin, another piece of fudge, that's simply an expression of your true desires, another preference revealed. In other words, conventional economics says that there should be no regret. But the truth is, regret is real.

Some behavioral economists argue that we should encourage government to deign policies that will nudge people into not having another snack or not making other choices that they may later regret. But this can involve significant government intervention — intervention that doesn't appeal to many people and may actually interfere with the choices of those who really *do* want to indulge in that chocolate bar.

So, what are those of us who would rather avoid choices that we'll later regret supposed to do? We have options, but the first step is to recognize that we lack self-control. Key to avoiding regrettable choices is avoiding situations that will result in our making such choices in the first place. So, if you don't want to smoke, don't hang out with smokers. If you don't want to drink, don't hang out at bars or with people who drink. If you don't want to eat hot dogs and fries and you know there's a hot dog vendor on your regular route home, take a detour.

People often think that they can resist temptation, but the reality is that they don't have the self-control to resist. When we put in place self-control mechanisms — things that prevent us from falling victim to our own lack of self-control — we can make better choices, choices we won't later regret.

Don't Blindly Follow the Herd

Conventional economics presumes that people think for themselves and aren't influenced by those around them. But behavioral economics recognizes that people often follow the leader when making decisions. This type of behavior is dubbed *herd behavior.* Some behavioral economists consider herd behavior to be a serious, irrational flaw. For others, following the leader is a longstanding piece in the evolutionary puzzle of human behavior, which often produces pretty good results. In the real world, information tends to be imperfect and uncertain, so people tend to follow others who appear to know what they're doing.

Herd behavior occurs with everything from investments to restaurants to fashion to films to computers to car purchases. Sometimes people follow the herd because they believe that, because so many others have made certain choices, those choices must be the right ones. All too often, such herd behavior can lead to serious errors in decision making.

Think twice before following the leader — especially if you have the time to think twice. Gather more information. Consult experts. Leaders don't always know what they're doing, and the crowd may be wrong.

You Can't Trust Everyone

Most people trust financial advisors to give them investment advice and do their investing. In a perfect world, this wouldn't be a problem. Every broker would be an honest broker. There would be no deceit in the system, no opportunity for moral hazard. But we don't live in the fantasy world assumed by many economic models.

Always check the credentials of any financial advisor. Check if the credentials are authentic — they sometimes aren't. Check the reputation and the track record of the financial advisor. Know whether your investments are guaranteed by the government — most investments aren't. If the rates of return appear to be too high, they probably are.

Educate yourself on financial matters so that you better understand the information you come across. No matter how good your information may be, if you don't understand it, you may be as lost as if the information were false.

Invest Simply

Many investors think that they can beat the market rate of return. Some can. But it's mathematically impossible for most people to do so. Most conventional economists would make this case. But they would also argue that careful calculation and the use of relevant formula based on mathematically sophisticated economic theory should produce the highest returns on investment. But this is typically not the case.

Some behavioral economists argue that simpler approaches to investing can produce higher returns. Organize your investments based on what Gerd Gigerenzer refers to as the *name recognition heuristic* or the *1/*N *heuristic.*

With the name recognition heuristic, you invest based on the companies you recognize. This approach tends to generate rates of return equal to or higher than what are typically produced by professionals.

The name recognition approach doesn't work so well if you have in-depth knowledge of financial markets — in that case, you know too much (at least to employ the name recognition heuristic).

With the 1/*N* heuristic, you divide the funds that you've allocated for investment purposes (given by 1) equally across a select number of stocks (given by *N*). As Gigerenzer points out, even Harry Markowitz, who won the Nobel Prize for his contribution to optimal asset allocation, apparently used the 1/*N* rule as opposed to his award-winning formulation for some of his personal investing. The 1/*N* approach typically outperforms the more complex approach recommended by conventional economics.

Unless you're an expert, you're better off using simple approaches to investing your income. Sometimes, even if you're an expert, you're better off using simple approaches as well.

Pay Attention to Sample Size

Every once in a while, you hear about someone who's a superb investor, poker player, manager, or CEO. And often, books on how to win the lottery or how to beat the odds in a casino top the bestseller lists. These stories often are based on one person's most recent or unique performance.

Often, you hear that a product is great for your health, increases your performance, or enhances your concentration. But these results are based on a very small number of studies or one study with only a few participants. They aren't representative of the wider body of studies or of the larger population.

Most consumers don't ask (or know to ask) about the empirical basis of these claims to fame. *Sample size* (the size of the sample relative to the total number of studies or to the total population, in the preceding example) and *sample selection bias* (when your sample does not represent the larger population) should make a big difference in whether consumers take these claims seriously.

When you're shopping for any kind of product or following anyone's advice, always ask how many people were involved in the study, if these people represent an accurate snapshot of the larger population, and whether the results of all the studies are being revealed. Just because something worked for one person doesn't mean it'll work for you.

Read the Fine Print

Conventional economics assumes that information is pretty much perfect and pretty well understood by everyone. Behavioral economics recognizes that the substance of many contracts is contained in the fine print at the end of the document. Often, the language is obscure, so you need a dictionary to make sense of it. So, given the cost in time and effort of getting through various important documents, most people just don't read them; instead, they trust the experts that everything is okay or that the government will protect them.

Think twice. You often aren't protected by anyone. If you don't understand the fine print, you can end up in all kinds of trouble financially. For example, you may sign a mortgage agreement that specifies that your 2 percent annual interest rate jumps to 6 percent after six months, which may spell bankruptcy.

Be careful when signing legal documents. Don't expect the information you need to be easily accessible or comprehensible.

Being Nice Pays

Most people are raised to believe that, in a market economy, being nice will cost you, especially if you own a company. Paying higher wages, improving working conditions, giving back to your community, making your company greener — all these things will cost your company and, therefore, reduce your profits. But this perspective hinges upon the assumption, central to the conventional economic wisdom, that the immediate costs of being nice can't positively affect productivity.

Behavioral economics reveals that niceness, fairness, and social responsibility often have positive effects on productivity. And these positive effects can offset (sometimes *more* than offset) the costs of being fair or nice. So, if you have a preference for being nice, you actually may be able to have your cake and eat it, too!

Educate Yourself

Some evidence suggests that providing people with appropriate and effective tools to make economic and financial decisions, as well as concrete examples of how their decisions are likely to pan out in the future, improves their decision making. Often, people think that their decisions will get them where they want to go, but they don't have the skill set to make that a reality.

Poorly designed tools can produce disastrous decisions. Many economists, especially those with a behavioral bent, now recognize that some of the tools used by many investment houses provided highly misleading advice, completely ignoring many of the serious risks involved in investing in a variety of high-yield stocks — now known as *toxic assets.*

Conventional economics assumes that people behave as if they're endowed with what they need to make error-free decisions, decisions that they're unlikely to regret in the near or even more distant future. But this is like assuming that if you give your kid a car to drive without any lessons, there's no risk that the kid (and a whole bunch of other people) won't end up dead or seriously injured.

Bottom line: Financial education appears to have some positive effects on decision making. So, if you want to make better decisions, learn all you can and don't trust everything you're told.

Index

• *F* •

finance, behavioral *(continued)*
  efficient market hypothesis, 111,
    261–262
  financial education, 273
  herding behavior and trust, 271
  implications of institutional failure,
    272
  irrational exuberance, 264–265, 271
  random walk hypothesis, 261,
    262–264
financial education, 273
financial markets, information deceit
  and, 313
financial services, 235
fine print, reading the, 338
fMRI (functional magnetic resonance
  imaging), 43
food and beverage companies, 235
food stores, 235
frames, repairing, 148–149
framing
  about, 131–132
  automobiles, 137–138
  cognitive illusions, 134–139
  as defaults, 144–147
  economic schools of thought on, 132
  effect on preferences and choices,
    133
  errors and biases approach, 133–134
  faces, 136–137
  as heuristics, 134
  market failure, 149–151
  options, 12–13
  in pictures, 134–139
  rational decision making, 148–149
  relationship with decision making,
    139–144
  relationship with loss aversion,
    140–142
framing effect, 100
framing of information, consumer
  rights and protection and, 312
Frank, Robert (professor), 88
free choice
  about, 91–92
  compared with paternalism, 13

constraining choice compared with,
  104–105
in economic decision making, 92–94
illusion of, 99–104
relationship with isolation
  economics, 156
revealed preferences, 94–99
free labor, 216–217
free will, 156
Friedman, Milton (economist)
  conventional view of ethical
    behavior, 230
  on free choice, 91
  on irrelevance of facts, 22–23
  unbounded computational
    capabilities, 34
frontal lobes, 46
functional magnetic resonance imaging
  (fMRI), 43
future
  compared with present, 57–58
  saving for the, 313–314
future contracts, 266
futures market, 267

• G •

Gage, Phineas (construction foreman),
  50–52
Galbraith, John Kenneth (economist),
  92, 265
gaze heuristic, 129–130
gender
  altruistic preferences of women,
    176–177
  conventional choice theory, 168–169
  effect on choice, 167–179
  effect on decision making of, 81–83
  household bargaining power, 169–171
  household choices, 171–172
  labor market discrimination, 177–179
  population growth, 172–174
  risk averseness of women, 175–176
  women on welfare, 174–175
  women's rights, 169–171

• *H* •

terrorism, 195
Thaler, Richard (economist)
  on behavioral finance, 259
  choice architect, 103, 316–317
  on decision making, 93–94
  endowment effect, 328
  on framing, 144–145
  on relationship between income,
    wealth, and happiness, 297
theory of advertising, 138
theory of relative positioning, 61
theory of the firm, 245–246
The Theory of Moral Sentiments
  (Smith), 39, 65, 73
Tip icon, 6
tipping, 74, 158–159
toxic assets, 339
traditional jobs, 211
transaction costs, 249
transparency, relationship between
    income creation, corruption,
    accountability and, 253–254
transportation industry, 235
travel industry, 235
true preferences, 96–98
trust
  about, 63
  impact on economic development,
    161–162
  linking with development, 161
  not trusting everyone, 336
  relationship with economic efficiency,
    319–320
  relationship with happiness, 305
  relationship with herding, 271
trustworthiness and reliability,
    334–335
Tullock, Gordon (economist), 248
Tversky, Amos (psychologist)
  on conventional economics, 118
  on economic psychology, 84

errors and biases approach, 38,
    116–117
on framing, 100, 140–142
on framing prices, 143–144
on happiness, 297
on prospect theory, 119
on sacrifice, 86

• *U* •

ultimatum game experiment, 321–323
Ulysses contract, 315
unbounded computational capabilities,
    assumptions about, 33
unbounded knowledge, 32
uncertainty
  in decision making, 271
  fear of, 85–87
underconfidence, as fuel for bubbles,
    272–273
unemployment
  effect of high wages on, 289
  effect on confidence and productivity,
    289–290
  involuntary, 287
  relationship with happiness, 304
utilities companies, 234
utility
  about, 95
  defined, 108, 322
  experiences, 58–60
  maximizing, 97, 293
  remembered, 58–60

• *V* •

value function, 119–122
Veblen, Thorstein (economist), 77
Veblen goods, 77
Veum, Jonathan (economist), 210
voluntary cooperation, 63

EDUCATION, HISTORY & REFERENCE

978-0-7645-2498-1

978-0-470-46244-7

Also available:

✔Algebra For Dummies
978-0-470-55964-2

✔Art History For Dummies
978-0-470-09910-0

✔Chemistry For Dummies
978-1-118-00730-3

✔English Grammar
For Dummies
978-0-470-54664-2

✔French For Dummies
978-1-118-27537-5

✔Statistics For Dummies
978-0-470-91108-2

✔World History For Dummies
978-0-470-44654-6

HOME & BUSINESS COMPUTER BASICS

978-0-7645-2498-1

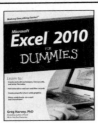

978-0-470-48953-6

Also available:

✔Office 2010 All-in-One Desk
Reference For Dummies
978-0-470-49748-7

✔Pay Per Click Search Engine
Marketing For Dummies
978-0-471-75494-7

✔Search Engine Optimization
For Dummies
978-0-470-88104-0

✔Web Analytics For Dummies
978-0-470-09824-0

✔Word 2010 For Dummies
978-0-470-48772-3

SPORTS & FITNESS

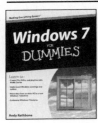

978-0-470-67659-2

978-0-470-73855-9

Also available:

✔Exercise Balls For Dummies
978-0-7645-5623-4

✔Coaching Volleyball
For Dummies
978-0-470-46469-4

✔Fitness For Dummies
978-0-470-76759-7

✔Golf For Dummies
978-0-470-88279-5

✔Mixed Martial Arts
For Dummies
978-0-470-39071-9

✔Wilderness Survival
For Dummies
978-0-470-45306-3

✔Yoga with Weights
For Dummies
978-0-471-74937-0

Available wherever books are sold. For more information or to order direct: U.S. customers visit www.dummies.com or call 1-877-762-2974. U.K. customers visit www.wileyeurope.com or call 0800 243407. Canadian customers visit www.wiley.ca or call 1-800-567-4797.

FOOD, HOME, & MUSIC

978-0-7645-9904-0

978-0-470-43111-5

Also available:

- 30-Minute Meals For Dummies 978-0-7645-2589-6
- Bartending For Dummies 978-0-470-63312-0
- Brain Games For Dummies 978-0-470-37378-1
- Gluten-Free Cooking For Dummies 978-0-470-17810-2
- Home Winemaking For Dummies 978-0-470-67895-4

- Home Improvement All-in-One Desk Reference For Dummies 978-0-7645-5680-7
- Violin For Dummies 978-0-470-83838-9
- Wine For Dummies 978-1-118-28872-6

HEALTH & SELF-HELP

978-0-470-58589-4

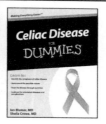

978-0-470-16036-7

Also available:

- Borderline Personality Disorder For Dummies 978-0-470-46653-7
- Breast Cancer For Dummies 978-0-7645-2482-0
- Cognitive Behavioural Therapy For Dummies 978-0-470-66541-1
- Emotional Intelligence For Dummies 978-0-470-15732-9

- Healthy Aging For Dummies 978-0-470-14975-1
- Neuro-linguistic Programming For Dummies 978-0-470-66543-5
- Understanding Autism For Dummies 978-0-7645-2547-6

HOBBIES & CRAFTS

978-0-470-28747-7

978-0-470-29112-2

Also available:

- Crochet Patterns For Dummies 978-0-470-04555-8
- Digital Scrapbooking For Dummies 978-0-7645-8419-0
- Knitting Patterns For Dummies 978-0-470-04556-5
- Oil Painting For Dummies 978-0-470-18230-7

- Quilting For Dummies 978-0-7645-9799-2
- Sewing For Dummies 978-0-470-62320-6
- Word Searches For Dummies 978-0-470-45366-7

INTERNET & DIGITAL MEDIA

978-0-470-44417-7

978-1-118-13060-5

Also available:

- ✓ Blogging For Dummies
  978-1-118-15194-5
- ✓ MySpace For Dummies
  978-0-470-27555-9
- ✓ The Internet For Dummies
  978-1-118-09614-7
- ✓ Twitter For Dummies
  978-0-470-76879-2
- ✓ YouTube For Dummies
  978-0-470-14925-6

MACINTOSH

978-0-470-87868-2

978-1-118-02444-7

Also available:

- ✓ iMac For Dummies
  978-1-118-20271-5
- ✓ iPod Touch For Dummies
  978-1-118-12960-9
- ✓ iPod & iTunes For Dummies
  978-0-470-52567-8
- ✓ MacBook For Dummies
  978-1-118-20920-2
- ✓ Macs For Seniors For Dummies
  978-1-118-19684-7
- ✓ Mac OS X Snow Leopard
  All-in-One Desk Reference
  For Dummies
  978-0-470-43541-0

GARDENING

978-0-470-58161-2

978-0-470-57705-9

Also available:

- ✓ Gardening Basics
  For Dummies
  978-0-470-03749-2
- ✓ Organic Gardening
  For Dummies
  978-0-470-43067-5
- ✓ Sustainable Landscaping
  For Dummies
  978-0-470-41149-0
- ✓ Vegetable Gardening
  For Dummies
  978-0-470-49870-5

PETS

978-0-470-60029-0   978-0-7645-5267-0

Also available:

- Cats For Dummies
  978-0-7645-5275-5
- Ferrets For Dummies
  978-0-470-13943-1
- Horses For Dummies
  978-0-7645-9797-8
- Kittens For Dummies
  978-0-7645-4150-6
- Puppies For Dummies
  978-1-118-11755-2

GREEN/SUSTAINABLE

978-0-470-84098-6   978-0-470-59678-4

Also available:

- Alternative Energy For
  Dummies 978-0-470-43062-0
- Energy Efficient Homes For
  Dummies 978-0-470-37602-7
- Green Building &
  Remodeling For Dummies
  978-0-470-17559-0
- Green Cleaning For Dummies
  978-0-470-39106-8
- Green Your Home
  All-in-One For Dummies
  978-0-470-59678-4